Samuel Bell Maxey

Senator Samuel Bell Maxey

Samuel Bell Maxey

A BIOGRAPHY

by Louise Horton

UNIVERSITY OF TEXAS PRESS, AUSTIN AND LONDON

Library of Congress Cataloging in Publication Data

Horton, Louise, 1916–
    Samuel Bell Maxey; a biography.

    Bibliography: p.
    1. Maxey, Samuel Bell, 1825–1895.
F391.M478H67   976.4'06'0924 [B]   73-17406
ISBN 0-292-77509-1

Composition by G&S Typesetters, Austin
Printing by The University of Texas Printing Division, Austin
Binding by Universal Bookbindery, Inc., San Antonio

To Letty and Robert Stone

CONTENTS

ILLUSTRATIONS

PREFACE

Samuel Bell Maxey is an important nineteenth-century Texas political figure of whom no biography has been written. His name is not recognized by historians and Texans in general because, until recently, his private papers have not been available to the public and, for some reason, he was dropped from consideration when the history of his period was written.

I have tried to use the voluminous correspondence of Maxey to emphasize the events of his life and to show his character. I have not been able to account for the fact that, although his letters mention close association with colleagues in the Senate and with many famous Texans, the writings of these men reveal little about Maxey—indeed it is as if he were present but unseen. I have treated Maxey's Mexican War and Civil War years briefly in order to devote a large part of this book to his major contribution, namely, his aid to his state and the nation during the Reconstruction. His life spanned that period and extended well into the period of the Progressive Movement. His political ideology was more advanced than is suggested by the term *Confederate Brigadier* that has been applied indiscriminately to him and his southern colleagues.

I had the extreme good fortune to profit from the advice of the late beloved Professor Allan Nevins, who, upon learning that I had access to the Maxey Papers and intended to write a biography, wrote me on March 4, 1969: "We badly need more light both on Confederate history, and on Congress during the Reconstruction, and the Grant-Garfield-Cleveland periods. You will be in a position to furnish it."

Urging me to make my story as human as possible and to paint good description scenes, he added, "A good biography which quotes vivid and interesting letters at length is always valuable." I have fallen short of Professor Nevins's admonitions but I have done my best.

Louise Horton

ACKNOWLEDGMENTS

I am happy to have this opportunity to thank Dr. Frank E. Vandiver for reading my manuscript and for offering advice and encouragement. I am grateful for the generous help and encouragement of the late beloved Allan Nevins.

I accept, with gratitude, the aid given me by Dr. Alwyn Barr. I thank Robert Moore Hill, Jr., my coworker, without whose assistance this book could never have emerged from its infancy.

I am indebted to the Maxey descendants—to the late Mrs. Sam M. Stone of Paris, Texas, donor of the Maxey Papers to the Texas State Library, and to Mr. Will H. Lightfoot of Paris, Texas, donor of the Lightfoot Family Papers to the Texas State Library. I wish to thank also Mr. Eugene Bray, curator of the Maxey Museum, Paris, who generously gave me all his research data for his intended biography of Maxey and who answered my many questions about the Maxey family.

To Dr. James M. Day and Mrs. Fischer Osburn, formerly of the Archives, Texas State Library, I owe a large debt of gratitude, for they first made me aware of the existence of the Maxey Papers and encouraged me to use them. I wish to thank Charles Corkran, who, while director of the Archives, Texas State Library, allowed me to arrange the Maxey Papers and to publish, under the auspices of the Texas State Library, an inventory of them. I thank John Kinney, present director of the Archives Division, and Ann Graves, director of the Reference and Loan Division. I could not have finished my research without the special help of the entire staff of the Archives, the Reference and Loan, and the Federal Documents divisions of the Texas State

Library. I thank also Sherry Hill, James Redell, Marilyn Von Kohl, Linda McWhorter, Melinda Wickman, and Elaine Schoenfeld.

Archivists Marie E. Keene (Thomas Gilcrease Institute of American History and Art, Tulsa, Oklahoma) and Chester Kielman (The University of Texas Library, Austin) were helpful, as were the staffs of the National Archives and the Library of Congress, especially Oliver H. Orr, Jr., and Robert H. Land. Chief Stanley P. Tozeski of the United States Military Academy at West Point, New York, supplied me with helpful interpretations of Maxey's performance as a cadet. I received generous help also from the following libraries: Ohio Historical Society, Western Reserve Historical Society, Mississippi State Archives, University of North Carolina, Duke University, West Virginia University, University of Georgia, University of the South and the Rutherford B. Hayes Library.

Last, but not least, I wish to thank my husband, Claude, who has been kind, helpful, polite, a good listener, and a reader of Maxey for the past four years.

Samuel Bell Maxey

1. The Kentuckian : Home in the Pennyrile

Harry Clay of old Kentucky
The industrious workman's friend,
He would exalt his low condition;
Protect his labor and defend
Him 'gainst all foreign competition.
Whig Song, 1842[1]

SAMUEL BELL MAXEY stood head and shoulders above any other congressman from Texas during the years from 1875 to 1887. An emigrant from Kentucky, he had practised law in North Texas, raised a regiment at the begnning of the Civil War, returned to Texas from 1863 to 1865, to defend the Indian Territory, and was elected on his first candidacy to be the first Democratic senator from Texas after the Civil War. After two years of office he became Texas's senior senator and held that position until replaced by John H. Reagan in 1887. Maxey's term of office spanned the turbulent period immediately following Reconstruction. White Southern Democrats were regaining power in the South but a great deal of Maxey's influence derived from his moderation. He was concerned that the Civil War remain ended and that the breach be healed. He was influential among Republican

[1] Whig Song about Henry Clay, sung to the air of "Roy's Wife of Aldovallock," *Cincinnati Gazette*, reprinted in the *Frankfort Commonwealth*, September 6, 1842.

congressmen from the North and aided substantially in Texas's regaining its full and equal participation as a state in the Union.

A lean, tall man with high cheek bones, a Roman nose, clear blue eyes, and sandy hair, Maxey was affable and genial with his fellow senators.[2] He bore himself with the military erectness acquired in his youthful days at West Point; nevertheless, he suggested the clergyman rather than the soldier, an impression that was reinforced by a certain dignity of speech he maintained on all occasions.[3] When he talked he spoke earnestly, emphatically, and at great length.

Maxey's parents were products of the western frontier, both having sprung from similar middle-class Virginia families newly transplanted to Kentucky. The Maxeys claimed descent from French Huguenots who had fled Maxcy, a small village south of Paris. The Bells, his maternal ancestors, were from Ireland. In America each generation of the family had striven for property ownership and for recognition as people of worth.

Radford Maxey, the first of Samuel Bell Maxey's ancestors born in the New World, became a tobacco planter of Dan River, Halifax County, Virginia.[4] It appears that he had some knowledge of bookkeeping, for he kept the accounts of John Randolph. He also served as a justice of the peace in Halifax County. After the Revolutionary War many of Radford Maxey's Virginia neighbors dreamt of greater prosperity farther west. William Wirt, a writer and lawyer who became attorney general of the United Stattes in 1817, remarked that "in the soil of Kentucky everything flourishes with rapidity."[5] He marveled that land was so cheap and fertile and that a new settler had so many choices of a way of life. Said Wirt, "He may farm it on his own country seat, or dash away, when his health will authorize it, in

[2] *New York World*, April 14, 1880, newsclipping, Maxey Papers, Archives Division, Texas State Library. Unless otherwise stated, all Maxey Papers referred to are in the Archives Division, Texas State Library.

[3] *Street's Monthly*, August 20, 1880, newsclipping, Maxey Papers.

[4] Maxey to William Storm, November 25, 1874, Maxey Papers; James Ray Andrews, *Genealogy of the Andrews-Maxey and Related Families*, p. 71; Eugene Bray, "Historical and Genealogical Notes on the Maxey Family," pp. 1–111.

[5] William Wirt to Dabney Carr, February 13, 1803, in J. P. Kennedy, *Memoirs of the Life of William Wirt*, p. 94.

the circles of the gay, or float his commercial speculations down the Mississippi River."[6] It was in Kentucky that Radford Maxey's son, William, took up the land grant that had been given to him in payment for his services in the Revolutionary War. In 1788, he settled on five hundred acres at Turkey Neck Bend on the Cumberland River in Lincoln County, Kentucky.[7]

William Maxey chose to "farm it on his own country seat." Worked by a handful of slaves, the gently rolling land of green grass, trees, and plenty of water yielded an abundance of corn, wheat, and tobacco, and Maxey soon prospered. He built a house in imitation of a respectable plantation house of Virginia. He engaged an itinerant cabinetmaker to use the cherry wood of the forest to make corner cabinets, blanket and sugar chests, tables, ladderback chairs, and four-poster beds.[8]

William Maxey apprenticed two of his sons, Radford and Rice, to Christopher C. Tompkins, a practicing attorney and chancery clerk of Barren County. By 1820 both sons had been admitted to the Kentucky State Bar. Rice Maxey accepted the post of county clerk in the newly established Monroe County, where he also conducted a private law practice. He chose as his wife Lucetta Pope Bell, the daughter of wealthy Samuel Bell of Barren County.[9] Bell, a former landowner in Culpeper County, Virginia, was the son-in-law of Nathaniel Pope.

Though the first Lucetta Pope, Samuel Bell's wife, had inherited very little of the wealth of her father, Nathaniel Pope, she had the manners and attitudes of the upperclass Virginian and passed them on to her daughters. That she was unusually proud of her name is shown by the fact that she gave both of her daughters the middle name Pope. She had met many of the affluent and political figures of Virginia, including her husband, Samuel Bell, in her father's home. She mingled with such people also in the homes of her brothers—Colonel Nathaniel Pope of Richmond (so favorably mentioned by William Wirt in

[6] Ibid.

[7] Willard Rouse Jillson, *Kentucky Land Grants*, pp. 22, 146; Franklin Gorin, *The Times of Long Ago*, p. 20.

[8] Mary Ida Williams, *Living in Kentucky*, p. 10.

[9] Andrews, *Andrews-Maxey and Related Families*, p. 71.

his life of Patrick Henry), and William Pope of Powhatan County, a brilliant jurist well known to all Virginians.[10] Upon their marriage, Samuel and Lucetta had established a home on Shockoe Hill in Richmond, but in 1800 they moved to Kentucky, settling in Barren County. Here Lucetta often visited her sister, the wife of Christopher Greenup, governor of Kentucky.

Lucetta Pope Bell Maxey (Samuel and Lucetta's daughter) was six years older than her husband, but this was not uncommon in frontier Kentucky, where the scarcity of eligible young men made it difficult to make a match. Rice and Lucetta were married on October 9, 1821.[11] Four children were born to them in quick succession, Samuel Bell Maxey, born March 30, 1825, being the third. Their household had the flavor of the typical upper-class Kentuckian. There were servants to do the menial tasks and leave the young wife time to devote to her children. Lucetta Maxey had been born in Richmond and had attended a young ladies' school, where, in addition to learning needlework and manners, she had read literature. She had a good memory and loved Byron and Campbell and could quote page after page from their works.[12] It may have been through her relatives, the Greenups, and Thomas Bell Monroe of Frankfort, an attorney, that Rice Maxey became acquainted with men like Henry Clay, Robert Wickliffe, John Crittenden, Thomas Marshall, and others of the Bluegrass region who were prominent in politics and law.[13] The Rice Maxey domicile was less than twenty miles from that of Lucetta's parents. When young Samuel Bell Maxey, or Sam Bell as he was known throughout his life, visited his grandmother she regaled him with stories of Richmond and life on Shockoe Hill, where her brother Nathaniel and other famous jurists lived, and where she had gone to live as a bride.[14]

[10] Maxey to William Storm, November 25, 1874, Maxey Papers.

[11] Andrews, *Andrews-Maxey and Related Families*, p. 71.

[12] *New York World*, April 14, 1880.

[13] For a discussion of men of the times see Alvin F. Harlow, *Weep No More, My Lady*, pp. 17–67. See also Lewis and Richard H. Collins, *History of Kentucky*, I, 350, 355, 409, 508, 543; II, 193, 303, 351; and the *Frankfort Commonwealth*, November 23, 1841, and March 14, 1843.

[14] For a description of Shockoe Hill see Maxey to Marilda Maxey, August 29, 1861, Lightfoot Family Papers; Ann Randolph to Maxey, May 29, 1895, Maxey Papers; William Pope Dabney to Maxey, May 1, 1882, Maxey Papers.

Albany, Kentucky, is associated closely with Sam Bell Maxey's childhood, for his family settled there in 1834 and this was the home he remembered with deepest affection in later years. A spur of the Cumberland Mountains called Poplar Mountain extended into Clinton County and in its windings produced a beautiful valley within which lay Albany. From the top of Poplar Mountain, some four miles from Albany, one could trace the meandering Cumberland River for miles and also overlook the fertile lands below. Albany was a mere hamlet consisting of a clerk's office over which Rice Maxey presided, a jail, a dry goods and grocery store, two taverns, and a water mill.[15] Here the nine-year-old Sam Bell Maxey formed lasting friendships with the sons of neighboring families. There was Thomas Bramlette, who became governor of Kentucky in 1866, and his brother William Bramlette, who later became a judge in Texas.[16] There was also the orphaned Preston H. Leslie, who came to live in the Maxey home and who, in 1871, became governor of Kentucky, and, Thomas Wooten, son of Kentucky pioneer Joseph Wooten. In later years, after receiving his medical degree from the University of Louisville, Thomas Wooten, moved to Texas to set up his medical practice.[17]

Kentucky in 1825, the year of Sam Bell Maxey's birth, was still a frontier state. It had been admitted to the Union thirty-three years earlier and its first state government had been organized to meet the needs of plantation owners and farmers. Only a generation separated Sam Bell Maxey from Kentucky's first settlers, among whom were his maternal and paternal grandparents. By 1825 Lexington and Frankfort were thriving towns where farmers, planters, hunters, and boatsmen came to purchase supplies and to attend land and slave auctions. Tompkinsville (Sam Bell Maxey's birthplace) and Albany were both more than a hundred miles south of Lexington, but the inhabitants of these villages, numbering some two hundred, kept up with the news of the state and participated in the political action.

Henry Clay held sway in Kentucky politics at that time and the

15 Collins, *History of Kentucky*, II, 145.

16 Ibid., p. 387; *Nashville Banner*, August 17, 1895, newsclipping, Maxey Papers.

17 *Nashville Banner*, August 17, 1895; Walter P. Webb and H. Bailey Carroll (eds.), *Handbook of Texas*, II, 934.

Whigs, of whom Clay was the foremost member, were active in developing a kind of frontier democracy. Clay had been appointed secretary of state under President John Quincy Adams, an honor that pleased most Kentuckians, although some opposed Adams's administration because they disliked New England and the old Republican party. The Whigs, including William Maxey and his sons, Radford and Rice, remained supporters of Clay and Adams. When the Democratic convention met in Frankfort in 1827, the Maxeys were effective in voting to send their Clay-supporting friends Christopher Tompkins and Joseph R. Underwood to Frankfort to represent the first electoral district.[18]

Radford Maxey, who had married the daughter of Governor John Adair of Kentucky, was elected in 1832 to the Kentucky legislature. At this time a cleavage took place between the Bluegrass Region and the Pennyrile, the less developed and exclusively farming south country where the Maxeys lived. (The Pennyrile Region took its name from a wild plant that grows throughout the south region of Kentucky.) The Lexingtonians of the Bluegrass Region were particularly disdainful of the homespun Pennyrile legislators, and when he attended the annual gathering at the state capitol, Radford Maxey had much to contend with from their arrogance. Soon, however, he joined forces with the two jurists Christopher Tompkins and Joseph Underwood.

Genial Rice Maxey became a prominent figure in Clinton County. He spoke before political groups and engaged in civic activities. The more prosperous farmers of the area had belonged in 1825 to the Anti-relief party, whose members were against the suspension of specie payments in the banks of Kentucky. When, in 1841, they wanted to establish a branch of the Bank of Kentucky in their own southern area, they chose Rice Maxey to present their resolution to his personal friend, the popular Whig Governor Robert P. Letcher.[19] Young Sam Bell became acquainted with Henry Clay, Robert Letcher, William and Bryan Owsley, and Charles Semple. Lucetta Maxey received with decorum and courtesy the distinguished Kentuckians her husband brought into their home.

---

[18] Collins, *History of Kentucky*, II, 771.
[19] *Frankfort Commonwealth*, December 21, 1841.

Sam Bell read the books contained in his father's modest library, and later he and his brother, William Henry, studied Latin and mathematics from a private tutor. In September, 1842, U.S. Senator Bryan Y. Owsley of Kentucky obtained an appointment for Sam Bell as a cadet at the U.S. Military Academy at West Point. Owsley had been so impressed by the letter he received from the seventeen-year-old Sam Bell stating his reasons for wishing to be a cadet that he forwarded the letter to Secretary of War J. C. Spencer with a note saying, "The letter speaks for itself and if any information be desired as to his [Sam Bell's] moral character I will most cheerfully give it."[20]

[20] Bryan Y. Owsley to J. C. Spencer, February 17 and February 21, 1842, Adjutant General's Office Records, National Archives, Record Group 94. Hereafter records in National Archives are indicated by the symbol NA followed by Record Group (RG) number.

2. Stonewall's Roommate

No man who was in that column will ever forget that narrow inverted crescent which connected the snowcapped mountains of Popocatepetl and Ixtaccihuatl, and the magnificent sight which burst upon his vision when he reached the summit of that ridge.[1]

Maxey proceeded to the Military Academy at West Point after making the customary call upon President John Tyler in Washington to thank him for the appointment. He passed the required oral and written examinations and was assigned to barracks. On March 13, 1843, after eight months of cadet training, he wrote his elder brother, William Henry, that he was becoming accustomed to the cadet life and was beginning to like it so well that he might stay in the army after graduation. "If a war breaks out between our nation and any other about 1844, I will most surely remain in the Army as I would then have the double opportunity of serving my country and being promoted," wrote Maxey, adding that if these plans did not suit his parents he would change them and study law.[2]

Throughout his four years at West Point, Maxey ranked near the

[1] Address of S. B. Maxey, in *Annual Meeting of the Soldiers of the Mexican War of the State of Texas, May 8, 1875*, p. 19, printed pamphlet, Maxey Papers.

[2] Samuel Bell Maxey to William Henry Maxey, March 13, 1843, Lightfoot Family Papers.

bottom of his class in nearly all his subjects. Perhaps the carefree attitudes of the Kentucky frontiersman persisted in him and kept him in the lower quarter of the class in general merit and conduct. He enjoyed the association of his classmates and participated in their extracurricular activities. His account book for 1844 lists fines for damaging public property in the mess hall, a purchase of dancing shoes, and a fee for dancing class in June and July of 1845. As for his studies, he lacked mathematical skill and did poorly in engineering, artillery, and infantry tactics. He did little better in philosophy, ethics, chemistry, mineralogy, geology, and drawing.[3] But he grew to like the dress parades and the guard mountings and was later to put great emphasis on this form of pomp and ceremony with his own troops during the Civil War. And he had the necessary flair for languages. He was able to read the French textbooks on artillery and infantry tactics, and later in Mexico he was to learn to speak and write Spanish.

Many of Maxey's classmates were destined to play conspicuous parts in their country's history: Ulysses S. Grant, Winfield S. Hancock, George Pickett, Edmund Kirby Smith, Barnard E. Bee, Dabney H. Maury, Fitz-John Porter, Earl Van Dorn, James Longstreet, Ambrose Burnside, and Cadmus M. Wilcox. During one of his West Point years, Maxey was the roommate of Stonewall Jackson.[4] A story has been handed down in the Maxey family that Cadet Maxey, who loathed rising before nine, actually asked the incorruptible Jackson to answer early morning roll call for him.[5] Jackson's reply is not recorded by Maxey heirs. Pennsylvanian Winfield S. Hancock was kind to lower classman Maxey, and Maxey described him as a "manly openhearted fellow."[6] When in later years some of Maxey's less noted

[3] Official Register of the Officers and Cadets of the U.S.M.A., West Point, academic years 1842 through 1846; Maxey's West Point Account Book, Maxey Papers; George W. Cullom, *Biographical Register of the Officers and Graduates of the United States Military Academy at West Point*, II, 304.

[4] Maxey to Marilda Maxey, July 11, 1862, Lightfoot Papers.

[5] Alice Stone to Mary Osburn, August 12, 1968. Mrs. Stone, an heir to the Maxey estate, states that Mrs. Sam Bell Long had told her of a favorite story that had been related by Maxey himself. This was the tale of how, allegedly, Stonewall Jackson answered roll call for Maxey, for, said Maxey: "I always liked to sleep. Indeed, I still feel that no gentleman transacts business before nine o'clock."

[6] Maxey to Marilda Maxey, November 30, 1875, Maxey Papers.

classmates called on him in Washington, he received them graciously, and if they had a favor to ask of him, he did his best to grant it.

When Maxey graduated in 1846 his low class standing consigned him to the infantry, an unpopular branch of the service. He was commissioned as a brevet second lieutenant and assigned to the Seventh Infantry Regiment.[7]

News of the American victories in Mexico in early 1846 had excited Maxey's class. On a three-month furlough after graduation, Maxey returned home to Albany, Kentucky. Here he learned that his brother, William Henry, had been admitted to the Kentucky State Bar in January, but that, enticed by talk of the war in Mexico, he had later volunteered for the Second Regiment of the Kentucky Volunteer Infantry. Distressed that both sons were about to depart, Rice Maxey had persuaded William Henry to remain at home temporarily. But, on May 6, 1847, the brother was fatally shot in New Orleans while on his way to Mexico to fight.[8]

In October, 1846, three weks after his furlough had ended, Maxey joined the Seventh Infantry Regiment quartered in the main plaza of Monterrey, Mexico. He remained with that regiment without a day's absence until the capture of Mexico City.[9] It was a grand experience for the twenty-two–year–old Maxey. His first taste of glory and excitement came when he helped to storm the heights of Cerro Gordo where Santa Anna waited with six thousand men. As the Americans spread out in battle line to attack Contreras, the gateway to the Valley of Mexico, Maxey was ordered to take his command of new recruits and to hold back the enemy cavalry that were threatening to break the line at one point. He skirmished with the enemy so successfully that he was commended by his superiors for his steady firmness with his troops, and the next day he and his company formed a part of the advance line.[10] They scaled the fortress under a murderous fire of

[7] Returns of the Regular Army, Seventh Infantry, September, 1846, NA, RG 391.

[8] Rice Maxey to E. D. Townsend, June 8, 1848, Adjutant General's Office Records, NA, RG 94.

[9] S. B. Maxey, *Address to the Annual Meeting of the Soldiers of the Mexican War of the State of Texas*; U.S. Congress, Senate, *Congressional Record*, Maxey speech, June 1, 1882.

[10] Justin H. Smith, *The War with Mexico*, II, 17, 25; Returns of the Regular

grapeshot and canister and captured Contreras. Maxey was commended again for his valor and was made a brevet first lieutenant.[11] He participated in the battles of Churubusco and Molino del Rey and later was placed in command of one of the five select companies that formed a city police guard in Mexico City. On June 6, 1848, Maxey left Mexico City for Jefferson Barracks, Missouri. The Seventh Infantry was scheduled to depart to Florida in August, 1849, but peacetime service in the army did not appeal to Maxey and he resigned.[12]

Twelve years elapsed from the date of this resignation from the regular army until his appointment in 1861 as a colonel in the Confederate army. During the interim he obtained his license to practice law, married, and moved to Texas, where he established a thriving law practice. Upon his departure from Jefferson Barracks on September 17, 1849, Maxey returned to his parents' home in Clinton County and soon entered, as a Whig, the race for the Kentucky House of Representatives. He outpolled his opponent in Clinton County but lost in the more populated counties.[13] He studied law under the tutelage of his father and, in April, 1851, joined his father's law firm, whose other members were Samuel Long and J. D. Wright.[14] In 1852 he was elected clerk of the circuit and county courts of Clinton County, and from 1852 to 1856 he practiced law in the adjoining counties of Kentucky and Tennessee.[15]

On June 19, 1853, Maxey married Marilda Cass Denton, the untutored daughter of George N. Denton, a poor farmer in Clinton County. Marilda's grandfather was a Kentucky Baptist preacher, well known in southern Kentucky for his fiery sermons.[16] The marriage

---

Army, Seventh Infantry, February, 1847, NA, RG 391; Frank E. Vandiver, *Mighty Stonewall*, p. 23; U.S. Congress, *Senate Executive Document* 1, 30th Cong., 1st sess., Report of J. Plympton, April 20, 1847, pp. 285–287.

[11] *Senate Executive Documents*, 30th Cong., 1st sess., Report of J. Plympton, August 22, 1847, and Report of B. Riley, August 24, 1847, pp. 88, 99.

[12] Returns of the Regular Army, Seventh Infantry, October, 1846, through September, 1849, NA, RG 391.

[13] *Frankfort Commonwealth*, August 20, 1850.

[14] Legal correspondence and legal accounts, 1854, 1855, Maxey Papers.

[15] Maxey to George Cullom, January 11, 1860, U.S.M.A., Historical File.

[16] J. D. Goodpasture of Livingston, Tennessee, wrote in the *Nashville Banner*, August 17, 1895, about the recently deceased Maxey. He recalled that he and Maxey

made no change in the business arrangement between Sam Bell and
his father, but despite the care and attention given to it, the law firm
did not thrive. There was little litigation in southern Kentucky and
the business of acting as bill collector paid small dividends.

The Maxey family had read with interest the glowing accounts of
life in Texas as described by their kinsman Varney Andrews, who had
settled in Fannin County some years earlier. They decided to post a
G.T.T. (Gone to Texas) notice on their Clinton County residence.
Though the slavery question was the most discussed subject in Kentucky, it seemingly had little, if anything, to do with the Maxeys'
move to Texas. Correspondence and records give some evidence that
their decision to come to Texas was primarily a result of their economic status.[17]

A strong wagon was made ready for the journey they would make
down through Arkansas, across the southeastern tip of the Indian Territory, and into the Red River valley of northeast Texas.[18] The travel-
ers reached Texas in October, 1857, and purchased five acres of prairie land south of the settlement of Paris. The fertile area of Lamar
County lay on the divide between the Red and Sulphur rivers. Paris
was situated on the margin of an extensive prairie, on the highest
ridge of land lying between the forks of the Sulphur and the middle
portion of the Red River. Here Rice and Sam Bell rented an office
from W. H. Milwee at five dollars per month, bought four common
chairs, one bucket and dipper, one broom, some sand and ink, a pair
of andirons, and then hung out their shingle advertising that they
were ready to practice law.[19] They engaged Charles DeMorse to print
legal cards for them and advertised in the *Clarksville Northern Standard* that S. B. Maxey was a commissioner of deeds for Virginia, Ken-

---

had both been in love with Henrietta Goodall of Clinton County and that she had
turned down Maxey's offer of marriage in 1850. For a description of Marilda Denton, see Henry Lightfoot, *In Memoriam of General Samuel B. Maxey.*

[17] Legal file and personal financial file, Rice and S. B. Maxey, 1855, Maxey Papers.

[18] Maxey to Marilda Maxey, May 19, 1884, Maxey Papers. The Maxeys, in 1857,
had left Kentucky and passed through Tahlequah, Indian Territory, near Fort Gibson,
then southward to Paris, Texas.

[19] Rice and S. B. Maxey Account Book, January 1, 1858, Maxey Papers.

tucky, Tennessee, Alabama, Arkansas, and Missouri. The Maxeys had a number of competitors—the legal notices of Epperson and Sims, Clarksville; C. C. Binkley, Sherman; Johnson, Williams, and Townes, Paris; Mills and Mills, Paris; Dillahunty annd Wright, Paris; John C. Easton, McKinney; and others also appeared in the *Standard*.[20]

Soon the Maxeys found it expedient to build their own office building. By May, 1860, when they moved into it, their law practice extended over several counties—Mount Pleasant, Clarksville, Bonham, Greenville, wherever state docket cases were tried. Too poor to buy a carriage for travel, Maxey mounted his mare named Prentice and traveled the circuit. A backache acquired from long marches in Mexico gave him so much trouble that he cheerfully accepted rides in the carriages of more affluent lawyers like Ben H. Epperson.[21] Rice Maxey remained in Paris, kept abreast of the local law business, and helped his daughter-in-law in the very important and immediate task of directing the slaves in tilling the five acres and in raising the fruit, vegetables, and animals.

In 1858, Sam Bell was appointed district attorney for Lamar County to fill out a vacancy.[22] He was reelected to the office in 1859 and again in 1860.[23] Though the job paid little, it placed his name before the public and furthered his plan to enter the race for a seat in the Texas Senate. He was elected to the Texas Senate in the summer of 1861, but in the interim there had occurred a number of important events that profoundly affected the nation and also changed Maxey's immediate goals.

In April and May of 1860, there were the national question of states' rights and the selection of the Democratic presidential nominee. In June, problems in Texas demanded Maxey's attention. Drouth and high temperatures across the state had caused crop failures, and people applied to the Texas Legislature for relief. During the sum-

---

[20] Item for May 28, 1859, ibid; *Clarksville Northern Standard*, March 3, 1860.

[21] Maxey to Marilda Maxey, April 28, 1859, and October 11, 1860, Maxey Papers.

[22] Maxey to George Cullom, January 11, 1860, U.S.M.A., Historical File.

[23] Maxey announced for reelection in the *Clarksville Northern Standard*, April 28, 1860.

mer there were reported rumors of incendiarism and poisoning throughout the state, the evil doings attributed to slave insurrections.[24] In September, overcome by all the rumors of expected violence and upset by a tiff with her husband and her indomitable mother-in-law, the homesick and childless Marilda returned to her kin in Clinton County. Sam Bell wrote her conciliatory letters and added a message which he hoped she would deliver to his friends. "Tell them," Maxey said, "that I am doing better than I ever did in my life, and getting big fees and as much business as I can attend to, all of which you know is true."[25] A week later he wrote the recalcitrant Marilda that "Mother talks about you all the time, I believe. She wants you to come back as soon as you get your brood out," and that "Mother says she is thinking of you all the time. She saw one of your dresses in the closet today, said it looked just like you and turned it all over every way."[26] Apparently the misunderstanding had to do with Marilda's right as head-mistress of the household to spend money and with Maxey's resolve to run for the Texas Senate in 1861. Maxey assured Marilda that he had settled down into a quiet, thirty-five–year–old citizen and liked home pleasure, and that all he wanted was to "make enough to have a snug little home with a snug little woman now in Kentucky to put into it and a sufficiency of property and money to live on out of debt and comfortable." He offered to come to Kentucky to take her to Louisville and Frankfort if she was not "tired" of his "sort."[27]

In November, as hysteria mounted daily and the cries of sectionalism brought the disruption of the Union nearer, Maxey agonized over the coming presidential election. The split in the Democratic party had resulted in two presidential candidates: Stephen A. Douglas for the Northern Democrats and John C. Breckinridge for the Southern Democrats. The Constitutional Union convention at Baltimore had further complicated the Southern choice by nominating John Bell of Tennessee. With so many choices, and in addition Abraham Lincoln,

[24] Ralph A. Wooster, *The Secession Conventions of the South*, p. 123; Ben H. Procter, *Not without Honor*, pp. 118–119.

[25] Maxey to Marilda Maxey, October 11, 1860, Lightfoot Papers.

[26] Ibid., October 17, 1860.

[27] Maxey to Marilda Maxey, October 22, 1860, Maxey Papers, Thomas Gilcrease Institute of American History and Art.

the Republican presidential candidate, would not the American votes be so scattered as to assure no candidate a victory?[28] Maxey cast his vote on November 6 for Breckinridge.[29]

When Marilda finally wrote that she would be content to come home if Maxey came to get her, he made the trip to Kentucky. He arrived during the lull after the dissension over the election. Bell had won out in Kentucky over Breckinridge by some 13,000 votes, and over Douglas by 11,000 votes; Lincoln trailed them all with a total tally of 1,366. Though there was a strong Union feeling among many of the people, the Democratic party had split between Douglas and Breckinridge.

Maxey wrote his father on November 27, 1860, "Times are exceeding hard. Negroes are at least 30 percent lower than they were four months ago. I have authorized [Preston] Leslie to hunt me up a likely girl and buy her if he can get her on fair figures."[30] Maxey had refused the request of one of the Bell's former slaves who wanted him to purchase her and her children. "I don't feel able to buy them all," Maxey wrote his father. As Sam Bell and Marilda visited friends they must have emphasized the attractive aspects of Texas, for by the time they arrived in Louisville to start homeward, they had arranged to meet two physicians, one being Maxey's nephew, Alfred Maxey, who wished to accompany them back to Texas. Aunt Sarah Maxey, who in later years loaned over $4,000 to Sam Bell, also became part of the Maxey entourage. They boarded a boat for New Orleans and then transferred to a steamer for the trip up the Red River to Jefferson, Texas.

Upon returning to Texas, Maxey learned that Governor Sam Houston had called a special session of the legislature to meet on January 21, 1861. One week later, at a secession convention held at Austin, a resolution was adopted that Texas secede from the Union. Lamar County delegates to the convention voted against the resolution.[31] In

[28] Gerald Mortimer Capers, *Stephen A. Douglas*, ed. Oscar Handlin, p. 205; Joseph Howard Parks, *John Bell of Tennessee*, pp. 351–352; Llerena B. Friend, *Sam Houston*, pp. 315–316; Procter, *Not without Honor*, p. 118, n. 81.

[29] *New York Weekly World*, April 14, 1880.

[30] Maxey to Rice Maxey, November 27, 1860, Lightfoot Papers.

[31] E. W. Winkler (ed.), *Journal of the Secession Convention*, p. 49.

a popular referendum on the secession ordinance, the Lamar County vote was 553 for, and 663 against secession, thus making it one of the fourteen counties in the state that gave a majority against the proposed action.[32] No extant Maxey correspondence has come to light showing Maxey's personal views of the issues dividing the nation in 1860, nor does there exist (to this writer's knowledge) any record of his opinion about the Lamar County votes against secession. But, from his actions it seems safe to assume that he retained some of his old feeling about the fame and fortune to be gained from a military career if war should come, and, in his own mind, he balanced that kind of future against the successful political career that he was also considering.

Although a majority of them had voted against secession, Lamar County citizens, Maxey among them, now prepared to do their part for the new Confederacy. Maxey wholeheartedly approved of the action of Lamar County officials when they appropriated $4,000 from county funds for the purchase of arms for Lamar County troops.[33] In May he organized a troop from the county to accompany W. C. Young and his Texas Cavalry across the Red River into the Indian Territory to lay claim, in the name of the Confederacy, to the recently abandoned U.S. Forts Arbuckle, Cobb, and Washita.[34] The venturesome Texans, under Young's leadership, pursued so closely the retreating federal troops that a sudden reverse movement enabled the federals to capture a few Texans, without bloodshed. They were held overnight, but after a conference the federal officers released them. The federals went on to Fort Leavenworth, Kansas, and the Texans occupied the Indian Territory forts.[35]

Maxey had his first encounter with Albert Pike, whom President Jefferson Davis had sent as a Confederate commissioner to negotiate

[32] Lamar County Election Returns, in Texas, *Records of the Secretary of State*, Secession Convention, 1861.

[33] A. W. Neville, *The History of Lamar County*, p. 111.

[34] Will of S. B. Maxey, May 3, 1861, Lightfoot Papers; Maxey to Marilda Maxey, May 8, 1861, Maxey Papers.

[35] Muriel H. Wright and LeRoy Fischer, "Civil War Sites," *Chronicles of Oklahoma* 44 (1966): 175, 176.

alliances with the Five Civilized Tribes of the Indian Territory.[36] A council of war, attended by whites and Indians, was held at Fort Arbuckle on May 7.[37] Among the whites who spoke to urge the Indians to join the secessionist cause was Maxey. He argued that the governor of Texas had the constitutional right to order Texas soldiers north of the Red River to repel federal invasion provided the Indians consented.[38]

Upon his return to Paris, Maxey completed the official organization of the hastily recruited company he had led into the Indian Territory and was officially elected its captain. Now dismounted, the company, called the Lamar Rifles, drilled daily behind an old brickyard north of Paris. They marched to the beat of a drum, with Maxey on a sorrel horse at their head. William H. H. Long, post-bellum law partner of Maxey, was orderly sergeant of the company. As summer approached, the company went into encampment in a field on the outskirts of the town, until sickness broke out and some of the infantry men died.[39] In June, George Wright, the founder of Paris, returned from New Orleans where he had purchased arms (mainly Hall's carbines and Mississippi rifles) and powder with the $4,000 appropriated from Lamar County funds.[40]

The Democratic state convention planned for April, 1861, in Dallas had not met, for, as the *Northern Standard* said, "to such a pitch has the public mind excited [*sic*] for the past three months that scarce a thought has been given to this convention, and the result is that no primary meetings have been held nor delegates appointed."[41] On June 8, the last day of the legislative session in Austin, the Democratic convention was called by a small squad of Austin officials. Naturally representation was meagre, but Maxey managed to get his name placed on the ballot as a candidate for a seat in the Texas Senate. By July he was campaigning in Tarrant and Sulphur Springs in Hopkins

[36] Albert Pike, *Report of Albert Pike on Mission to the Indian Nations*, reprint ed., p. 7.
[37] Maxey to Marilda Maxey, May 8, 1861, Maxey Papers.
[38] Maxey to Henry McCulloch, June 8, 1864, Letterbook A, Maxey Papers.
[39] Neville, *Lamar County*, p. 117.
[40] *Clarksville Northern Standard*, June 1, 1861.
[41] Ibid., May 4, 1861.

County, sister county to Lamar. He reported the crowds as fair in
number.[42] The election was held in August, but the news of General
P. G. T. Beauregard's victory at Bull Run on July 18 and 21 so over-
shadowed everything else at that time that many weeks passed before
the election results were made known.[43] The *State Gazette* complained
that "very many papers in the state, published a week after the election very complacently inform us that 'the election passed off quietly'
but that they 'have not yet learned how the county voted.' " When on
September 14 the *Gazette* finally published a list of those who would
be newcomers in the Senate when it met on November 4, Maxey's
name was included as senator representing Lamar and Hopkins counties.[44] But when the Ninth Legislature met in November, Maxey was
not present. By February, 1862, his father, Rice Maxey, had been
elected to the Texas Senate in his place.[45]

Maxey had made other plans. On August 19, he had left Paris for
Richmond, hoping to obtain permission from President Davis to form
a Texas regiment. He journeyed from Shreveport to Vicksburg and
on to Knoxville. As he neared Richmond he wrote, "I have never seen
the amount of military excitement that has been exhibited all the
way from Vicksburg to this place. The cars have been crowded with
troops for Virginia and the roads lined with them. Whenever the
train passed an encampment, cheers were given the troops inside answered by those on the cars. . . . I don't know that you can read this—
a bad pen and a crowd all round."[46] The trip was very tiring for
Maxey, who suffered from chills and fever during the journey. He
purchased newspapers at every large city where the train stopped,
avidly read the war news, and then mailed the newspapers back to his
family in Paris with the admonition that after they had read them
they should pass them on to J. D. Crooks, editor of the Paris newspaper.

[42] Maxey to Marilda Maxey, July 9, 1861, Maxey Papers.
[43] *Clarksville Northern Standard*, August 3, 10, 17, 1861.
[44] *State Gazette*, September 14, 1861.
[45] Neville, *Lamar County*, p. 120.
[46] Maxey to Marilda Maxey, August 24, 1861, Lightfoot Papers.

On the train to Richmond he visited with Simon B. Buckner, an old acquaintance from West Point; George W. Johnson, soon to be elected provisional governor of Kentucky; Thomas Clay, son of Henry Clay, Jr.; and Professor George W. Bayless of Louisville, all of whom were going to Richmond to offer their services to the Confederacy. Upon his arrival in Richmond, Maxey, armed with credentials from Texas lawyer Samuel A. Roberts (a West Point classmate of Jefferson Davis) and from Postmaster General John H. Reagan, attempted to call on President Davis. Unfortunately, Davis was ill and could not receive visitors. On August 29, Maxey submitted to L. P. Walker, Confederate secretary of war, a letter in which he requested permission to "raise a regiment of cavalry (or mounted men) in northern Texas to serve for a space of twelve months" and gave the names of Senator W. S. Oldham, General T. N. Waul, William B. Ochiltree, and John Gregg as persons who could vouch for his standing in Texas.[47] He was disappointed that he had not been able to add the name of Louis Wigfall to the list, but ex-Senator Wigfall, helpful aide of P. G. T. Beauregard during the bombardment at Fort Sumter, now commanded a Texas brigade and had left Richmond for Manassas.[48]

Maxey would have liked to go to Manassas but learned that the generals in charge had found it necessary to prohibit any nonarmy person from crossing the lines. It was difficult to ascertain the future plans for army movements because, as Maxey wrote Marilda, "Generals Lee, Beauregard, and Johnston keep their counsels to themselves as they ought to."[49]

Maxey visited Reagan, who advised him that the authority to raise a regiment would more likely be forthcoming if he could arm and equip his men. Reagan explained that the government was not prepared to furnish arms.[50] At the end of August, Maxey, accompanied by Senator W. S. Oldham, had an interview with Secretary of War

[47] Maxey to L. P. Walker, August 29, 1861, Maxey Papers, Gilcrease Institute.
[48] Robert Underwood Johnson and Clarence Clough Buel (eds.), *Battles and Leaders of the Civil War*, I, 72–73, 78–79, 83.
[49] Maxey to Marilda Maxey, August 27, 1861, Lightfoot Papers.
[50] Ibid., August 31, 1861.

Walker who expressed the opinion that no more troops ought to leave Texas except to repel invasion. William Ochiltree, a member of the Provisional Congress of the Confederacy, had recently received the same admonition when given permission to return to Texas to raise a regiment. Congress sat in closed-door sessions, which made it difficult for Maxey to enlist the aid of members of the Texas delegation, but he visited them after the daily sessions and was received with marked courtesy by each of them, including the great John Hemphill. He was promised that the delegation as a whole would file an endorsement of his application to raise a regiment of infantry. General Waul, who had been detailed to remain in Richmond as a part of a five-man advisory committee to the War Department, also promised to do all he could for Maxey.[51]

On September 3, Maxey wrote Marilda, "I have succeeded in getting authority to raise a Regiment of Infantry to be armed with the double barrel shot gun and common rifle and musket. The Secretary of War in granting the authority is quite complimentary. . . . it seems that the War Department has quite a different opinion of me to some of my special friends."[52] Maxey did not name the special friends (the objecting Paris citizens) but perhaps the politically and financially powerful George W. Wright of Paris had someone else in mind to command the regiment now being formed by Maxey.

Before he left Richmond to return to Texas, Maxey learned of the Confederate fight in western Virginia against the Union forces of General Daniel Tyler.[53] At the same time the Confederates had suffered a reverse at Fort Hatteras when General Butler, with a force of four thousand men and a large naval fleet, captured the fort, twenty pieces of cannon, and several hundred prisoners. It was therefore particularly cheering to learn that the British ship *Alliance* had successfully run the blockade into Port Beaufort, North Carolina, and brought contraband articles much needed for war, including percussion caps and guns. Stephen Tyler, an old acquaintance, invited Maxey

[51] Ibid., August 30, 1861.
[52] Ibid., September 3, 1861.
[53] Johnson and Buel, *Battles and Leaders of the Civil War*, I, 175, 178.

to visit the Ordnance Department in Richmond, where he showed him through the works and gave him a pair of Minié molds.[54]

Back in Texas, Colonel Maxey set to work organizing his regiment and by October 29 he had set up camp at Camp Benjamin, near Paris, with eight companies of infantry, two others being nearly ready.[55] The merchants of the area made every effort to outfit the regiment. Colonel W. C. Young, who had also received permission to form a Texas regiment, returned from Richmond with requisition permits from the quartermaster and commissary department for himself and Maxey. He stopped at Jefferson, Texas, and drew needed groceries, which he shared with Maxey's regiment upon his arrival in Paris.[56] Maxey sent home for his West Point diploma and his certificate of brevet commission in the Mexican War and hung them up in his staff tent.[57] By December he had almost completed the raising of the Ninth Texas Infantry Regiment, which was finally to consist of 1,120 men. On December 18, 1861, he was ordered by General P. O. Hebert, commander of the Department of Texas, to proceed with his regiment to camp at Sim's Bayou near Harrisburg. But Maxey was determined to join General Albert Sidney Johnston, and a telegram to him at Bowling Green, Kentucky, elicited new orders for Maxey. He was to take his regiment to Memphis.[58]

Johnston had placed himself at Bowling Green, the center of his line of defense against the Union armies advancing southward. The

[54] Maxey to Marilda Maxey, August 27, 30, September 3, 1861, Lightfoot Papers. A Minié mold was a mold for making Minié balls to be shot from a muzzle-loading rifle. Designed in 1849 by French Army Captain Minié and quickly adapted by the U.S., the bullet greatly improved small arms fire (Mark Mayo Boatner, *Civil War Dictionary*, III).

[55] *Clarksville Northern Standard*, October 19, 1861. The *Standard* stated, "Colonel Maxey received a communication from the War Department offering him control of the coast defences if his regiment would enlist for the war." See also Maxey's Marching Orders No. 15 from Camp Benjamin Headquarters, December 18, 1861 (signed by S. B. Maxey, Colonel Commanding), Maxey Papers, Gilcrease Institute.

[56] *Clarksville Northern Standard*, October 19, 1861.

[57] Maxey to Marilda Maxey, October 29, 1861, Maxey Papers.

[58] See Marching Orders, December 18, 1861, Maxey Papers, Gilcrease Institute; *Clarksville Northern Standard*, December 21, 1861; Will of S. B. Maxey, January 5, 1862, Lightfoot Papers.

Union plan of campaign in 1862 called for a steady drive toward the Confederate capital at Richmond and, in addition, a push in the west to open the Mississippi River and allow a march through the center of the western area on the way to Richmond. Johnston's line of defense extended from eastern Kentucky through Bowling Green to Columbus, Mississippi.[59] Maxey hoped to join the southern end of that line.

[59] Thomas Lawrence Connelly, *Army of the Heartland*, pp. 65–77.

3. Civil War Years

I would rather you and I were both reposing quietly beneath the green turf of my beautiful Texas with her native flowers and green prairies, than live the taxed slaves of a Northern despot.[1]

MAXEY LEFT CAMP BENJAMIN for Memphis in January, 1862. When some of his men became sick in Arkansas he left them in places where he knew they would receive good care, planning to send back ambulances from Little Rock. The weather was good, and the men, in general, well behaved. Maxey did allow some pressing of provisions when Arkansas residents did not treat the men fairly or did not want to accept a quartermaster receipt for their goods.[2] By January 18 the regiment had marched 199 miles in twelve days. Five days later, on the Saline River about twenty-seven miles from Little Rock, Maxey experienced a taste of the bad luck that was to dog him throughout his military career east of the Mississippi. The weather grew inclement, a heavy rain turned to sleet, and he decided to dismantle his wagons and put them and his men on a train. The load was so heavy that a second engine had to be sent for. Meanwhile Maxey's men waited in open cars. The second engine, when it arrived, was improperly at-

[1] Maxey to Marilda Maxey, February 20, 1862, Lightfoot Family Papers.
[2] Maxey to Marilda Maxey, January 18, 1862, Maxey Papers, Thomas Gilcrease Institute of American History and Art.

tached to the rear of the train so that it came loose when the train moved forward, and then caught up at such a high speed that it rammed the last car. Twelve men were injured and a large number of guns damaged.[3]

Maxey was finally able to take his men by railroad to White River, forty-five miles beyond Little Rock, and then they were forced to walk again. He reached Memphis on February 13, expecting to march north to Bowling Green to help General Johnston hold the line against Grant's push into Mississippi and Tennessee.[4] But at Memphis, Maxey was instructed to wait for new orders, the delay affording him time to rest his men and repair his broken guns.

The Confederate loss of Fort Henry had forced Johnston south of the Tennessee River and endangered the Memphis and Charleston Railroad, which was within eight miles of the river at Iuka, Mississippi. Maxey was ordered from Memphis east to Iuka to protect the railroad, the last means of communication with Nashville and Bowling Green.[5]

In early 1862, Confederate fortunes in the Tennessee-Kentucky-Missouri area were declining. The Union commander of the Department of the Missouri, Henry Halleck, threatened Columbus, Kentucky, and the Tennessee and Cumberland rivers. Capturing Fort Henry on February 7 and Fort Donelson on February 16, he extended the threat to western Tennessee. A Union amphibious force under Grant moved south up the Tennessee River as far as Florence, Alabama, in early February.[6]

Maxey's position at Iuka placed him within range of this Union activity. At 4 A.M. on February 22, he received orders to send his regiment by railway to Florence to protect a bridge threatened by Union gunboats. But later that morning he was informed that the

[3] Maxey to John Adams, February 14, 1862, Maxey Papers, Gilcrease Institute.

[4] Maxey, in his letters to Marilda, spelled General Albert Sidney Johnston's name "Johnson." See Maxey to Marilda Maxey, February 15, 1862, Lightfoot Papers.

[5] Charles P. Roland, *Albert Sidney Johnston*, p. 289; Maxey to Marilda Maxey, February 15, 1862, Lightfoot Papers.

[6] Robert Underwood Johnson and Clarence Clough Buel (eds.), *Battles and Leaders of the Civil War*, I, 368; Thomas Lawrence Connelly, *Army of the Heartland*, pp. 106–107, 120–125; Stephen E. Ambrose, *Halleck*, pp. 23–26, 34–36.

gunboats had passed and that he was not to proceed until he received further orders.[7]

In the west, Halleck's subordinate, General Samuel R. Curtis, drove the Confederates under General Sterling Price from Springfield, Missouri, on February 12, and by the twenty-first had driven them to within thirty miles of Fort Smith, Arkansas.[8] When news of Price's setback reached Maxey and his men at Iuka, they became concerned for the safety of Texas. Maxey and a Captain Dickson journeyed to Richmond with a petition from the Ninth Texas Regiment asking that they be sent to aid in resisting Curtis's threatened invasion of Texas. But when Maxey arrived in Richmond he discovered that he had been nominated by the president and confirmed by the Senate to the rank of brigadier general.[9] At this point his interest in the petition apparently waned—after he reached Richmond his voluminous correspondence with Marilda fails to mention it. Instead, having just ordered a new uniform, he wrote, "I think you have a pretty good looking General for a husband, what do *you* think?"[10]

He was ordered to report to General Albert Sidney Johnston at Decatur, Alabama, and from there was assigned to General John B. Floyd's command at Chattanooga. When he returned to Iuka on March 14 to collect his baggage and bid his men goodbye, he learned that the Ninth Texas Regiment had left to join Beauregard at Corinth, where a battle was expected with Union forces under Halleck and Grant. Maxey's mind was divided. He wrote Marilda on March 14: "I learn from the sick left behind that great anxiety was manifested for me to be with the regt. and shall join them by tomorrow's train if it is not stopped by the flood that has been pouring down since about ten o'clock today, and shall take command of the regt. which I know is their will, and which I have the right to do as I have not formally accepted the brigadiership."[11] But in the same letter he stressed the

---

[7] D. C. Ruggles to J. R. Chalmers, February 20, 1862, U.S., Congress, House, *War of the Rebellion*, VII, 894; Maxey to Marilda Maxey, February 23, 1862, Lightfoot Papers.

[8] Ambrose, *Halleck*, p. 22; Johnson and Buel, *Battles and Leaders*, I, 275.

[9] Maxey to Marilda Maxey, February 26, March 7, 1862, Lightfoot Papers.

[10] Ibid., March 14, 1862.

[11] Ibid.

importance of Chattanooga and outlined his plans for its defense. He chose, fatefully and typically, to accept the brigadiership and the assignment at Chattanooga, where, in a task similar to that he had had at Iuka, he guarded the railroad and the river and helped send supplies to Atlanta. The Ninth Texas Regiment went on to suffer heavy losses at the battle of Shiloh on April 5 and 6—a battle Maxey participated in only by watching General Don Carlos Buell's departure westward to assist Halleck.

Maxey arrived at Chattanooga on March 15 and was placed in charge of the meagre force of 2,300 men left there, the other forces under General Floyd having moved north to guard the Cumberland Gap. Enemy forces threatened Chattanooga from the direction of Nashville, but the arrival of Georgia troops reinforced Maxey and there was no attack. Buell had some 50,000 Union troops at Nashville, but by March 24 it was clear, to Johnston at least, that Buell would reinforce Grant at Pittsburg Landing.[12] Buell was to take with him some 25,000 men.[13]

On April 6 Maxey telegraphed from Bridgeport to his assistant adjutant general back at Chattanooga that the minor enemy force he had been hunting "has taken the back track," and when he returned to Chattanooga he found where the action had been.[14] He had missed it. He expected another battle at Corinth and hastily maneuvered his way into Beauregard's command. He wrote Marilda, "Knowing that our forces would need reinforcements for the next fight, I telegraphed to General Beauregard my strength, and being in Maj. Gen. E. K. Smith's Department, and having no right to leave without his authority, I telegraphed to him for authority to come here [Corinth] and got it on Wednesday."[15] He went on to describe what he had learned of the battle at Shiloh: "The fights here on Sunday and Monday last were terrific. The victory on Sunday was complete. In both engage-

[12] Joseph Howard Parks, *General Edmund Kirby Smith, C.S.A.*, pp. 156–165; E. K. Smith to S. Cooper, March 31, 1862, *War of the Rebellion*, X, pt. 2, p. 376; Connelly, *Army of the Heartland*, pp. 149–150.

[13] Ambrose, *Halleck*, pp. 41–43.

[14] Maxey to T. M. Scott, April 7, 1862, *War of the Rebellion*, X, pt. 2, p. 398.

[15] Maxey to E. K. Smith, April 7, 1862, ibid., pp. 405–406; Maxey to Marilda Maxey, April 13, 1862, Lightfoot Papers.

ments I am proud to say that my old Regt. behaved gallantly, gloriously, fully sustaining the honor of the Rgt. and of our state. . . . The Regt. has suffered terribly from sickness and the loss in the fight was great."[16] Maxey did not try to conceal his anticipation as he wrote further to Marilda: "Whether the fight will take place here or at some other point I can't say but another battle will unquestionably be fought which I think will be the greatest on the American continent. Beauregard's dispatch to me on Wednesday last, was, 'How many men can you bring for the *coming fight*.' I am willing to devote every energy of mind and body, risk all for the preservation of the liberties of our people. I think the fight cannot come off here, for several days past on account of the marshes there having been continual rain here almost ever since the battles."[17]

The battle Maxey expected never occurred; instead Beauregard was besieged at Corinth until May 30, when he finally retreated to Tupelo. Maxey, having missed Shiloh, chafed at the bit, "It is not reasonable that two contending armies the size of these would lie so close together long without doing something."[18] He was again at work guarding bridges and railroads, but after an abortive attempt to prevent the enemy from burning a bridge at Bear Creek and his failure to clear the railroad tracks near Corinth, Beauregard transferred him north to duty at Bethel, Tennessee. Here he was occupied with obstructing roads.[19] Each day Maxey rode ten to fifteen miles out from Bethel to check on the work on the roads, returned to Bethel to drill a regiment in double-quick time for over an hour, did his paper work, and went to bed at one in the morning. Until his personal servant arrived, Maxey also did what was most unusual for him—got up in

[16] Maxey to Marilda Maxey, April 13, 1862, Lightfoot Papers.

[17] Ibid.

[18] Ibid., April 18, 24, 1862; Alfred Roman, *The Military Operations of General Beauregard*, I, 568.

[19] For a Federal report on the expedition to Bear Creek, Ala., see *War of the Rebellion*, X, pt. 1, pp. 644–646. See also Special Orders No. 20, April 13, 14, 1862, Army of the Mississippi, Maxey Papers, University of Texas Archives; P.G.T. Beauregard to Maxey, April 26, 1862, and Beauregard to Leonidas Polk, May 1, 1862, *War of the Rebellion*, X, pt. 2, pp. 451, 476, 477; T. Harry Williams, *P. G. T. Beauregard*, p. 151.

time for breakfast with the other officers. He continued to believe that a battle was imminent for Beauregard's force and became convinced of it when he learned of the fighting going on around New Orleans. New Orleans fell to the Federals on April 29. On May 15 Maxey wrote to Marilda: "There has been a good deal of skirmish and picket fighting but nothing decisive. A success here would re-inspire the whole South."[20]

Beauregard's retreat to Tupelo averted the expected battle, and on June 1 Maxey was stationed at Baldwin to the north. He was by this time back with the Ninth Texas Regiment. Still wishing for fighting action, he grumbled to Marilda: "I think it extremely doubtful whether Halleck follows us here at all. If he does not then the Army should be put in motion and put in contact with the enemy somewhere. . . . If we can do no better we should be sent to Virginia to help Johnston and Jackson, or force our way across the Mississippi and up to Saint Louis."[21]

On June 13, General Braxton Bragg replaced the inactive Beauregard as commander of the Army of the Mississippi, and Bragg's first move, when it came in the middle of July, was to Chattanooga.[22] Maxey accompanied him and, being separated again from the Ninth Texas Regiment, was given a new command and assigned to watch the movements of those forces of Buell stationed around Bridgeport. This time he found action. Minor though it was, it was the high point of his career to date. He captured Union commissary supplies at Bridgeport after a two-day battle on August 24 and 25. On August 31 he successfully assaulted strong fortifications at Stevenson.[23]

[20] Maxey to Marilda Maxey, May 15, 1862, Lightfoot Papers. See also, Roman, *Beauregard*, I, 388; William M. Polk, *Leonidas Polk*, II, 117.

[21] Maxey to Marilda Maxey, June 11, 1862, Lightfoot Papers.

[22] Don C. Seitz, *Braxton Bragg: General of the Confederacy*, p. 124; Connelly, *Army of the Heartland*, pp. 197–199.

[23] Grady McWhinney, *Braxton Bragg and Confederate Defeat*, p. 219; J. P. McCown to Maxey, July 28, 1862, and Maxey to Charles Stringfellow, August 29, 1862, Maxey Papers, Gilcrease Institute; Maxey to Marilda Maxey, September 18, 1862, Lightfoot Papers; Samuel Jones to Maxey, August 24, 1862, *War of the Rebellion*, XVI, pt. 2, pp. 776–777.

But in the meantime, on August 28, Bragg had left Chattanooga for a Kentucky campaign that included Maxey's old Ninth Texas Regiment, but not Maxey. He was left behind until September 16, when Bragg, heading toward Louisville, sent orders for Maxey to bring additional troops and supplies to General Edmund Kirby Smith in Kentucky. Faced with another major opportunity, this time in his home state, Maxey had his customary difficulty in proceeding. In October he was in Knoxville still collecting troops and supplies. The route Maxey had been ordered to take through Cumberland Gap and London, Kentucky, was bare of supplies for man or beast. Everything had been taken from the Knoxville area, including a large quantity of ammunition. And the hostile Unionist country around Knoxville did not take kindly to Maxey's efforts to gather up materials, such as corn and fodder.[24] Maxey wrote home of his difficulties, saying: "East Tennessee is filled with Tories, traitors and bushwhackers—those right are as true as steel, but the bad predominates. I had two men killed and one wounded by bushwhackers last Saturday about thirty-five miles from here in Frost's Valley."[25] There were other difficulties also not of his making. His two superiors, Generals John McKown and Samuel Jones, unable to cooperate and feuding over the jurisdiction of East Tennessee, failed to forward the men and supplies Maxey was to take to Kentucky.[26]

Maxey was to wait and accompany General John B. Breckinridge but Breckinridge was delayed, first by General Earl Van Dorn, who tried to keep him in West Tennessee, and then by General Jones, who tried to keep him at Knoxville and attach some of his forces. It was not until October 11 that Maxey, with his command of five thousand men and one battery, was transferred to Breckinridge's division. He was dispatched the following day via Cumberland Gap to Kentucky. Breckinridge followed him immediately, but on October

24 Frank Vandiver, *Their Tattered Flags*, p. 158; B. Bragg to Maxey, September 16, 1862, Maxey Papers, Gilcrease Institute; Maxey to Marilda Maxey, September 18, 1862, Lightfoot Papers; Stanley F. Horn, *The Army of the Tennessee*, p. 75.
25 Maxey to Marilda Maxey, October 10, 1862, Lightfoot Papers.
26 Connelly, *Army of the Heartland*, pp. 271–273.

15, when only twenty-eight miles from Knoxville, Breckinridge received orders from Bragg to halt the column—Bragg was falling back from London.[27] As Maxey was about to enter Kentucky he received Breckinridge's order to halt. Maxey mourned: "I can but look on the Kentucky campaign as very unfortunate. The State is lost to us forever. . . . It was a cherished ambition with me to aid in redeeming my native State. That dream has fled. I was at the head of a large well appointed Force. . . . I was ordered to Danville just where I wanted to go, and just at the threshold of the State, Cumberland Gap, I was ordered back. From the highest point in the Gap, I could see men and wagons for miles coming this way. The whole tale was told and my fondest hopes crushed."[28]

Maxey retreated with Bragg to Murfreesboro. He shared the general disappointment of his men and wrote Marilda: "What the campaign will be now I do not know. If I thought it was to be a mere commissary campaign I should want to go home and try to get there, but if it is to be an active one then I prefer remaining at my post."[29] On December 14, it looked again as though it would be an active campaign for Maxey since his brigade was ordered to form part of a force of eight thousand sent from Bragg's army to help Pemberton at Vicksburg. But Maxey was sent to Port Hudson, a little over a hundred miles south of Vicksburg.[30] His life settled into a routine of drills and parties until May, 1863, when the no-nonsense Grant crossed the Mississippi between Vicksburg and Port Hudson and moved toward Jackson, the rail center for supplies to the Confederate army in the west. Pemberton ordered Maxey north to help repel the oncoming Union troops.[31] Maxey and his troops were rushed forward by rail to Brookhaven, twenty-five miles south of Jackson, where they were relegated to expediting the shipping of ordnance and other sup-

[27] John Breckinridge to Maxey, October 18, 1862, Maxey Papers, Gilcrease Institute; B. Bragg to L. Polk, October 16, 1862, *War of the Rebellion*, XVI, pt. 2, p. 951.
[28] Maxey to Marilda Maxey, November 11, 1862, Lightfoot Papers.
[29] Ibid.
[30] Ibid., January 14, 1863.
[31] J. C. Pemberton to Frank Gardner, May 4, 1863, *War of the Rebellion*, XV, 1071.

plies. Shipments were slowed because there was only one engine and ten cars, the rest having been destroyed by Union troops on May 2.[32]

On May 23, Maxey was incorporated into a newly formed division under General Joseph E. Johnston, since May 9 the commander of all troops in the Vicksburg area. Maxey was part of Johnston's plan to form a semicircle around Vicksburg, and he was sent to Canton, Mississippi, and then on June 24 to Livingston.[33] Camp life resumed a leisurely pace. Though Vicksburg was under siege, Maxey could write from Livingston: "Last Sunday I had a very fine Review. I invited Generals Gregg, Ector and McNair—McNair was late—Gregg and Ector rode round with me and participated in the Review and expressed themselves highly pleased. I gave a tolerably good dinner and they both stayed with me. A great many ladies were present. . . . I gave General French a Review one day last week. He was also present Sunday, but as it was my own affair, was simply a spectator. It passed off splendidly."[34]

On June 30, Maxey received orders to march north of Vicksburg to the Big Black River, where Johnston was concentrating 25,000 men. But scouting reports over the next few days convinced Johnston that there was no way he could help.[35] Pemberton surrendered Vicksburg to Grant on July 4 and Johnston's army began to retreat. Maxey participated in a battle near Jackson that ended in a Confederate retreat on July 17 and Maxey's thoughts turned toward home. From an encampment on Robinson's Creek near Morton he wrote Marilda on July 23: "I do not believe there will be an active campaign with this army this summer. If I can get across the river (between ourselves) I intend to do it—I am now at work making the effort. I think I could breathe freer and be better satisfied."[36]

[32] Joseph E. Johnston, *Narrative of Military Operations Directed during the Late War between the States*, ed. Frank E. Vandiver, pp. 176–178; John Adams to John Pemberton, May 13, 1863, *War of the Rebellion*, XXIV, pt. 3, p. 871.

[33] J. E. Johnston to James Seddon, May 23, 1863, *War of the Rebellion*, XXIV, pt. 3, p. 222; Maxey to Marilda Maxey, June 3, 24, 1863, Lightfoot Papers.

[34] Maxey to Marilda Maxey, June 30, 1863, Lightfoot Papers.

[35] Horn, *Army of the Tennessee*, p. 218; Johnston, *Narrative of Military Operations*, pp. 202–203; Vandiver, *Their Tattered Flags*, p. 218.

[36] Maxey to Marilda Maxey, July 23, 1863, Lightfoot Papers.

On August 6, Maxey was ordered to Enterprise, Mississippi, where forces were being gathered to send to aid General Dabney H. Maury at Mobile.[37] Then, on August 18, he received from Richmond his awaited special orders transferring him to the Trans-Mississippi Department. He was going home. He was to report to General T. H. Holmes at Little Rock. But by the end of the month, Maxey, with 1,987 men, was in Mobile, angry that he had been sent there despite his new orders from Richmond and "exceedingly anxious to be relieved."[38] Maury wrote Johnston that "Maxey's brigade arrived this morning. Ordered it to Portersville where change of air and scene will do all hands good. . . . Maxey tells us he is going across the river."[39] Johnston wrote to Richmond requesting that an officer be sent to relieve Maxey.[40]

In October, Maxey reported to General Kirby Smith, commander of the Trans-Mississippi Department at Shreveport. There he obtained leave for a month to return to Paris and was notified that his orders might be changed by the time he reported back for duty.[41] On December 11, 1863, Maxey was appointed commander of the Indian Territory, replacing Brigadier General William Steele.[42] In his new post he was faced with vaster problems than those he was accustomed to handling, and he must have obtained a great personal satisfaction in solving them as well as he did. In Kirby Smith's opinion the Indian Territory was "one of the most complicated commands in the Confederacy."[43] Maxey was following no less than four unsuccessful commanders.

In 1861 Union troops had abandoned the forts in the Indian Ter-

[37] General Order No. 148, Johnston's Headquarters, August 6, 1863, and Johnston to D. H. Maury, August 13, 1863, *War of the Rebellion*, XXIV, pt. 3, p. 1048.
[38] Maxey to Marilda Maxey, September 4, 1863, Lightfoot Papers.
[39] D. H. Maury to J. E. Johnston, August 31, 1863, *War of the Rebellion*, XXVI, pt. 2, p. 190.
[40] J. E. Johnston to S. Cooper, September 1, 1863, ibid., XXX, pt. 4, p. 576.
[41] Special Order No. 172, E. K. Smith to Maxey, October 24, 1863, Maxey Papers, Gilcrease Institute.
[42] S. S. Anderson to Maxey, December 11, 1863, ibid.
[43] Maxey quoted Smith in Maxey to Henry E. McCulloch, March 21, 1864, Letterbook A, Maxey Papers.

ritory, but during 1862 and 1863 they had moved slowly southward from Kansas until they had recaptured more than half of the vacated area.[44] By April, 1863, they had occupied Fort Gibson on the Arkansas River. The Confederates under Steele held Fort Smith a few miles down the river, but growing discouraged about the lack of guns, powder and supplies and about the lack of discipline among his troops, he evacuated the fort in November. A few weeks later, after very little fighting, General James G. Blunt and his Union forces took over the post. Thus, when Maxey assumed command in December, the Unionists held both Forts Gibson and Smith. Maxey's self-interest as well as his duty lay in preventing Union forces from invading North Texas through the Indian Territory. He faced pressure from General Nathaniel P. Banks in Louisiana and from General Frederick Steele in Arkansas. Both of these forces were parts of Halleck's winter campaign, planned to destroy the Confederate forces west of the Mississippi.[45]

Before he could meet these threats Maxey had to mold effective fighting forces from his white and Indian troops. He had no infantry—his white troops, under Colonel Richard M. Gano, were all cavalry, and the Indians would not serve unless mounted. The white troops were plagued by low morale among the men and petty jealousies among the officers, and the six thousand Indian troops had scattered because of recent Confederate reverses. After regathering his Indian allies, Maxey had to convince them that the Confederacy would keep its hitherto unmet treaty obligations and supply them with money and arms. Not the least of his worries concerned supplies. All the troops were poorly armed—some of his white troops were equipped with shotguns, small squirrel rifles and mammoth Belgian muskets; the Indians were so poorly armed and had so little ammunition that they were generally ineffective as a fighting force. Maxey complained to his wife that "the great trouble, and the one about which I have

---

[44] Gary N. Heath, "The First Federal Invasion of Indian Territory," *Chronicles of Oklahoma* 44 (Winter 1966–1967): 410; William J. Willey, "The Second Federal Invasion of Indian Territory," *Chronicles of Oklahoma* 44 (Winter 1966–1967): 420.

[45] Ambrose, *Halleck,* pp. 168–169.

more anxiety than any other is arms. Oh! for five thousand *good* guns, and I would place Northern Texas in safety."[46] Supplies of food and horses were also a problem. These had to be drawn from Texas, and because Maxey's position required him to act as superintendent of Indian affairs, he found himself responsible for feeding hundreds of indigent Indians.

Maxey established his headquarters on the Red River at Fort Towson, an old army post with only a hospital and one barracks left standing. When Banks and Steele began to move toward Shreveport, Kirby Smith ordered Maxey to put himself in communication with General Sterling Price (newly appointed commander of the District of Arkansas) at Arkadelphia. He was to be ready to cover Price's crossing of the Red River at Fulton should Price have to fall back. Maxey requested arms for his men but never received any.[47] Leaving Brigadier General Douglas H. Cooper in command of the Indian Territory, and accompanied by Tandy Walker's Choctaw Brigade, which had agreed to go outside the Indian Territory, Maxey took a portion of Gano's brigade to Price's headquarters twenty-three miles northeast of Fulton. Maxey was anxious to get into battle. He wished to gain some honors, "while others were getting honors conferred," and felt that he could work himself "to a skeleton in the district and not do so much in that way as in a single day with opportunity in the field."[48] He kept an alert eye on movements within the Indian Territory and planned to return immediately if an emergency, or opportunity, arose.

Steele planned to take his Union forces to Shreveport by way of Camden, Arkansas. With the main part of his army, he left Little

[46] Maxey to Marilda Maxey, February 25, 1864, Maxey Papers, Gilcrease Institute. See also, Maxey to H. E. McCulloch, March 21, 1864, Letterbook A, Maxey Papers. For a general discussion of conditions in the Indian Territory prior to Maxey's arrival see Annie H. Abel, *The American Indian as Participant in the Civil War*, pp. 243–306.

[47] Ludwell H. Johnson, *Red River Campaign*, p. 160; Parks, *Edmund Kirby Smith*, pp. 371–402; James Monaghan, *Civil War on the Western Border, 1854–1865*, pp. 298–299; Maxey to E. K. Smith, March 26, 1864, Letterbook A, Maxey Papers; Maxey to E. K. Smith, April 3, 1864, *War of the Rebellion*, XXXIV, pt. 3, pp. 728–730.

[48] Maxey to W. R. Boggs (General Kirby Smith's chief of staff), April 7, 1864, *War of the Rebellion*, XXXIV, pt. 3, pp 745–746.

Rock and crossed the Little Missouri, although not without harass-
ment from Confederate forces under Generals Joseph Shelby and J. S.
Marmaduke. Steele's strategy was to try to force the Confederates to
converge in front of him and his plan succeeded, for Price gathered
his forces at Prairie D'Ane on April 12, in time for a confrontation
with a part of Steele's command. After skirmishing briefly, Steele's
Unionists withdrew and marched to occupy Camden.[49]

When Steele's forces occupied Camden—the most important Confederate military center in southern Arkansas—Union success appeared complete, but soon the securing of food and forage became a
major problem for them too. A combination of circumstances cut off
supplies from Pine Bluff and forced Steele to send out forage groups
to gather up corn and other food within an eighteen-mile radius of
Camden. On the morning of April 18, 1864, Confederate forces inter-
cepted an enemy escort of 198 wagons at Poison Spring, fourteen
miles west of Camden. General Marmaduke, who had the forage
train under surveillance, called for reinforcements when he saw the
number of the enemy.[50]

Price ordered Maxey to proceed to Poison Spring and take command. Maxey had some 1,335 men plus four small pieces of artillery,
and as he arrived General William L. Cabell's troops, which had been
detached from General J. F. Fagan's division, were forming their
line of battle. Marmaduke's cavalry was already in place.[51] The heavy
forage train, supported by 1,170 Union troops, advanced along an old
military road between Washington and Camden and stopped on high
ground in front of the Confederate forces. Marmaduke tendered his
command to Maxey at once, but Maxey declined to issue new orders,
saying that, since Marmaduke had "put on foot the expedition" and

---

[49] Johnson, *Red River Campaign*, pp. 178–179.

[50] Ira Don Richards, "The Battle of Poison Spring," *Arkansas Historical Quarterly* 18 (Winter 1959): 339–342; Albert Castel, *General Sterling Price and the
Civil War in the West*, p. 185; Stephen B. Oates, *Confederate Cavalry West of the
River*, pp. 140–141; Alwyn Barr, "Confederate Artillery in the Trans-Mississippi,"
masters thesis, pp. 171–175.

[51] Maxey to J. F. Belton, April 23, 1864, *War of the Rebellion*, XXXIV, pt. 1,
pp. 841–844; Richards, "The Battle of Poison Spring," pp. 339–342.

knew the position of affairs, he should continue to "make disposition of the troops."[52]

Marmaduke placed Maxey's division, now dismounted, on the left, forming a line nearly at right angles to Marmaduke's line and paralleling the main road to Camden. Maxey moved forward rapidly and turned the enemy's flank. While the flank was turning, Marmaduke moved forward, as did Cabell who had been placed in front and to Maxey's right.[53] Fifteen minutes after the whole force was put in motion, the enemy was routed and the train captured. The Confederate troops pursued the fleeing Union soldiers until Maxey ordered a halt. Maxey reported that, with not more than 1,800 men, he had taken 170 wagons and routed an enemy that he numbered at 2,500.[54]

The most important result of the victory was the effect on the Confederate troops. Knowing that his own troops' morale had been raised tremendously, Maxey wanted to take advantage of their ebullience to make a dash at Forts Smith and Gibson, thus clearing the territory of Jayhawkers and stray Union troops. He was prevented from doing so by new orders to return to the Indian Territory.[55] Maxey returned on April 29, leaving Smith and Price to pursue the retreating Steele. At Fort Towson, he was stunned to learn that his name had been left out of a recommendation that the brigadier generals involved in Price's campaign be promoted to major generals.[56] He indignantly tendered his resignation, which was returned to him with a personal letter from General Kirby Smith assuring him that he too had been recommended for the promotion.[57] Kirby Smith sent copies of his orders to Richmond but did not wait for President Davis's written approval before placing the recommended officers on duty with in-

[52] J. S. Marmaduke to J. F. Belton, April 21, 1864, Letterbook A, Maxey Papers; Ernest Wallace, *Charles DeMorse*, pp. 149–150.

[53] Maxey to J. F. Belton, April 23, 1864, *War of the Rebellion*, XXXIV, pt. 1, p. 841.

[54] Ibid., pp. 842–844. Kirby Smith estimated the enemy at 2,700 and "Maxey's forces" at 2,000 (Document 38, Steele's March, 1864, Edmund Kirby Smith Papers).

[55] George Williamson to Maxey, April 28 , 1864, *War of the Rebellion*, XXXIV, pt. 1, p. 845.

[56] Maxey to S. S. Anderson, May 20, 1864, Maxey Papers, Gilcrease Institute.

[57] E. K. Smith to Maxey, June 8, 1864, ibid.

creased rank. It was not until December, 1864, that he received Davis's negative reply to his request.[58] Only after the war did Maxey learn from Texas Confederate Senator H. C. Burnet that the assignments made by General Kirby Smith had been nominated and confirmed by the Senate.[59]

With the matter of the promotion presumably settled, Maxey turned to directing the movement of his troops and the operations of his spies in North Texas and Arkansas. With the aid of Henry McCulloch of Bonham, Texas, he placed spies around Fort Smith and Fort Gibson. Other spies kept an eye on the strong, disaffected element in North Texas. Unionism in North Texas had lost some of its blatancy after executions at Gainesville and the arrest of Union sympathizers in Wise, Grayson, and Denton counties. The current of dissension still lay beneath the surface, however, and men disloyal to the Confederacy hid out in the brush of North Texas, particularly in the wooded section of Collin, Grayson, Fannin, and Hunt counties known as Five Corners.[60] Jefferson Mears, a Choctaw who had volunteered to infiltrate the North Texas sympathizers, reported that the brushmen were determined not to fight for the South and that they hoped to leave for the Union lines as soon as spring arrived.[61] Maxey wrote to General Smith: "Sometime ago I captured and killed most of a party of scoundrels armed and organized into a company with a captain en route from Fannin Co. Texas to the Yankees. Some of these were deserters from my command."[62] Albert Pike, called a great humbug by Maxey's father, added to his unpopularity with some Texans by using his influence to prevent the execution of at least one of the Union men captured by Maxey.[63]

[58] Parks, *Edmund Kirby Smith,* pp. 417–418.

[59] Maxey to Marcus J. Wright, February 18, 1881, Marcus J. Wright Papers.

[60] Claude Elliott, "Union Sentiment in Texas, 1861–1865," *Southwestern Historical Quarterly* 50 (April 1947): 449–477; Abel, *The American Indian as Participant in the Civil War,* p. 303; J. Lee Stambaugh and L. J. Stambaugh, *A History of Collin County, Texas,* pp. 62–63.

[61] Maxey to H. E. McCulloch, January 20, 1864, Maxey Papers, Gilcrease Institute.

[62] Maxey to S. S. Anderson (Assistant adjutant general to General Kirby Smith), February 27, 1864, Letterbook A, Maxey Papers.

[63] Rice Maxey to Henry and Dora Lightfoot, December 14, 1862, Lightfoot Pa-

In mid-June Maxey's Indian forces, under General Stand Watie, captured a Union steamboat loaded with supplies near Pleasant Bluff, a way station at the junction of the Canadian and Arkansas rivers. The next day the same Indian forces routed the Unionists at Iron Bridge on San Bois Creek. Although the raids were militarily insignificant, they raised the morale of the Indians to such a point that they began to reenlist in the Confederate army.[64] Some six hundred of Gano's men attacked the Sixth Kansas Cavalry within five miles of Fort Smith on July 27, defeating the Kansans and capturing four hundred six-shooters, two hundred Sharps rifles, a number of horses, and some sutler's stores, all badly needed supplies.[65]

Kirby Smith warned Maxey not to make any rash attacks on Fort Smith or Fort Gibson. Maxey agreed that the idea of an attack on Fort Smith could not be entertained, because of his extended communications and supply lines—all supplies, including breadstuffs, were being brought from Texas. But he wrote in August that he would like to plan a campaign to regain Little Rock and Pine Bluff in the fall. Quoting Cooper, he mentioned the rumors that the Unionists could not winter on the subsistence in upper Arkansas and that they planned to try to reach Texas for the winter.[66]

Maxey received permission to send Stand Watie northward as far as central Kansas to raid isolated army installations and to attempt to secure the assistance of the western Indians. Kirby Smith warned Maxey to plan the raid to take place before the first of October so that it would coincide with General Price's attack upon Missouri.[67] Maxey was pleased to cooperate, for he felt that, although his men were dismounted, barefoot, and unarmed, they were better satisfied

pers; Robert L. Duncan, *Reluctant General,* pp. 256–257. For details of the life of Albert Pike see also Walter L. Brown, "Albert Pike, 1809–1891," doctoral dissertation.

[64] Stand Watie to D. H. Cooper, June 17, 1864, Maxey Papers, Gilcrease Institute; Monaghan, *Civil War on the Western Border,* p. 301.

[65] Maxey to W. R. Boggs, July 30, 1864, *War of the Rebellion,* XLI, pt. 1, p. 29.

[66] Maxey to D. H. Cooper, June 28, 1864, ibid., XXXIV, pt. 4, pp. 697–698; Maxey to E. K. Smith, August 18, 1864, Letterbook A, Maxey Papers.

[67] Marvin J. Hancock, "The Second Battle of Cabin Creek, 1864," *Chronicles of Oklahoma* 39 (Winter 1961–1962): 416.

when actively employed than when idling in camps, and that on the raids there would be plenty of chance to capture arms, horses, and clothing. In fact, in August he felt so pressed by the need for clothing for his men that he published appeals in the *Dallas Herald*. Citizens were asked to contribute clothing and to send the contributions to specified towns, from which Maxey arranged to transport the supplies to his men in the Indian Territory. Similar appeals continued to appear in the Texas press during September and October.[68]

The last major engagement of the war in the Indian Territory came in September, 1864, with the battle of Cabin Creek. Although the white troops had been unhappy during July and August, the Indian troops had not. They were anxious for action. At Cabin Creek the Confederates encountered a large Union supply train enroute from Fort Scott, Kansas, to Fort Gibson. Encircling the 610 Union soldiers guarding the train, they captured nearly all the supplies in the wagons and took some prisoners. On returning to Fort Towson, Gano presented Maxey with some of the captured supplies: two bolts of calico, five dozen star candles, and some cans of pineapples and oysters. He also sent a bolt of calico from the captured wagon train to Mrs. Edmund Kirby Smith.[69]

In October General Price advanced with his troops into Missouri as planned, and General John B. Magruder took over the district command of Arkansas, with the task of backing up Price's expedition. Maxey was displeased when, without his knowledge or consent, Magruder ordered Gano's brigade to move south of the Arkansas River to shore up the defenses of Washington and Fulton. Maxey maintained that the removal of the brigade from north of the Arkansas River would prevent the enforced evacuation of the Unionists from Forts Smith and Gibson.[70]

Price's advance into Missouri lacked proper support and by mid-

[68] James L. Nichols, *The Confederate Quartermaster in the Trans-Mississippi*, p. 40.

[69] R. M. Gano to Maxey, October 4, 1864, Maxey to Marilda Maxey, October 12, 1864, Maxey Papers, Gilcrease Institute.

[70] Maxey to E. K. Smith, November 8, 1864, *War of the Rebellion*, XLI, pt. 4, p. 1036; Maxey to Marilda Maxey, November 1, 1864, Maxey Papers, Gilcrease Institute; Maxey to W. R. Boggs, November 6, 1864, Letterbook A, Maxey Papers.

November he was forced to retreat, pursued by the enemy and in great need of supplies. General Kirby Smith directed Maxey to forward supplies to Magruder's rear, where they would be sent on to Price, and to allow Gano's brigade to join the cavalry forces that were moving to Price. Smith was careful to add that General John A. Wharton, as senior officer, would command the expedition.[71]

Maxey began the new year by arguing with Magruder over the control of Gano's brigade, and on January 23 the brigade was put under the command of General H. P. Bee and sent to Rusk, Texas.[72] Smith tried to end the wrangling and ordered Magruder to come to Maxey's assistance should the enemy attempt to raid North Texas.[73] The loss of Gano's brigade at this time displeased Maxey, and he wrote Smith that since he had been stripped of his best troops he saw no particular service that he could render any longer in the Indian Territory. Smith replied that Maxey's administrative duties in the Indian Territory were very extensive and that it was sometimes necessary to "strip one district of its best troops and throw the mass of troops into another district."[74]

The need for supplies for the starving Indians and the troops was of paramount importance, and the only hope lay in the ability of North Texans to provide food. Maxey wrote his friend B. H. Epperson of Clarksville to ask what he thought could be expected from North Texas in the way of food supplies for the spring and summer. Epperson's reply was depressing. He pointed out that the conscription of many of the slaves had substantially reduced the labor forces; thus, the number of crops actually planted would be fewer than in the previous spring. Also, Joseph Shelby's division of Missourians had appeared in Red River County and had requisitioned wagons and teams to haul corn and provender to their camps in Arkansas. Without

71 E. K. Smith to Maxey, November 4, 1864, *War of the Rebellion*, XLI, pt. 4, pp. 1028–1029.
72 Maxey to J. B. Magruder, January 15, 1865, ibid., XLVIII, pt. 1, p. 1347; J. B. Magruder to Maxey, January 19, 1865, ibid., p. 1348; W. R. Boggs to J. B. Magruder, January 20, 1865, ibid., pp. 1335–1336; W. R. Boggs to Maxey, January 23, 1865, ibid., p. 1340.
73 W. R. Boggs to J. B. Magruder, January 25, 1865, ibid., p. 1345.
74 W. R. Boggs to Maxey, February 9, 1865, ibid., p. 1372.

teams, the farmers could not plant crops, and Shelby's men were removing so much corn that there would be none left to plant. The farmers were bitter, also, because Shelby's troops were not Texas troops. They felt that the Missouri raiders scorned them and took their supplies without thanks. To cap the list of problems, all the public blacksmiths had been conscripted and General Smith declined to release them to repair farm implements. Epperson intimated that Maxey would have to use his influence, and quickly, if spring crops were to be planted.[75]

During 1864, General D. H. Cooper had made repeated efforts to gain command of the Indian Territory. In May he accused Smith of having misinterpreted an earlier order from President Davis. Cooper insisted that he was to have been given command of all the troops in the Indian Nation, not just the Indian troops.[76] On July 21, the Confederate War Department explicitly ordered Cooper to be placed in command of the Indian Territory, but perhaps Smith felt that the long delay in communications between Richmond and Shreveport justified procrastination in carrying out these orders, for the following month Maxey wrote his wife that General Smith had decided on Cooper's third application "the same as the others. No telling when the next will be made."[77] On October 1, Smith wrote the War Department and asked that the order to place Cooper in command of the Indian Territory be revoked.[78] General S. S. Cooper of the War Department replied that the order was "deemed imperative and must be carried out."[79]

By mid-October Smith, anticipating orders to place D. H. Cooper in command of the Indian Territory, began the organization of a new division to be placed in Lieutenant General Simon B. Buckner's corps and to be commanded by Maxey. Smith directed his chief of staff to

[75] B. H. Epperson to Maxey, January 30, 1865, Maxey Papers, Gilcrease Institute.
[76] D. H. Cooper to W. R. Boggs, May 29, 1864, ibid.; Larry L. West, "Douglas H. Cooper, Confederate General," *Lincoln Herald* 81 (Summer 1969): 75; Frank Cunningham, *General Stand Watie's Confederate Indians*, p. 167.
[77] Maxey to Marilda Maxey, August 9, 1864, Maxey Papers, Gilcrease Institute.
[78] E. K. Smith to S. S. Cooper, October 1, 1864, *War of the Rebellion*, XLI, pt. 3, p. 971.
[79] Endorsement of S. S. Cooper on letter from E. K. Smith, October 1, 1864, ibid.

write Maxey an unofficial letter explaining that "no matter what may be the ruling in regard to the Indian Territory you will have the command of a major general."[80] Maxey wrote his wife soon after receiving the letter: "I have been detached from command of the district of the Indian Territory. . . . I had drawn my own conclusions as to the reason for it and yesterday morning I received an unofficial note from General Boggs . . . as General Smith's reasons are private, of course you will say nothing about it. I am very glad this has been done, for should trickery . . . succeed in giving command to General Cooper which however I do not believe, I nevertheless have a splendid division of all Texians."[81] On February 21, Cooper was officially put in command of the Indian Territory.[82] Smith wrote once more to the War Department and expressed his dissatisfaction in being forced to remove Maxey from the Indian Territory, saying that the change did not have "the concurrence of my judgment, and I believe will not result beneficially."[83]

Maxey was given a division of infantry and ordered to report to Beauchamp Springs near Houston.[84] Since Generals Johnston and Lee had surrendered, Maxey had felt that the only remaining hope of the Confederacy lay within the Trans-Mississippi Department. He maintained that, if the people would give assurances "of support to the soldiers in the field and to their families at home as would make them contented to remain, an army of 100,000 men could be kept constantly in the field. . . . To overcome this would require an exertion on the part of the North they would be unwilling to undertake, and we would thus be in condition to extort better terms than by any other possible course, besides having all the chances resulting of any difficulty that might spring up between the United States and Foreign Powers."[85]

---

80 W. R. Boggs to Maxey, October 15, 1864, Maxey Papers.
81 Maxey to Marilda Maxey, October 18, 1864, Maxey Papers, Gilcrease Institute.
82 Special Orders No. 45, Trans-Mississippi Department, February 21, 1865, *War of the Rebellion*, XLVIII, pt. 1, p. 1396.
83 E. K. Smith to S. S. Cooper, March 2, 1865, ibid., p. 1408.
84 W. R. Boggs to J. A. Wharton, February 17, 1865, ibid., pp. 1392–1393.
85 Maxey to Marilda Maxey, May 11, 1865, Lightfoot Papers.

But on May 22, Maxey, discouraged beyond hope at mass desertions of the soldiers in his division, asked to be relieved from command. He went home to Paris, and on July 15 he formally surrendered as a prisoner of war to Major General E. R. S. Canby.[86]

[86] Maxey to Andrew Johnson, August 22, 1865, Adjutant General's Office Records, NA, RG 94.

4. United States Senator
Samuel Bell Maxey

It is such men as he [Maxey] whose ideas determine the character and direction of a great political measure and the fields
upon which a party's battles are fought.[1]

AFTER THE WAR Maxey found himself hamstrung by restrictions
placed on his political and legal activities by both President Andrew Johnson and Texas Provisional Governor A. J. Hamilton. Men
like Maxey, who had held important offices in the Confederacy, were
excepted from Johnson's general amnesty and required to receive
special presidential pardons.[2] Hamilton proclaimed further that without this pardon no ex-Confederate should be allowed to practice as an
attorney or a counsellor in the courts.[3]

In October, 1865, Maxey began the first of several unsuccessful
efforts to gain such a pardon. He took the oath of allegiance required
by the amnesty proclamation and included an affidavit to that effect
with a letter addressed to President Johnson. He sent the letter and
affidavit to Hamilton with the request that Hamilton add his recom-

[1] *New York World*, February 10, 1875.
[2] M. S. Lomask, *Andrew Johnson*, pp. 85–86; Eric L. McKittrick, *Andrew Johnson
and Reconstruction*, pp. 142–143.
[3] A. J. Hamilton, Proclamations of 1865, November 25, 1865, pp. 137, 138.

mendation. To Maxey's chagrin Hamilton returned the papers to him with the remark, "I cannot recommend the pardon of anyone who was educated at West Point."[4] Maxey's next tactic was to send the papers directly to President Johnson. When this elicited no response, he sought the help of influential acquaintances from Kentucky, among whom were U.S. Congressmen James Guthrie, Henry Grider, and Aaron Harding, and from his kinsman Thomas Bell Monroe, the law partner of U.S. Attorney General James Speed.[5] None was able to help. In January, 1866, a trip to Washington to see President Johnson brought Maxey no pardon but did result in Johnson's overriding Hamilton's restriction on the lawyers.[6] Success was finally achieved when Maxey asked his old West Point classmate Ulysses S. Grant to help. Grant wrote Johnson: "I knew him [Maxey] well as a cadet at West Point and afterwards as a lieutenant in the Mexican War. I believe him to be well worthy of Executive clemency and heartily recommend it."[7] Maxey received his pardon on July 20, 1867.[8]

Maxey's personal life also had its new developments after the Civil War. In 1863, he and Marilda had adopted a little war orphan, eight-year-old Dora Rowell, whose father, Thomas Rowell, had been killed at the battle of Shiloh.[9] Though this adoption had somewhat appeased Marilda's desire for a child of her own, it had not satisfied Maxey,

[4] A. J. Hamilton to Maxey, October 11, 1865, Adjutant General's Office Records, NA, RG 94.

[5] Guthrie, Grider, Harding, and Kentucky Governor Thomas Bramlette, old friends of the Maxey family, wrote Johnson on Maxey's behalf. Monroe's mother was Ann Bell, a cousin to Maxey's mother, and Monroe's father was a grandnephew of President James Monroe. See Maxey to B. H. Epperson, October 28, 1865, Epperson Papers; Maxey Pardon Records, Records of the Office of the Adjutant General; Lewis Collins and Richard H. Collins, *History of Kentucky*, I, 409.

[6] In a letter to Grant, Maxey describes his visit with President Johnson (Maxey to Ulysses S. Grant, March 23, 1867, Adjutant General's Office Records, NA, RG 94).

[7] Ulysses S. Grant to Andrew Johnson, January 16, 1866, ibid.

[8] Henry Stanberry, U.S. attorney general, wrote on the back of Maxey's brochure of letters, "I recommend a pardon in this case." It is dated July 20, 1867 (ibid).

[9] On March 31, 1863, Maxey petitioned to be appointed Dora's guardian. In 1870, when Dora was fourteen and entitled to choose in open court, she named Maxey as her guardian. But in 1875, Maxey had to file an answer to Dora's relatives who had petitioned for a final settlement of her estate. See Records of the Probate Court, Lamar County, Texas, Book E-1, p. 249; Book F, pp. 35–36, 120–121.

who wrote her from Fort Towson in 1864 that he had dreamed he had a baby son. "I thought I went to a cradle and got out a real live baby boy which I thought was ours. I nursed him for an hour or two and thought him very smart, and very heavy for a little one," wrote Maxey, and added sadly, "I awoke and found it all a dream."[10]

In August, 1869, Maxey rejoiced in the birth of a son to his niece, Mary Susan Gatewood, who had married Maxey's law partner, William H. H. Long. When Long died in 1871, the Maxeys informally adopted the boy, who had been named Samuel Bell Maxey Long. The doting forty-five–year–old Maxey now had his longed-for son. By the time the boy was three Maxey was saying: "I have an earnest desire to do my part in bringing Sam up right. He has undoubted talent and if his mind is properly trained there is no good reason why he should not make a very useful and distinguished man."[11]

Meanwhile, at the age of thirteen Dora started to school and did not like it, but Maxey urged her to study hard. "An ignorant person has a poor way of getting along through the world," he wrote, adding righteously that it was important to be cheerful and tidy and to learn to work with a hearty good will. "A lazy person is always selfish and useless for any good purpose," he advised further. He was beginning to accept Dora as his own, for he signed his letters to her "Your affectionate Father."[12]

In 1868, Maxey began the final stages of his eleven-year-old plan to build a new home on his five acres in Paris. The house was patterned after the new Greek Gothic Revival houses in Louisville.[13] Though her mother-in-law had died in 1866, leaving Marilda the undisputed mistress of the household, she was still a pessimistic person and given to moods. She wrote Maxey, away at court in Sherman, that she had resolved to do better in her new home. "There shall never be one unhappy hour spent by us on account of anything that I shall say or do," wrote Marilda,[14] but she was not able to keep her resolve for

---

[10] Maxey to Marilda Maxey, January 13, 1864, Lightfoot Family Papers.

[11] Maxey to Marilda Maxey, May 15, 1872, Maxey Papers.

[12] Maxey to Dora Maxey, March 18, 1868, ibid.

[13] A Louisville architect drew the plans for the house (Maxey to Marilda Maxey, September 2, 1867, ibid.).

[14] Marilda Maxey to Maxey, December 16, 1868, Lightfoot Papers.

long. Maxey replied that he was glad that she had got settled in their new home, where he hoped they could live many happy years, and then continued, "I never expect to be rich and don't care much about it but I want enough to get what we want, live comfortably, and have a competency for old age."[15]

Maxey's first law cases after the war concerned privately owned cotton that had been confiscated by the U.S. Treasury agents along with that belonging to the Confederate government. One of Maxey's most illustrious clients was cotton plantation owner R. M. Jones, a wealthy Choctaw Indian, who had built a fine mansion in Paris.[16] By 1867, Maxey's practice was sufficiently large to keep him from home almost all the time. While Rice Maxey and William H. H. Long occupied themselves with the law office in Paris, Maxey formed an additional partnership at Bonham with Judge M. A. Knight and James Q. Chenoweth. Maxey was strangely smitten with Chenoweth, a young ex-senator from the Harrodsburg district of Kentucky, whom Marilda later grew to dislike heartily because he borrowed money from Maxey and never repaid it. The Bonham firm of Samuel A. Roberts, J. W. Throckmorton, and Thomas J. Brown also often hired Maxey to assist with their cases. Maxey traveled from court to court— to Sherman, Bonham, Tarrant, Sulphur Springs, Gainesville—and sometimes roomed with fellow lawyers Judge Oran M. Roberts and D. B. Culberson.[17]

Maxey became politically active in the East Texas Democratic party, which, with the state Democratic party, was working hard to overthrow Republican rule in Texas. When the Lamar County Democrats met, Maxey, Silas Hare, James M. Hurt, James Chenoweth, and others in the party urged that, though there were many possible ways to defeat the Republicans, the best way was to make common cause with the national Democratic party and let alone such irrelevant matters as party affiliation and Negro suffrage.[18] But, unlike the still disen-

[15] Maxey to Marilda Maxey, December 23, 1868, ibid.

[16] Maxey to Marilda Maxey, December 25, 1865, ibid. (Maxey was in New Orleans attending to Jones's claims of wrongfully confiscated cotton.)

[17] Maxey to Marilda Maxey, September 23, December 7, 1868; January 2, February 14, 27, August 9, 1869, Maxey Papers.

[18] Ibid., October 4, 1870.

franchised but very popular John H. Reagan, Maxey did not wish the national Democratic party to back Horace Greeley for presidential nominee. Greeley was the choice of the Liberal Republican party at their meeting in Cincinnati in May, 1872. Said the very mistaken Maxey about this choice: "The Democratic party will never march under his banner and it would be a fatal day for the country should the national party so direct. I do not believe it will commit so criminal a blunder."[19]

Maxey had his own plans for counteracting the Republicans in the U.S. Congress. Though it was not perhaps seemly, Maxey, Democratic party chairman of the Congressional Committee of the Second Congressional District, placed his own name in nomination as a candidate to the U.S. House of Representatives.[20] On July 27, his own Lamar County instructed its delegates to the forthcoming convention at Mc-Kinney to cast their vote for Maxey.[21] But even here, Maxey's opinions did not coincide with some leading Texas Democrats, such as Reagan, Throckmorton, Ashbel Smith, and Epperson. They objected to Maxey's endorsement of Hoosier-turned-Texan John C. Conner, then seeking a second term in the House of Representatives. Maxey defended his stand by saying: "Whilst I infinitely prefer our own peoples, we are sometimes forced by circumstances to take those from the North. I think Conner is a better man than any man of the South who can swear that he did not aid or countenance us in the late war."[22] But at the McKinney convention in August, Maxey ran a poor third to D. B. Culberson and W. P. McLean for the coveted nomination.[23] Though Republican Grant won over Democrat Greeley in the 1872 presidential election, Texas successfully put her Democrats both in Congress and in the Texas legislature.

In March, 1873, Maxey was nominated as Judge of the Eighth Judicial District of Texas and was confirmed by the Texas Senate and Governor E. J. Davis. Maxey refused the commission on the grounds

[19] Ibid., May 12, 1872.
[20] Maxey political circular, June 25, 1872, ibid.
[21] *Clarksville Northern Standard*, July 27, 1872.
[22] Maxey to Marilda Maxey, July 28, 1872, Maxey Papers.
[23] *State Gazette*, January 29, 1874; *Sherman Daily Courier*, August 29, 1879.

that he was too involved in all the major law cases on the docket in the Eighth Judicial District. He argued that, since he was involved in most of the cases, either a special judge would have to try them, or the cases would have to be moved to a county out of the district.[24] Various newspapers reported that Maxey had declined for "financial considerations" and that he believed "the office should seek the man."[25]

In August, 1873, the *Galveston News* published a list of some twenty possible candidates for governor in the coming December election, and Maxey was included.[26] But, since Maxey had been in Kentucky since July, it is probably safe to say that he had no serious ambition for the governorship race. He had gone, ostensibly, to place Dora in the Caldwell Institute at Danville, a girls' private school that had been recommended by Chenoweth. He also found time though for a brief visit with his boyhood friend Preston Leslie, in the governor's mansion at Frankfort, and with other friends around the state. He talked politics wherever he went and it is not unlikely that his Kentucky friends urged him to try for a seat in the U.S. Senate.

On returning to Texas, and learning of Richard Coke's and Richard B. Hubbard's nominations for governor and lieutenant governor, Maxey wrote Marilda: "Coke was my choice. He is a sound lawyer, an honest man, clear of railroad rings and opposed to repudiation.[27] Whilst not an accomplished stump speaker according to reports he is a sound argumentation speaker, which is more important now. There his moral character will weigh immensely with the people. Hubbard is a good stump speaker. I shall write to Coke expressing my gratification at his nomination."[28] In early October, unaware that Maxey was away at court at Sulphur Springs, Coke and Hubbard called on Mrs. Maxey at Paris. Hubbard praised Marilda's hospitality and was captivated by the luxury and beauty of the Maxey home. Lat-

[24] *Clarksville Northern Standard*, March 22, 1873.

[25] *Houston Age*, January 20, 1874; *Sherman Register*, January 29, 1874, newsclipping, Maxey Papers.

[26] *Galveston News*, August 29, 1873. See also, Claude Elliott, *Leathercoat*, p. 213.

[27] During Davis's governorship, there had been widespread refusal to pay taxes. Coke felt that the state debt should not be repudiated and proposed issuing high interest bonds to meet the payments (Alwyn Barr, *Reconstruction to Reform*, pp. 8–9).

[28] Maxey to Marilda Maxey, September 7, 1873, Maxey Papers.

er Marilda complained to Maxey of the strain and embarrassment she suffered from having to entertain such dignitaries alone, but the unsympathetic and ambitious Maxey replied, "These troubles our social position forces upon us."[29] Coke and Hubbard went on to Sulphur Springs, where they visited with Maxey and were assured of his support.

Coke and Hubbard won the December election. Shortly thereafter, Maxey wrote John Ireland, a Kentuckian by birth like Maxey, and also nearly the same age. Ireland was now serving in the Texas House of Representatives, and Maxey asked his opinion about Maxey's attempting to represent his district in the coming U.S. senatorial race. Ireland replied that he did not regard James Flanagan or Morgan Hamilton (the incumbent Republican senators) as chargeable to either Maxey's section or the western section of the state, and that it was conceded by the Democratic party that these two sections should furnish the senators.[30] Maxey decided to enter the race.

In early January, 1874, while at Bonham, Maxey learned of the Texas Supreme Court decision in the Rodriguez case. Joseph Rodriguez of Harris County had been arrested on the charge of voting twice in the election of December 2, 1873. The court decision against Rodriguez put the entire political situation in Texas at issue because it invalidated all the Texas elections of December, 1873, including that of Richard Coke as governor.[31] The situation was considered to be a last-ditch effort by Republican Governor Davis to keep control of the Texas government. Cried the impassioned Maxey: "It is simply infamous. It is the highest handed, most bald-faced and unscrupulous effort to subvert the government and the fairly expressed will of the people known to history. I blush for humanity. It is a dizzy height in crime I did not believe the court would have the audacity to attempt to reach."[32]

The fact remained that Davis still controlled the Texas government

[29] Ibid., October 18, 1873.
[30] John Ireland to Maxey, December 14, 1873, ibid.
[31] *Texas Reports*, XXXIX, 706–776; George E. Shelley, "The Semicolon Court of Texas," *Southwestern Historical Quarterly* 48 (April 1945): 449–469; Walter P. Webb and H. Bailey Carroll (eds.), *Handbook of Texas*, II, 497.
[32] Maxey to Marilda Maxey, January 6, 1874, Maxey Papers.

and that the Democrats must devise some method, short of bloodshed, to oust him. Maxey's plan for removing Davis involved organizing the newly elected Democratic houses of the legislature on January 8, 1874, and having them ratify the amendments to the constitution that had also been voted on December 2, 1873. These amendments gave the legislature the sole power to suspend the laws in Texas and to control appointment of justices to the Supreme Court. Maxey further suggested that Governor Coke should nominate five Supreme Court judges, who would set to work immediately to undo the harm that Davis and his "semicolon" court had done. He advocated that a committee be appointed to prepare an address setting forth the facts, as the Democrats saw them, to the people of the United States.[33] But Coke had plans of his own when he learned on January 12 that Davis planned armed resistance at the state capitol.[34] By the time Maxey arrived in Austin on January 19, Coke's coup, which involved his possession of the second floor of the capitol and the wresting of control of the militia from Davis, was completed.

The legislature began its work and had so much business to transact that the election of the U.S. senator from Texas had to be postponed for a week.[35] Maxey used the time to persuade influential men like Houston real estate dealer William Wagley, *State Gazette* editor J. D. Elliott, and ex-Chairman of the State Democratic Executive Committee Austinite William Walton to take a stand for him. From the way things were shaping up, it appeared that the senatorial race would be between Maxey, John H. Reagan, and Texas ex-Governor James Webb Throckmorton. Maxey felt sure that he could win if the race were just between him and Reagan but was unsure in the case of a three-way choice.[36] He believed that Throckmorton had a good chance since he was an attorney for the Texas and Pacific Railway and would have the backing of that powerful group. There was a great deal at stake for the railway company, which had been forced into a receiver-

[33] Louise Horton, "Samuel Bell Maxey on the Coke-Davis Controversy," *Southwestern Historical Quarterly* 72 (April 1969): 522–523.
[34] Webb and Carroll, *Handbook of Texas*, I, 370.
[35] Maxey to Marilda Maxey, January 19, 1874, Maxey Papers.
[36] Ibid.

ship and wished to reorganize and continue to build its road from
Marshall, Texas, through Fort Worth, and on to San Diego, California.[37]

On January 27, the House and Senate of the Texas legislature met
separately to elect a senator to replace Republican James W. Flanagan,
whose term was to expire in March, 1875. Neither house was able to
select a man and, as a matter of fact, Maxey was not even among
those nominated.[38] But, on January 28, when the legislature met in
joint session, the names of Maxey, Throckmorton, and Reagan were
placed in nomination. Senator John Ireland of Seguin and Representative Frank Rainey of Houston County placed Maxey's name before
the legislature. The Republicans nominated Edward T. Randle. On
the first ballot, Maxey received a majority of the votes—thirteen in the
Senate and forty-six in the House, a total of fifty-nine—and won.[39]

Maxey returned to Paris and wrote to Dora at school in Kentucky:

I was elected United States Senator on the 27th[40] of January by a very
handsome vote. I received fifty-nine, Governor Throckmorton forty, Randle
(radical) thirteen and two scattering. So far as I can judge from the papers
I have seen the people are well satisfied with the result. There was a grand
demonstration here the night of the election Wednesday last surpassing
anything ever known in Paris—bonfires, illumination, speechmaking, and
rejoicing generally. I was in Austin at the time but saw the account of
it in Thursday morning papers. Certainly I have great reason to be thank-
ful and proud of the esteem in which I am held by my neighbors.[41]

The Texas press had a variety of comments on the election. The
State Gazette endorsed Maxey warmly:

While the contest was spirited, it was conducted in a dispassionate manner
and without the slightest indication of bitterness of feeling. . . . General
Maxey has for years been the leader of a straight Democracy of North
Texas and at the Corsicana convention won the applause of the country

---

[37] Webb and Carroll, *Handbook of Texas*, II, 752.

[38] Texas Legislature, House and Senate Journals of the 14th Legis., 1st sess., January 27, 1874.

[39] Ibid., January 28, 1874.

[40] Maxey was mistaken about the date. He was elected on January 28, 1874.

[41] Maxey to Dora Maxey, February 2, 1874, Maxey Papers.

for his uncompromising devotion to principle. His abhorrence to the new departure and the Greeley movement won our highest admiration. . . . In the district convention at Dallas he came within a few votes of securing a two-thirds majority in a contest with the distinguished Culberson for Congress and it was in consequence of this close contest between these giants of Democracy that McLean[42] was taken up as a third man and nominated for Congress. . . . Senator Maxey is about fifty years old—spare built—six feet tall—and of commanding mien. He will be a suitable colleague of the chivalric Gordon of Georgia.[43]

Houston's *Age* commented that "the majority of the Democracy of Texas are not prepared to endorse ex-Governor Throckmorton as a fair representative of their views upon railroad matters. . . . His advocacy of the railroad combination upon the treasury and public domain of Texans . . . is in violation of the first and best principle of Democracy. . . . The people desire a man in the United States Senate who has no connection with railroads. . . . We endorse General Maxey . . . he belongs to the district which we think is entitled to one of the senators."[44] The *Galveston News* also endorsed the election of Maxey "though he was chosen in deference to a great extent to his identification with Northern Texas."[45]

But Throckmorton's supporters did not accept defeat lightly, and, as late as March 4, the *Austin Statesman* charged that the legislators had indulged in "bargain and trade" and "log-rolling" to bring about the election of Maxey and that Maxey had been foisted upon the country "at the expense of the great public interests."[46] But the *State*

[42] William P. McLean was elected to the United States House of Representatives in 1872 to serve from 1873 to 1875 (Webb and Carroll, *Handbook of Texas*, II, 120).

[43] *State Gazette*, January 29, 1874, newsclipping, Maxey Papers. John Brown Gordon did somewhat resemble Maxey but the problems of Texas were so distinct from Georgia's that the two senators had little in common in Congress. For a description of Gordon see Frank E. Vandiver, *Their Tattered Flags*, pp. 304–305; H. J. Eckenrode, *Rutherford B. Hayes*, p. 207.

[44] *Houston Age*, January 28, 1874, newsclipping, Maxey Papers.

[45] *Galveston News*, January 29, 1874.

[46] *Austin Democratic Statesman*, March 4, 1874. General Dodge of the Texas and Pacific had announced that Throckmorton was devoted to the railroad's interests and was a very valuable man to them (C. Vann Woodward, *Reunion and Reaction*, p. 74).

Gazette answered these charges by stating: "The friends of Judge
Reagan, finding that they could not secure a sufficient vote to insure
his election, joined the supporters of General Samuel Bell Maxey and
by a united vote the latter was elected. This action was certainly legitimate. There were no promises made, or hopes of preferment held
out to secure this action."[47] *The Austin Daily State Journal*, however,
used an unfortunate expression to describe Maxey: "Anyone would
have been better than this ultra-simonpure–secession–anti-reconstruc-
tion Democrat Maxey."[48] This quote has been used often since; Rupert Richardson, for example, used it in *Texas: The Lone Star State,*
and David Gracy II used it in his edited publication of *Maxey's
Texas.*[49]

During the balloting in caucus on January 27, the Democrats had
given John Ireland fifteen votes, and had Ireland remained in the
race for the Senate seat he probably would have been nominated.
But believing that North Texas was entitled to the office, he withdrew
his name and gave his support to Maxey. On February 7, perhaps at
Maxey's prodding, the *Paris Press* expressed its admiration of Ireland's spirit and pointed out that he was the logical Democrat to represent West Texas and to succeed Morgan Hamilton when his term
in the U.S. Senate expired.[50] But two years later when the matter came
up, Maxey refused to pay his debt to Ireland and failed to back him
for Hamilton's seat.

Maxey's election to the Senate was a matter of interest outside the
state too. The *Louisville Courier-Journal* noted: "The party in Texas
could send no sounder Democrat nor truer nor cleverer man than
General Samuel Bell Maxey nor any who deserves more at its
hands. . . . We should both as Kentuckians and Democrats be glad
to see the General elected to the position to which so many of our
ablest contemporaries in Texas seem unequivocally to call him."[51]
The *New York World* published a list of the seven new senators:

47 *State Gazette*, March 4, 1874.
48 *Austin Daily State Journal*, March 4, 1874.
49 Rupert Norval Richardson, *Texas*, 3d ed., p. 227; David B. Gracy II, ed., *Maxey's Texas by Samuel Bell Maxey*, p. 21.
50 *Paris Press*, February 7, 1864, newsclipping, Maxey Papers.
51 *Louisville Courier-Journal*, January 10, 1874, ibid.

Thurman of Ohio, Eaton of Connecticut, Edmunds of Vermont, Bruce of Mississippi, Whyte of Maryland, Withers of Virginia, and Maxey of Texas. It noted that several of the junior senators—Cockrell of Missouri, Withers, and Maxey—were soldiers of the Confederacy and that their public services had been local rather than national. Of Maxey, the article stated: "Senator Maxey will be one of the most marked men of the new senate. His capacity is distinctly of the states-manlike kind. It is such men as he whose ideas determine the character and direction of a great political measure and the fields upon which a party's battles are fought. His attainments will be of the greatest service in the financial legislation of the next six years."[52]

Since Maxey's term in the Senate did not begin until March 3, 1875, he returned to Paris in February, 1874, and resumed his law practice. Most of his court cases were held at Bonham, but he complained that he was collecting no money and also getting very much disgusted. Having neglected his family during the hectic days of the election though, he was glad of the brief respite so that he could attend to matters at home.

Dora, at the Caldwell Institute in Kentucky, was lonesome and wished to come home. Sympathetic Kentucky Governor Preston Leslie knew from experience what it was like to be an orphan and lonely. He had sent Dora a box of food, which included a large silver cake on which was written, Eat This and Don't Cry. The governor had also written the Maxeys that he would see to it that Dora lacked for nothing and that he would bring her to the governor's mansion as often as her teacher would permit.[53]

Maxey's own letters to Dora provided an insight into his philosophy of work and study. He entreated Dora: "Make it a point to learn thoroughly whatever you undertake. Whilst your studies should be systematically carried on you should not fail to take plenty of exercise. Always treat your teachers and schoolmates with becoming courtesy. Politeness is characteristic of every true lady and gentleman. You should respect the opinions and feelings of others. By so doing every one whose friendship is worthy of having will in like manner res-

[52] *New York World,* February 10, 1875, ibid.
[53] Preston H. Leslie to Maxey, August 18, 1873, Lightfoot Papers.

pect your opinion and feelings."[54] He was perplexed as to why Dora
was not being taught mathematics and wrote, "A fair knowledge of
mathematics so far at least as concerns the ordinary affairs of business are important to a woman as well as to a man and the study has
the merit of expanding the intellect, cultivating the reasoning faculties
and systematizing thought."[55] He warned that her position in society
would demand "intelligence and refinement," that the graces of music
and painting would be expected of her, and complimented her by
saying, "You have an unusually fine voice and should take care of it
and cultivate it."[56] When Dora continued to be homesick and begged
to come home, Maxey replied firmly to her entreaties: "It is to your
interest to be thrown for a time amongst strangers, where you can
learn something of the world and where you will acquire something
of self-reliance which you would not be so apt to do at home, where
you would have us to consult. . . . You are not at Danville in search
of young men but of education and refinement that you may be an
ornament to your Texas home and the society in which you will
move."[57] When he learned that Dora in Danville and Thomas Woot-
en's son, Dudley, at Princeton were corresponding, Maxey chided her,
"Correspondence with young men should never be carried on. A polite note should be answered, of course, but a schoolgirl has no business with correspondence with young men."[58]

Dora wrote Dudley to explain that she could no longer write to
him; in Paris, Dudley's mother, Etta, visited Marilda, whereupon the
two ladies discussed the futures of Dora and Dudley. Marilda then
wrote Dora: "Mrs. Wooten was here yesterday evening and spent
some time with me and had a good deal to say about Dudley and asked
many questions about you. Said she went up to old Mrs. Brames' a few
days since and the old lady told her that she understood that your
father and Dr. Wooten had made every arrangement—that all the
ground work had been layed for you and Dudley to marry. . . . Mrs.

[54] Maxey to Dora Maxey, September 7, 1873, Maxey Papers.
[55] Ibid., September 29, 1873.
[56] Ibid., October 27, 1873.
[57] Ibid., November 7, 1873.
[58] Ibid., February 18, 1874.

Wooten just replied that she had been told that the arrangements had been made and so left the woman without telling her any better."[59] If there were plans for this marriage, something went wrong with them. Soon, despite his admonition to Dora about corresponding with young men, Maxey was encouraging his law partner, Henry William Lightfoot, eleven years Dora's senior, to write Dora and send her new pieces of music for voice and piano. The surprised Dora wrote her parents to ask if they ever saw what Lightfoot wrote her.

In May, 1874, Marilda, having felt keenly the year's separation from Dora, wrote her that soon her father would go to Kentucky to "bring my treasure to me. How happy I shall be to once more look upon and take in my arms my dear darling child. I could never have borne the separation had I not felt that it was for your good and that I ought to do all that was in my power to advance you in the world and right here."[60] After time at home, the recalcitrant Dora refused to return to school. In October, Maxey urged her to accept Lightfoot's proposal of marriage and she did.

The wedding was set for November 3. The wedding guest list included several of Maxey's boyhood friends—Kentucky Governor Preston Leslie, past Kentucky governors Thomas Bramlette and Beriah Magoffin, and Jilson P. Johnson, owner of the Galt House hotel in Louisville. Magoffin reputedly had been highly successful in the management of his business affairs. He was regarded as a millionaire and among the wealthiest of Kentuckians, having gained his wealth through judicious investments in Chicago.[61] Other notables who were invited were Texas Governor Richard Coke, General Albert Pike, Major Andrew J. Dorn, Attorney Thomas J. Brown, General William Steele, General W. L. Cabell, Congressman John H. Reagan, Attorney John A. Alexander, and Colonel William Wagley.[62]

[59] Marilda Maxey to Dora Maxey, May 8, 1874, ibid.
[60] Ibid.
[61] Collins and Collins, *History of Kentucky*, II, 537.
[62] Wedding Guest List, Maxey Papers. Pike, Steele, Dorn, and Cabell were Maxey's old Indian Territory friends; Brown was Throckmorton's and Samuel Roberts's law partner at Sherman; Reagan was newly elected to the United States House of Representatives; Alexander was a Houston attorney; Wagley was a Houston real estate dealer and a leader in the Texas Democratic party.

Maxey had been making unceasing efforts to learn all the problems of Texas that required the attention of Congress. In February he had written to Governor Coke outlining proposals he hoped to make in the Senate. Coke replied: "I will take great pleasure in conferring with you and making suggestions as may occur to me of measures looking to the advantage of the people of Texas which may be urged by you in the Federal Congress. You say rightly that frontier protection and coast improvement are the most prominent objects affecting the interests of the people of Texas demanding the action of the Federal government."[63]

When border troubles between Mexico and Texas became acute in September, 1874, Coke ordered Texas forces to cross the Rio Grande into Mexico in pursuit of Mexican marauders who had escaped with stolen Texas property. U.S. Attorney General George D. Williams ordered Coke to bring his troops back, but Coke insisted that Mexico was not a friendly power, because it did nothing to help capture the marauders and, therefore, the act of Congress of April 20, 1818, which prescribed penalties for the breach of the neutrality laws of the United States, did not apply.[64] Coke wrote Maxey, "I suggest that affairs on our Mexican border should also receive prompt attention from the general government."[65]

The civil rights bill that was to come up in the next session of Congress was another matter of grave concern to Coke, to Maxey and to newly elected Congressman Reagan. They all thought the bill contained faults that would harm the South. Reagan wrote Maxey that he believed the bill was unconstitutional. On the general approach of the Texas Democratic delegation in Congress, Reagan concurred with Maxey that great prudence and caution would be necessary on the "part of the Democracy and especially on the part of those from southern states to secure us the full benefits of the brilliant political victory we have just won in so many states and in the election of a majority of members to the lower branch of Congress." He further

[63] Richard Coke to Maxey, February 20, 1874, Maxey Papers.

[64] Ibid., September 7, 1874. See also *Austin Democratic Statesman*, October 17, 1874.

[65] Richard Coke to Maxey, September 7, 1874, Maxey Papers.

cautioned that "we must . . . overcome our sectional prejudices and passions and ally ourselves firmly with the national democracy. . . . We must especially not forget that the recent elections were, among other things, a protest against extravagance and high taxation in both the Federal and state governments."[66] Reagan looked askance at the many new schemes to secure aid from the federal government for such things as the building of railroads and canals. Perhaps his remarks were a gentle reprimand to Maxey and through him to others like Ashbel Smith and Guy M. Bryan for their plans to improve Galveston harbor with federal aid, and to Thockmorton, also a new member of the House, who was greatly interested in having the federal government grant aid to the Texas and Pacific Railroad. Reagan felt, and on general principle Maxey agreed with him, that these enterprises would "Swamp the Democratic, as they have the Republican party in corruption and debt and dishonor."[67]

As the time grew nearer for his departure for Washington, a great many people suddenly wanted something of Maxey. For instance, his law partner, James Chenoweth, asked for, and received, his help in securing an appointment as special district judge of the criminal courts of Fannin, Lamar, and Red River counties. "Pull me through on this," said Chenoweth to Maxey, "and I am yours for life."[68] U.S. Congressman Samuel S. Cox of New York wrote Maxey asking him to use his influence with the Democratic Texas delegation to vote Cox the speakership of the House. Cox added that he knew John Hancock was already against him because Cox had returned his back pay and voted against the bill for increased pay for the House members. "But in my conscience," Cox wrote, "I could not keep it and I would leave politics if I could not obey some better instinct or ambition than greed. There is something good in the air for you in Texas!"[69]

In January, 1875, Congressman Throckmorton wrote from Washington to Maxey in Paris and asked him to come early to Washington

[66] John H. Reagan to Maxey, December 4, 1874, ibid.
[67] Ibid.
[68] James Q. Chenoweth to Maxey, January 28, 1875, ibid.
[69] Samuel S. Cox to Maxey, November 9, 1874, ibid. Cox was referring to John Hancock, Texas Unionist, who had been elected to the House of Representatives on the Democratic ticket.

to aid in solidifying the southern Democratic vote (especially that of the lukewarm Kentucky Democrats) for federal aid to the Texas and Pacific Railroad.[70] Although Throckmorton sent along a free railroad pass, and although Maxey had been instructed in May by the Texas legislature to help obtain such aid for the Texas and Pacific, he didn't arrive in Washington until February 27, 1875, only four days before the opening session of Congress.

On March 1, Maxey handed his credentials to his colleague Morgan C. Hamilton, who was to present him to the Senate. Strict courtesy would have required Maxey to allow the departing James W. Flanagan to do the honor, but Maxey did not like Flanagan, a Whig, a friend of Sam Houston, and an opponent of secession. Flanagan had been a delegate to the Republican national convention in 1872 and had voted consistently with the Radicals since his election to the Senate.[71] Although Maxey had no intimation that any objection would be raised to his being sworn in, he was anxious, for he was aware that the Radicals wished to be rid of the Democrats. With great relief he later wrote Marilda:

The long agony is over. . . . I was sworn in without the slightest objection from any quarter. It was thought by the Radicals that an effort would be made to unstate Texas by refusing to swear me in. The other point I know was a question of law utterly frivolous, still in a matter of such great importance where every vote counts, I did not know. . . . Cockrell of Missouri, Withers of Virginia, Jones of Florida, and myself had to take what Senator McCreary of Kentucky calls the "diluted oath" suited to rebels.[72]

I have a very good seat which you may tell by taking the diagram of the senate chamber, place yourself in the chair of the President of the Senate and mine is in the middle tier to his right and the second seat from the end of the semi-circle. The first is occupied by Senator Jones of Florida, the second by me, the third by Senator Dennis of Maryland. Right back of me sits Andy and the Constitution.[73] . . . As Senator Johnson walked

[70] J. W. Throckmorton to Maxey, January 21, 1875, ibid.

[71] Webb and Carroll, *Handbook of Texas*, II, 609.

[72] The "diluted oath" was an oath to support the Constitution and also the special oath that had been prescribed by an act of Congress, July 11, 1868, and which, in the main, was a promise not to take up arms against the government.

[73] Andrew Johnson was elected to the Senate in 1874. He attended the special

down the aisle to take the oath he was received with a good deal of applause from the galleries and he found a handsome bouquet on his table.[74]

Maxey was disappointed that the Senate immediately adjourned for a long weekend. He assumed that it was to give the "old senators" some rest.

Shortly after his arrival in Washington, Maxey had gone to the Capitol and called upon Congressman John Hancock of Texas, and upon the elderly Congressman Samuel S. Cox of New York. He also visited Senator Thomas F. Bayard of Delaware and, after observing the amount of work he did, Maxey ventured the opinion to Lightfoot that it was a great mistake to think that a senator had a leisurely life. "In addition to the legitimate work of the senate in session and in committee there is a larger amount of labor in interview on business with citizens and in reply to correspondence, visiting departments, etc."[75]

Maxey had admired Bayard of Delaware since 1869 when Bayard had first shown a deep sympathy for the South in its struggles against Republican misrule. In January, 1875, Maxey had written Bayard expressing his concern that General Philip Sheridan had asked Congress to pass a bill declaring unruly whites in Louisiana banditti. Bayard had replied that the Democrats must use "discretion and perseverance in those localities where Federal outrages encourage violent resistance—a resistance justified by everything except the hope of success (and that is the test)."[76] Although an ardent and popular Democrat, Bayard had the ability to rise above partisan considerations, and he had won the respect of leading Republican senators. In Congress he propounded the axiom that any program designed to destroy the liberties of the southern voters would, in the end, react adversely upon

---

short session in March, 1875, and delivered a speech attacking Grant and defending the Constitution. Soon afterward he returned home, had a paralytic stroke and died. See Wirt Armistead Cate, *Lucius Q. C. Lamar*, p. 230.

[74] Maxey to Marilda Maxey, March 5, 1875, Maxey Papers.

[75] Maxey to Henry Lightfoot, March 11, 1875, ibid.

[76] Thomas F. Bayard to Maxey, January 19, 1875, ibid. See also Charles C. Tansill, *The Congressional Career of Thomas Francis Bayard, 1869–1885*, p. 92; Allan Nevins, *Hamilton Fish*, pp. 748–749.

every section of the Union. After having dined with Bayard in Washington, Maxey wrote enthusiastically to Marilda: "The more I see of him the better I like him. He is a plain, unassuming and a thorough gentleman and has an unostentatious winning way about him that I admire greatly. I feel sure that he and I will be good friends as he says we are bound to be. . . . Bayard is not far from my age."[77] Allan Nevins, in his biography of Grover Cleveland, describes Bayard as a "man of high culture, with a grave stately courtesy and a polished if heavy eloquence."[78] The second most influential Democrat in the Senate was Allen G. Thurman of Ohio, an older man than Maxey and Bayard, who was described by Maxey as "a blunt, outspoken, honest man of immense sledge hammer force."[79]

Maxey renewed his acquaintance with a number of old friends in Washington. General Ambrose Burnside, now a senator from Rhode Island, was one. The two West Point classmates, who had not seen each other in twenty-five years, expressed the hope that the two of them could, in some measure, help to unite the estranged sections of their country.[80] Upon meeting Tom Ochiltree, his former aide in the Indian Territory, Maxey commented that Tom seemed to know everybody. Ochiltree, the *bon vivant*, teller of tall tales, and adventurer, had been to New York, where he had been installed as president of the Torpids, a gentleman's club at Delmonico's, whose motto was Take Things Easy.[81] Among others Maxey met in the capital were several Kentuckians: ex-State Treasurer Richard Wintersmith and Harry I. Todd, the latter being the son-in-law of ex-Governor John Crittenden. By invitation Maxey had breakfast with John W. Stevenson, another ex-governor of Kentucky, who was now a senator.

Maxey called on ailing Alexander H. Stephens, representative from Georgia, whom he had met during the Civil War when Stephens was vice-president of the Confederacy. Maxey found him to be now "a mere shadow but full of animation." Maxey was relieved to find that

[77] Maxey to Marilda Maxey, March 2, 1875, Maxey Papers.
[78] Allan Nevins, *Grover Cleveland*, p. 194.
[79] Maxey to Marilda Maxey, March 2, 1875, Maxey Papers.
[80] Ibid.
[81] Claude H. Hall, "The Fabulous Tom Ochiltree: Promoter, Politician, and Raconteur," *Southwestern Historical Quarterly* 71 (1968): 359, n.

Stephens's wartime secretary, William H. Hidell, was no longer barring access to the great man. Upon inquiry Maxey learned from Stephens that Hidell was attempting to practice law in Memphis and Stephens remarked further that Hidell had some talent but was impractical. In Maxey's opinion this estimate gave a fair analysis of Hidell's abilities.[82]

Senator Theodore Randolph of New Jersey invited Maxey to dine, and Mrs. Randolph, a hospitable and amiable Mississippian, encouraged him to call at their rooms whenever he felt like it. Senators Randolph, William Eaton of Connecticut, Francis Kernan of New York, William Whyte of Maryland, and Maxey were all staying at the exclusive Arlington Hotel. They liked to walk to and from the Senate each day, and as they walked together they gave Maxey polite and sincere assurances that Texas would come out of the Reconstruction phase and become a coequal state in the Union.[83]

When Secretary of War William Belknap left his card, Maxey returned his call but was reserved about promising to serve him. Maxey knew well Belknap's wife, the ambitious Amanda Tomlinson of Glasgow, Kentucky, and wrote Marilda of his feelings about Belknap, "He has the appointing power and I think I could serve him, but I have no right nor would my recommendation be of avail, outside of Texas, unless in fortifying a recommendation from the immediate representative."[84] Maxey was thinking of the fact that the War Department maintained closer relations than any other with Southern affairs but he disliked Belknap's closeness to the Radicals, who believed that Belknap would do what they wished to keep Mississippi, Texas, and other states Republican.

Among other calls Maxey made in Washington was one on President Grant, who received him quite graciously but not familiarly. Maxey also visited with a group of his Indian Territory friends who were in the capital to argue a case before the Supreme Court. Generals Albert Pike and Douglas H. Cooper, and Elias Boudinot, the Chero-

[82] Maxey to Marilda Maxey, March 2, 1875, Maxey Papers.
[83] Ibid., March 6, 1875.
[84] Ibid.

kee delegate to the Confederate Congress, welcomed Maxey and urged him to sit in on the case they were presenting.

After the first flurry, Maxey's social life in Washington became considerably calmer, almost to the point of seclusion. His rooms were plain and he lacked the money to entertain or even to hire a cab to ride to the daily sessions of the Senate. When, in June, 1876, he received an invitation to dine at the White House with President and Mrs. Grant, he had to borrow the swallow-tail coat of his fellow boarder, the elderly Senator Allen T. Caperton of West Virginia. Considering Grant's previous kindness, Maxey's attitude toward this invitation is curious. He wrote Marilda: "Yesterday I received the enclosed invitation from the Grand Gyascutus[85] and his old woman to dine with them socially Saturday evening at 7 P.M. According to etiquette in such cases provided I had to accept or tender a note of regret, etc. As he had asked me last year to call socially whenever I felt like it and as I had never done it and had no excuse, I was bound to accept, so I armed myself with some of this note paper and acknowledged the honor, etc., done up in a blue rag."[86] Maxey also accepted the informal invitations of bachelor Ambrose Burnside from time to time, possibly because there was no obligation to return the favor.[87]

The Senate had opened on March 4 and, in addition to the assignment of committee work, took up the Civil Rights Bills, the Force Rights Bill, and the long-standing question of whether P. B. S. Pinchback of Louisiana should be permitted to take his seat in the Senate. When the Democratic caucus was held on March 6 to determine committee assignments, Maxey expressed his eagerness to serve on those committees of immediate interest to the people of Texas. Since the Republicans still had the majority, there were few places left for the Democrats. Maxey would have preferred appointment to the Committee on Commerce so that he could press for federal aid for the

[85] A gyascutus is an imaginary large four-legged beast with legs on one side longer than on the other that enable it to walk around steep hillsides (*Webster's International Dictionary*, 3d ed.).

[86] Maxey to Marilda Maxey, June 1, 1876, Maxey Papers.

[87] Benjamin Perley Poore, *The Life and Public Services of Ambrose E. Burnside*, p. 330.

improvement of Texas harbors, or to the Committee on Indian Affairs where he could urge frontier protection for Texas. These two and the Committee on the Texas and Pacific Railroad were the only ones he believed had a special significance for the people of Texas. He was assigned to none of these, although every effort was made to get an opening for him on the Committee on Indian Affairs. Unluckily, it had no vacancy on the Democratic list, since Democrats McCreary of Kentucky and Bogy of Missouri were already on it. Senator Thurman, a member of the Committee on Arrangements, promised to try to place Maxey on the Indian Affairs Committee at the beginning of the next session. Meanwhile, he was assigned to the Committee on Post Offices and Post Roads, the Committee on Territories, and the Committee on Education and Labor. He explained these positions to Marilda: "The first is one in which everybody is interested and is an unusually strong committee with an ex-President and Vice-President on it.[88] Our people are vitally interested in this matter, more so perhaps than anybody else as there will be a constant demand for new [Post] offices and [Post] routes. . . . The Committee on Territories is not especially important to Texas except in case the Indian Country should be converted into a Territory."[89] Although the Radicals believed the Committee on Education and Labor to be highly important and had made it a strong committee with Senators Morton, Gordon, Eaton, and Ferry, Maxey could not perceive that the Federal government had any special concern with these subjects. He believed them to be matters of concern and decision of the individual states. He had discussed his position on this matter with Reagan and Coke, who both agreed with him.[90]

Washington was a rich man's city. Many of the senators were very wealthy and many of them spent much more than they earned. Maxey spent the nineteen days of the special session of the Forty-fourth Congress at the exclusive Arlington Hotel where wealthy New York-

[88] Maxey was speaking of Hannibal Hamlin of Maine, vice-president under Lincoln and president of the Senate, 1861–1865 (*Biographical Directory of the American Congress, 1774–1961*, p. 998).

[89] Maxey to Marilda Maxey, March 10, 1875, Maxey Papers.

[90] Richard Coke to Maxey, September 7, 1874; John Reagan to Maxey, September 12, December 4, 1874, ibid.

ers, titled foreigners and rich lobbyists stayed, but he realized that
when he returned for the regular session he must find cheaper lodg-
ings.[91] The economic depression in Texas was severe. Maxey had
borrowed $3,000 from his Aunt Sarah Maxey for his stay in Wash-
ington. Lightfoot was unable to collect any of the money owed to the
law firm. There was little new law business for the firm, partially because Lightfoot did not inspire the confidence of his clients as Maxey
had.

Marilda, hostile to Maxey's devotion to politics, tended her house
and gardens and wrote wistfully to Maxey: "Sam [Sam Bell] Long
talks about you every day. He woke up after you had been gone some
time and missed you and turned over to me and said in a low tremu-
lous tone, 'Uncle is gone, Mufoda.' He then began to cry and the little fellow cried for a long time and somebody else cried too."[92] Maxey
replied that he missed Sam Bell very much, "Tell him I have no one
to sleep with me and I want my boy every night to warm my back."
He continued to Marilda, "Be a good girl and don't take on because
I am not at home."[93]

On March 18, Maxey wrote Marilda that he wanted her to return
to Washington with him for the congressional session in December,
explaining:

The idea of staying home for six or seven months whilst I am here is perfectly absurd and I don't propose to stand for it. There is not a woman
I have seen here better qualified to perform her part than you are. I don't
blame you for not wanting to engage in the frivolities of Washington life.
I have not the slightest taste that way—have not been out but once since
here and that was a special invitation to Senator Bayard's. . . . My idea is,
and that is followed by many, to either get good rooms at a hotel or at a
private house and live quietly.[94]

But Marilda realized that there was not enough money to do as Maxey
wished. Although his wardrobe, according to his own pronouncement, was "on the average with the balance in the senate which is

91 For a description of Washington during this period, see Nevins, *Fish,* p. 553.
92 Marilda Maxey to Maxey, February 28, 1875, Maxey Papers.
93 Maxey to Marilda Maxey, March 1, 1875, ibid.
94 Maxey to Marilda Maxey, March 18, 1875, ibid.

not a dressy body very particularly,"[95] she had not the equivalent wardrobe. This expense, added to the cost of her fare to Washington and her room and board there, was prohibitive for them in their present economic position. Too, the idea of living in a boardinghouse with nothing to occupy her time was repugnant to her.

[95] Ibid., March 2, 1875.

5. Forty-fourth Congress
First Session

> The Republicans consider me a strict partisan but entirely fair
> and are personally kindly disposed. It is very greatly to our
> interest to have it so.[1]

AFTER THE CIVIL WAR the Texas Whigs had been forced slowly
and surely into the Democratic party though they did not find
it always congenial. The conservative Maxey was an old Henry Clay
Whig, but there was no room left in either the Republican or Democratic party for the Whig notion of moderation and compromise. In
1872, when the northern Democrats had failed to back appropriation
bills and internal improvement measures for Texas, some of the Texas
Democrats, led by Reagan, had cooperated with liberal Republicans
by supporting Horace Greeley with all "his brands of socialism, spir-
itualism and radicalism and his long record of South baiting."[2] But
Maxey had opposed the move toward Greeley.[3]

The panic of 1873 and the deep depression that lasted well into
1877 prostrated Texas economically and spiritually. Although the
drive for federal aid to build Texas railroads and to improve Texas

---

[1] Maxey to Marilda Maxey, April 14, 1876, Maxey Papers.
[2] V. Vann Woodward, *Reunion and Reaction*, p. 47.
[3] Maxey to Marilda Maxey, May 12, 1872, Maxey Papers.

harbors and frontier defenses was largely inspired by individuals who sought their own gain, like W. L. Moody, William P. Ballinger and Guy M. Bryan, all of Galveston, the improvements they demanded attracted wide support among Texans. This Maxey discovered when he returned to Texas at the end of the special session of the Senate on March 24, and began a tour of the state with his wife and daughter, addressing agricultural groups and laying cornerstones, having contact with community leaders and with a large cross section of the population.

In September, Maxey was invited to a floor seat at the convention that met in Austin to form a new constitution for Texas. He was dismayed that the prevailing trend of the convention seemed to be overreaction against Republican abuses during Reconstruction, but he was encouraged that quite a number of men whom he considered very able had been sent as delegates. When the report of the legislative committee was brought before the convention, it was clear that many restrictions were to be imposed on the legislature. "Whilst certain guards are essential against hasty legislation," Maxey complained "the convention should remember that it does not embody all the present and future wisdom of the state."[4]

During this month in Austin, Maxey was treated royally. Governor Coke received him cordially, as did Assistant Attorney General Andrew J. Peeler. He accepted the invitation of State Treasurer Andrew J. Dorn (an old friend from the Mexican and Civil War days) to use the state treasurer's office. Perhaps if he had foreseen the favors the failure-prone Dorn would be seeking in the future, he would not have accepted the offer to receive guests in Dorn's state office and to use the state treasurer's official stationery.[5]

The constitutional convention met for eleven weeks, and the new constitution did not come before the people for voting until February 15, 1876, after Governor Coke stumped the state explaining it. The anxious Maxey wrote from Washington: "I trust Coke made a favorable impression on our people. It would be most unfortunate for the

4 Ibid., September 26, 1875.
5 Ibid.

Democratic party and the country to have the new constitution defeated."[6]

Maxey had returned to Washington and taken rooms at Number 1412 I Street, Northwest. The first session of Congress opened on December 5, 1875, and lasted nine months, during which time its paramount consideration were tariff reform and the monetary standard. Both the House and the Senate delayed passing the appropriation bills as long as possible. The Democrat's very human desire for revenge manifested itself in penetrating investigations of the corruption in Grant's administration, but they sapped their own energy and only added fuel to the fires of Republican presidential aspirants who hoped to dump Grant.[7] For instance, Senator Oliver Morton of Indiana, eager for the presidency and one of the oldest champions of the Republican policy in the South, took advantage of the atmosphere of reform created by the Democrats and sought to have a committee appointed to investigate the alleged frauds in the recent Mississsppi elections. Since the Democratic candidates had won, naturally the Democrats opposed the move and many of them spoke out against it. Maxey, though he had no fear of holding his own in the Senate, saw the futility of hasty action and did not believe it "policy to strike out too brash," and so he remained silent on the question.[8] But Reagan, in the House, was doing enough speaking out for the entire Texas delegation.[9] Congress was filled with such acrimony and tension that when Maxey was invited to visit both Senators Kernan of New York and Randolph of New Jersey for the Christmas holidays, he was pleased to escape to the hospitality of the Randolphs.

Maxey was back in Washington when news came that Governor Coke had decided to run for the Senate seat of Morgan C. Hamilton.

6 Ibid., February 17, 1876.

7 Conditions under Grant's administration are described in Allan Nevins, *Hamilton Fish*, pp. 747–780, and in William B. Hesseltine, *Ulysses S. Grant*, pp. 393–394.

8 Maxey to Marilda Maxey, December 18, 1875, Maxey Papers. See also, Edward Stanwood, *James Gillespie Blaine*, pp. 177–178.

9 Ben H. Procter, *Not without Honor*, p. 212; U.S. Congress, *Congressional Record*, 44th Cong., 1st sess., January 12, 1876, and June 22, 1876, pp. 389–390, 4035.

Other Democratic candidates for the seat were John Hancock and John Ireland, and though Maxey owed Ireland a favor for his help in 1874, he preferred to remain neutral and speak for neither Coke nor Ireland. But things were brought to a head when Coke visited Paris during his campaign and was invited to stay at the Maxey home. Marilda explained to Maxey that she had only wanted to treat Coke as well as he had treated them during their stay at the Governor's mansion in Austin in June, 1875. Her hospitality was misinterpreted by Ireland, however, who complained to O. M. Roberts that Maxey owed his election to the Senate in 1874 largely to him, and that he also resented the fact that Lightfoot and Chenoweth had spoken in Austin to support Coke. The angry Ireland claimed that Maxey's actions were a result of fear that Coke might be an antagonist for Maxey's own seat in the Senate in 1881.[10] Ireland further confided to Roberts that he felt Maxey was a trickster and double dealer. Coke won the election.

Until February, Maxey's demeanor in the Senate was cautious. He veered from controversial subjects and restricted his comments to legal arguments, but when the bill relating to the centennial celebration of American Independence came up, he was overcome with patriotic zeal and delivered a speech on the spur of the moment. He was justifiably pleased with his oration and with its reception. It was printed, without revisions, in the *Congressional Record*.[11]

On George Washington's birthday Maxey took an excursion boat to Mount Vernon and was surprised, upon his arrival, to be asked to give an impromptu speech before his fellow excursionists. The *New York World* reported the text of his extemporaneous speech, which was filled with fervor for the Federal Union of coequal States.[12] In Austin, attorney Thomas Duval, after reading the *New York Tribune*'s account of the speech, wrote enthusiastically to Maxey, "If such patriotic sentiments were felt and uttered by our politicians,

[10] John Ireland to O. M. Roberts, October 23, 1879, Oran Milo Roberts Papers.
[11] Maxey to Marilda Maxey, February 24, 1876, Maxey Papers; *Congressional Record*, 44th Cong., 1st sess., Feb. 9, 1876, pp. 970–971.
[12] *New York World*, February 23, 1876, newsclipping, Maxey Papers.

North and South, there would soon be an end to all the sectional bitterness."[13] In Paris, Marilda's reaction to the New York newspaper accounts was more bitter than enthusiastic: "I hope you may gain some reputation whilst you are in the senate for the Lord knows there is nothing else that is good in being a member of the senate to compensate one for the necessary separation from one's home and family."[14] The word reputation agitated Marilda, who had written earlier in March to Maxey: "Reputation is a good thing in its place but I think that six years away from home and wife is paying a little too dear for it. But you don't look at it that way or you would never have been there."[15]

On March 31, while Morton's resolution to investigate the Democratic victory in Mississippi was before the Senate, Boutwell of Massachusetts took the floor to make an assault upon the South. Among those who made effective replies were Withers of Virginia and Maxey. Boutwell had charged that all the statesmen of the South for the past seventy years had been enemies of the Union. When Maxey stood to speak he attacked this statement by reminding the senators of the contributions of James Madison, Andrew Jackson, James Monroe, Zachary Taylor, Winfield Scott, and many others—all southern men who had done much for their country. He depicted Boutwell as a false guide who was not supported by the people he represented when he made accusations against the South and chided him saying, "Every true patriot, be he Republican or Democrat, from the North, South, East or West, knows that a restoration of fraternal feeling is necessary to a real Union.[16]

The Democrats considered Wither's and Maxey's speeches such effective and positive answers to Boutwell that they arranged to print and distribute ten thousand copies of the three speeches. Northern newspapers of the Democratic and Independent persuasion also liked Maxey's reply to Boutwell; the *Baltimore Sun* was one that praised

---

[13] Maxey quotes from Duval's letter in Maxey to Marilda Maxey, March 19, 1876, ibid.

[14] Marilda Maxey to Maxey, March 22, 1876, ibid.

[15] Ibid., March 9, 1876.

[16] *Congressional Record*, 44th Cong., 1st sess., March 31, 1876, pp. 2075–2076.

him.[17] Bayard reported to Maxey that in Boston alone five hundred copies of the speeches had been distributed. In Texas the *Sherman Courier* applauded Maxey's speech and favorably compared him with Rusk, Hemphill, and Houston.[18] Maxey basked in his success and commented to Marilda: "Although I say it myself, I think I am able to hold my own now, which I propose to do. In any nonpartisan measure I can do as much as any man in the senate. The Republicans consider me a strict partisan but entirely fair and are personally kindly disposed. It is very greatly to our interest to have it so."[19]

When the vote was taken on Morton's resolution to investigate the Mississippi election, Maxey wrote of his part in the proceedings:

[Morton's Mississippi resolutions] provide for a committee of five. Of these three will be Republican and two Democrats. Yesterday evening the President of the Senate called me and told me if I would accept he would appoint me. I declined. This morning we had a caucus in relation to the two we should have. Thurman thought that they should be from the South —I think from the North. We selected Bayard and McDonald [of Indiana]. . . . The investigation will not have the slightest effect on the South one way or the other nor will it affect prominent Democrats or Republicans in the North but will weigh with the Independents.[20]

Preparations for the coming presidential election began in the spring of 1876. On May 20, Maxey wrote of his disappointment that Allen Thurman had lost his bid for the presidential nomination in his home state: "I have been much pained to notice the proceedings of the Democratic convention of Ohio. Thurman who is as true a man as ever lived, honest beyond question, able by universal concession, has been slaughtered in his own household, stabbed under the fifth rib with a 'how is it with thee brother?' "[21] Maxey added that he believed the nomination possibility was reduced to Thomas Bayard, Governor Samuel Tilden of New York, and wealthy Hoosier Thomas

[17] Maxey remarks on the *Sun* article in Maxey to Marilda Maxey, April 14, 1876, Maxey Papers.
[18] *Sherman Courier*, April 8, 1876.
[19] Maxey to Marilda Maxey, April 14, 1876, Maxey Papers.
[20] Ibid., April 1, 1876.
[21] Ibid., May 20, 1876. See also John S. Hare, "Allen G. Thurman," doctoral dissertation, pp. 261–262.

Hendricks. He felt that Bayard would run as strongly in New Jersey or Connecticut as Tilden and much stronger in the doubtful states of Mississippi, Louisiana, and Florida. But Maxey's father wrote to disagree, insisting that most Texans believed Tilden a safer man for the nomination.[22]

On June 11, James G. Blaine of Maine, a hopeful candidate for the Republican presidential nomination, fell down unconscious on the steps of his church. In 1872, Blaine had been found guilty of indiscretion and dishonesty in the Credit Mobilier scandals. Shortly before his collapse he had been accused of being involved in manipulating worthless bonds in a shady deal with the Union Pacific Railroad. On June 5, he had defended himself before a House committee in a long and angry harangue that, no doubt, took a heavy toll on his mental and physical energies and probably contributed to his collapse a few days later.[23] He was removed to his home, just a few steps away from Maxey's boardinghouse. Maxey, observing the steady stream of visitors to the Blaine home and pondering over the unlucky man, wrote home to Marilda: "The attack, I suppose, resulted from the terrible mental strain under which he has necessarily been laboring for sometime past. My opinion is he has made his money by dark and tortuous methods. He has been deep about it but the developments already have shown him that he was walking on the thin crust of a volcano liable at any moment to belch forth its consuming fires. I think he has been satisfied throughout his desperate game that he could not be nominated."[24] The next day Maxey learned that Blaine was recovering, and perhaps feeling somewhat remorseful about his earlier remarks, he wrote further, "Whilst I have no earthly use for him, I want him to get well."[25] The Republicans, deciding that Blaine had rendered himself too controversial to become a presidential candidate, announced on June 14 that Rutherford B. Hayes was their choice. The popular William A. Wheeler of New York was announced as the vice-presidential candidate, thus forming a very strong ticket that,

[22] Rice Maxey to Maxey, May 28, 1876, Maxey Papers.
[23] Hesseltine, *Grant*, pp. 310–311, 399–401.
[24] Maxey to Marilda Maxey, June 11, 1876, Maxey Papers.
[25] Ibid., June 12, 1876.

said the worried Maxey, "will require a first rate nomination on our part to give us any show of success."[26]

One fervent plea Maxey made on the Senate floor was that the pay of the professors and cadets at West Point *not* be reduced.[27] Probably as a result of this he was invited to attend the June 16 graduation ceremonies at the academy. He later described his trip:

I left here [Washington] on the 9:30 A.M. train and just before reaching Philadelphia, Senator [John] Sherman and his brother General [William T.] Sherman came into the car where I was and the Senator introduced me to his brother. General Sherman is a brusque, quick spoken, quick moving, very plain, slender man not at all handsome but still with character strongly marked in his face. I would take him to be an honest man. Reaching New York we remained overnight and went up the next morning on the 8:30 train. General Sherman in the meantime having telegraphed for a room for me as well as himself. Seeing that he wanted to be friendly I met him halfway not only because it was right but because it is to the interest of Texas with her immense frontier to be protected that I should be on good terms with the General of the Army.[28]

Although the Senate was behind schedule on granting appropriations, other matters were taken up. On June 20, Maxey spoke urging that the charge of Indian Affairs be placed under the War Department instead of the Interior and amplifying his belief that the Indians respected army officers more than they did civilians.[29] Some of the senators complimented him by saying that his speech was the best he had made since coming to the Senate.[30]

On July 4, while visiting a resort in West Virginia, Maxey learned of General Custer's defeat at the hands of the Sioux and wrote Marilda, "I suppose, of course, the account is greatly exaggerated but it is believed here that a fight took place and that Custer was very badly worsted and most people think was killed."[31] This event reinforced

[26] Ibid., June 16, 1876.
[27] *Congressional Record*, 44th Cong., 1st sess., Feb. 25, 1876, p. 1283.
[28] Maxey to Marilda Maxey, June 16, 1876, Maxey Papers.
[29] *Congressional Record*, 44th Cong., 1st sess., June 20, 1876, p. 3904.
[30] Maxey to Marilda Maxey, June 21, 1876, Maxey Papers.
[31] Ibid., July 6, 1876.

Maxey's opinion that it was imperative to place the Indians under strict military control. When he returned to Washington, Maxey talked with Senator Isaac P. Christiancy of Michigan, a close friend of Custer, and was promised Christiancy's help in passing an act to place the Indian Bureau under military control. The act was defeated, however.

The Army Appropriations Bill came before the Senate in July. One of its many amendments provided for increasing the military strength of the army in order to protect the western frontier more effectively. Back in December, 1875, Senators Hamilton and Maxey and Congressmen Schleicher, Hancock, and Reagan had called on President Grant to discuss the Texas frontier, especially the Rio Grande. Grant had suggested that the most feasible and expeditious plan for protection would be to increase the cavalry to one hundred enlisted men to a company, and he had added that if this could be effected he would give Texas two full regiments.[32] When voting time came in the Senate, Maxey alone among the Democrats voted with the Radicals to increase the number of men in each cavalry unit.[33] Later General Sherman thanked Maxey for his efforts in increasing the army by 2,500 men and assured him that recruits would be sent to Texas.[34]

As the time neared for the Democratic national convention in St. Louis, Maxey, still an enthusiastic supporter of Bayard despite his father's arguments to the contrary, wrote home to inquire whether Henry Lightfoot, a Texas delegate to the convention, had left for Saint Louis:

I trust that the St. Louis convention which meets tomorrow will be governed by wisdom and prudence. Tilden goes there with a great sounding

[32] Maxey to William T. Sherman, August 27, 1876, published in the *Waco Examiner*, September 22, 1876, newsclipping, Maxey Papers. In September, 1875, while attending the Texas constitutional convention, Maxey interviewed General E. O. C. Ord, commander of the frontier troops in Texas, who emphasized the great need for increased troops. In December, Maxey presented to the U.S. Senate a petition from the Texas convention requesting an increase of troops on the Rio Grande. See Maxey to Marilda Maxey, December 10, 1875, Maxey Papers.

[33] *Congressional Record*, 44th Cong., 1st sess., July 14, 1876, p. 4140.

[34] William T. Sherman to Maxey, September 1, 1876, published in *Waco Examiner*, September 22, 1876, newsclipping, Maxey Papers.

of brass and tinkling of cymbals. Much of his reputation and supposed popularity is of the newspaper variety. The *best* nomination for success is Bayard. To try to win Republican votes by ignoring our true friends for fear of the bloody shirt is the veriest nonsense. No bloody shirt man ever intended to vote the Democratic ticket. We had better solidify our own ranks by putting out the best possible men to satisfy Democrats. . . . I would be entirely satisfied with Thurman but Bayard will create more enthusiasm.[35]

From Saint Louis, Lightfoot reported on June 27 that the convention had met and organized quietly and harmoniously, and that there was a great deal of pulling and buttonholing for different candidates—but that at the same time all claimed they would support the nominee of the convention, whoever he might be. Lightfoot added that the Tammany ring of New York was actively opposing Tilden at the convention and that Winfield Scott Hancock was running a close second in strength to Tilden, leaving Bayard in third place.[36]

Ultimately, the Texas delegation voted for Tilden with W. S. Herndon of Texas making a speech to second his nomination. Bayard trailed behind Tilden, Hendricks, Hancock, and Thurman on the first ballot and fared little better on subsequent ones. Tilden won a final majority vote and Hendricks was chosen as vice-presidential nominee.[37]

Rutherford B. Hayes's letter accepting the Republican nomination was published on July 10. As Maxey watched for Tilden's acceptance speech he wrote bitterly to Marilda: "Tilden is said to be worth several million dollars. I suppose he will bleed freely." He added: "I read Hayes's lettter of acceptance last night. It is a shrewdly written paper. Uncle Sammy's [Tilden] has not come out yet. He is very cool and wonderfully plausible and I suppose his letter will be a good one. A man who showed such consummate tact as he did at St. Louis ought to be able to write a good letter. Uncle Sammy is very old.[38] J. B. is sly. Devilish sly is John B."[39] J. B., or John B., was John Bigelow,

35 Maxey to Marilda Maxey, June 26, 1876, Maxey Papers.
36 Henry W. Lightfoot to Dora Lightfoot, June 27, 1876, Lightfoot Family Papers.
37 Alexander C. Flick, *Samuel Jones Tilden*, pp. 289–290.
38 Tilden was 62 years old, Maxey was 51. (Tilden's age from Flick, *Tilden*, p. 1.)
39 Maxey to Marilda Maxey, July 11, 1876, Maxey Papers.

who polished the style of Tilden's letter of acceptance, but Tilden's acceptance speech was not delivered until almost three weeks later.[40]

The River and Harbor Bill came before the Senate on July 13. Maxey made a bold fight to prevent the removal of the appropriations for Texas. He pleaded with the Senate to give Texas the same aid other states had received from the federal government, and he added: "I belong to the younger class of men who believe in developing the great resources of the South and the new Southwest. I live in a progressive state and among progressive people."[41] Later he wrote Marilda: "It [the bill] is fought very bitterly by Edmunds of Vermont and Eastern men generally, and is supported by the South and a majority of the West. . . . If we can get a good harbor at Galveston we will, I think, secure a good portion of the trade of Kansas and West Missouri."[42] On July 31 the bill was recommended to a conference committee on appropriations, thus endangering its passage, for, Maxey reported, the chairman and some others of the committee were inimical to any appropriation for rivers and harbors.

As a parting gift to Bayard at the end of the session on August 15, Maxey sent a piece of Texas-made white flannel from the New Braunfels mills with the information that the Texas Rangers had summer uniforms made of it. The pleased Bayard wrote Maxey that "the cloth is beautiful enough to turn all the old Texas Rangers into dandies and stimulate a love of dress quite fatal to industry."[43] About this time, too, the generous Caperton, whose dress suit Maxey had worn to the dinner party given by President and Mrs. Grant, died quietly and suddenly in Maxey's rooming house.

On September 20, a Democratic convention at Longview, Texas, endorsed "with pride and admiration" Maxey's course in Congress. The *Galveston News* recorded this and went on to say, "Having entered the senate untried in public life as a civil officer it is no disparagement to say that he has surprised many of his friends by the high

---

[40] See Flick, *Tilden*, p. 297.
[41] *Congressional Record*, 44th Cong., 1st sess., July 17, 1876, pp. 3926; 5107.
[42] Maxey to Marilda Maxey, July 28, 1876, Maxey Papers.
[43] Thomas F. Bayard to Maxey, August 15, 1876, ibid.

rank which he so soon acquired in that body."[44] Said the *Honey Grove Independent*, "We must have the General [Maxey] in Mr. Tilden's Cabinet if the senate can spare him for no man has the interest of Texas more at heart than he."[45]

Maxey met with the other Texas Democratic congressional delegates—Reagan, Throckmorton, Culberson, Mills, Hancock, and Schleicher—to make plans for their campaign for Tilden, and Maxey spoke for him at Paris, Clarksville, and other towns in North Texas. The populace asked him, "What does Tilden suggest? Will he stand up?"[46] but Maxey had no answer because Tilden had not outlined his campaign. On November 7, Maxey reluctantly cast his vote for Tilden and on the twenty-third left for a visit to New York before returning to Washington and a new session of Congress.

As the time for the election approached, President Grant had sent federal troops to South Carolina, Florida, Louisiana. Their duty was to protect Negro voters from the Ku Klux Klan and thus gain support for the Republican party. Nevertheless, the early returns seemed so unfavorable for the Republicans that the newspapers at first stated that Tilden had won. Hayes wrote in his diary that "the election has resulted in the defeat of the Republicans after a very close contest."[47] The Democratic campaign committee was timid about claiming victories in South Carolina, Florida, and Louisiana, but the Republican leaders, in a bold move, used the *New York Times* to influence public opinion, announcing in it that a canvas of the returning boards of Florida, South Carolina, and Louisiana showed a majority vote for Hayes, thereby making him the winner.[48] The Democrats demanded that Tilden be declared the rightful winner, but as the debate grew louder, each party insisting that it had won in the contested states, the more thoughtful southern Democrats separated themselves from

---

[44] *Galveston News*, September 21, 1876, newsclipping, ibid.

[45] *Honey Grove Independent*, October 27, 1876.

[46] *Galveston News*, November 1, 1876.

[47] T. Harry Williams (ed.), *Hayes*, p. 47.

[48] C. Vann Woodward, *Reunion and Reaction*, p. 18; Charles C. Tansill, *The Congressional Career of Thomas Francis Bayard, 1869–1885*, pp. 136–138.

the northern Democrats, who were demanding that troops be raised to enforce their rights. Tilden insisted that he had won and that therefore no compromise of any kind was necessary. Maxey, like Bayard and Thurman, disliked Tilden, but not to the point of desiring his defeat. In New York, Maxey learned that Bayard had annoyed Tilden's agents by refusing to go to New Orleans to review the contested Louisiana vote on behalf of the Democrats.[49] When Thurman arrived on December 2, Maxey was still in New York and was invited to accompany Thurman to visit Tilden. Maxey pondered over the resultant indecisive conversation with Tilden, "It is impossible to tell just now what will be the program as it is impossible to say what will be the facts, as events of great importance are transpiring every day."[50] On the train back to Washington with Senators Thurman, Conkling, Randolph, Kernan, and Eaton, the main topic of conversation was whether the count of the electoral vote would really settle the matter or instead further inflame the already agitated people.

In Republican quarters there was talk of trying to win over prominent southerners to Hayes by offering them assurances of assistance to their section. There was also a great deal of indignant reaction to the fact that Senator Roscoe Conkling of New York, head of the powerful Republican congressional oligarchy, was showing signs of listening to the pleas of the Democrats for the formation of a special committee to decide what should be done about the election count.[51]

The second session of the Forty-fourth Congress opened on December 4. On December 6 the electoral votes of the states were cast, two sets of conflicting votes being cast by Florida, Louisiana, and South Carolina.[52] Both Houses began an immediate discussion on the question of whether the president of the Senate or the two Houses should count the electoral vote. When John Sherman of Ohio declared in the Senate on December 21 that Hayes did not want other than the honest vote of the disputed states, Maxey rose to point out that question-

---

[49] Tansill, *Bayard*, p. 139.
[50] Maxey to Henry Lightfoot, December 2, 1876, Maxey Papers.
[51] Tansill, *Bayard*, pp. 154–155.
[52] Ibid., p. 142.

able integrity of past examining boards and to propose that a better and fairer method was needed.[53]

Back in Texas, Guy M. Bryan, intimate college friend of Hayes but a Tilden backer, read the news report of Maxey's response to Sherman and wrote Hayes enclosing a copy of a letter he had sent Maxey. Bryan wrote Hayes, "There is no doubt, my friend, that the South thinks Tilden is elected," and he proposed that Hayes and Tilden get together in a private conference, being careful not to presume that they could dispose of the office but agreeing between them that they would look into the facts themselves. He felt this would lend a nonpartisan and patriotic turn to the affair that was by then at civil war intensity, with northern Democrats declaring that they would organize troops to ensure that Tilden took his rightful place as President.[54] "I have written Maxey (senator from this state) to that effect, and said to him I know that you are chivalrous, patriotic and noble," wrote Bryan to Hayes.[55] In his letter to Maxey he urged him to approach Sherman and Congressman Lucius Q. C. Lamar of Mississippi for help in getting Hayes and Tilden together.[56] But Hayes replied to Bryan: "Your suggestions are in good spirit and, with the light you have, timely and wise. But one fact, not known to you, puts it completely out of the question. Whatever the result, I will someday when we meet name it to you. I *know* you will regard it as I do."[57]

It is assumed, for no letters are extant, that Maxey did all he could to carry out Bryan's request. He also kept in almost hourly touch with Bayard, Thurman, and Lamar and was as disappointed as any of the

---

[53] *Congressional Record*, 44th Cong., 2nd sess., December 21, 1876, p. 767.

[54] Woodward, *Reunion and Reaction*, pp. 32–34.

[55] Guy M. Bryan to Rutherford B. Hayes, December 30, 1876, Rutherford B. Hayes Papers.

[56] Guy M. Bryan to Maxey (enclosures), ibid.

[57] R. B. Hayes to Guy M. Bryan, January 6, 1877, Guy M. Bryan Papers. Perhaps Hayes already had some intimation about the coded telegrams that later proved so incriminating to Tilden. These showed that Tilden's nephew who was acting secretary of the Democratic national committee had some abortive dealings with the Louisiana canvassing board. See H. J. Eckenrode, *Rutherford B. Hayes*, p. 190; Tansill, *Bayard*, pp. 220–221.

Democrats when Bayard and Lamar's visit to see Tilden at the end of December brought forth from Tilden no advice.[58] On January 16, Maxey, with Bayard, Thurman, and Lamar, attended a meeting of twenty-three Democratic representatives to discuss final plans for a proposed electoral commission, which was to decide which votes should count for Hayes and which for Tilden. Bayard and Thurman, the two Democratic senators on the special committee for deciding the commission's make-up, were committed to the formation of a neutral electoral commission composed of selected members of both Houses along with selected judges of the Supreme Court.[59] Many worried Texans wrote Maxey for his opinion on the explosive political situation, and, on January 19, he replied to a letter from James B. Simpson, editor of the *Dallas Herald*, saying that he believed that a peaceful solution could be arrived at now that a special committee had been appointed for devising a way to count the electoral votes. He praised the Republican members of the committee—Senators George F. Edmunds of Vermont, Roscoe Conkling of New York, and Frederick Frelinghuysen of New Jersey—calling them "able lawyers and able men," and said that members Bayard and Thurman were too well known as lawyers and statesmen to need comment. He wrote: "I have never doubted, and I do not doubt, that Tilden and Hendricks were fairly elected. I believe Tilden will be duly inaugurated and that our country will rapidly recover from the paralysis into which it was thrown by the grave complications surrounding the Presidential question.[60] Following a week's debate, the Electoral Commission Bill was passed in the Senate on January 25 and in the House on the twenty-sixth. Among the Texas delegation only Republican Senator Morgan Hamilton and Democratic Congressman Roger Q. Mills voted no to the formation of the commission.[61] Grant signed the bill on January 29 and the Electoral Commission consisting of five representatives, five senators, and five Supreme Court justices was formed. Because

[58] Tansill, *Bayard*, pp. 155–156.

[59] Flick, *Tilden*, p. 369.

[60] Maxey to James B. Simpson, January 19, 1877, as printed in the *Dallas Herald*, January 27, 1877. See also Maxey to W. W. Stell, January 12, 1877, printed in *Sherman Courier*, January 20, 1877.

[61] *Congressional Record*, 44th Cong., 2nd sess., January 25, 1877, p. 913.

the Democrats controlled the House, three of the five representatives were Democrats, but since they were a minority in the Senate, only two Democrat senators, Bayard and Thurman, were placed on the commission. Thus the commission was evenly divided between the two parties. It was supposed that the justices would be neutral and that the investigation would be objective. Hayes, still prepared to lose, wrote in his diary that he would not be so mortified by a defeat resulting from a decision of such a commission.[62] But when one of the chosen justices, David Davis, was elected to the Senate, another justice had to be chosen, and all the remaining justices were Republicans. Thus the Electoral Commission turned out to be partisan after all.

Debate began immediately in a joint meeting of the Houses of Congress as the Florida votes were retallied. Though Bayard and Thurman both spoke to persuade the Electoral Commission that it had the power to thoroughly investigate the state returns, they lost to the majority opinion that the votes should go to Hayes without further action. This decision greatly perturbed the Democrats, and Thurman began to suspect that they had been misled in believing that the Electoral Commission would be nonpartisan. Though Bayard attempted to persuade him to remain, on February 26 Thurman resigned from the commission, Kernan taking his place.[63] Maxey was infected with Thurman's dismay, but because he could see no alternative, he voted, along with Bayard, to accept the Florida votes going to Hayes.[64] The Democrats became even more restless when the Louisiana votes were also given to Hayes, and Maxey attacked the decision as a judgment that "exalts fraud, degrades justice, and consigns truth to the dungeon"; he voted not to accept the decision.[65] By February 28, when

---

[62] Williams, *Hayes*, pp. 70–71.

[63] Tansill, *Bayard*, p. 180; *Congressional Record*, Electoral Commission, pt. 4, vol. 5, 44th Cong., 2nd sess., pp. 56–57.

[64] *Congressional Record*, 44th Cong., 2nd sess., Feb. 10, 1877, p. 1477. Thurman was at home sick on the day of the vote.

[65] Ibid., Feb. 19, 1877, p. 1675. Thurman also spoke out against the decision but refrained from voting, remarking that he was paired with Edmunds and that if Edmunds voted yea, Thurman would vote nay. Pairing is an agreement between two members on opposite sides of an issue that if one is absent, the other will also be absent, or refrain from voting. Senator Edmunds was absent that day.

the Senate voted on South Carolina, the Wormley Conference had occurred. At this conference agents of Hayes and southern Democrats had arrived at a compromise giving southern support to Hayes in return for an end to carpetbag rule in Louisiana, Florida, and South Carolina.[66] Bayard, Thurman, Gordon, Conkling, and even Hamilton were absent from the Senate on February 28, but Maxey, Kernan, and Eaton quietly and sadly voted to accept the South Carolina votes for Hayes.[67] On March 3, Hayes was sworn in as president.

Texans were unhappy with their congressmen who, they thought, had capitulated to the Republicans. "And so Hayes is the President, and a new Southern party, designed to weaken the Democratic party, is to be established, with Ben Hill at its head in Georgia and John Hancock its leader in Texas," bewailed the *Carthage Panola Watchman*, referring to two of the representatives who had been loudest in their support of accepting the compromise.[68] In April, when each Texas congressman returned home from Washington, he gave out publicly his reasons for voting as he had. The papers of North Texas generally supported the actions of the Texas delegation, Maxey's views being published both locally and as far away as Austin.[69] "Every prominent man I have met fully endorses my course," Maxey wrote from Austin, "and cordially agrees that we were exactly right on the electoral bill. The general impression is that the little blaze of glory over those voting against the bill will soon end in smoke."[70]

Together with Governor Hubbard and Guy M. Bryan, Maxey sought an immediate favor from Hayes by asking that Bryan be appointed minister to Mexico.[71] Though Bryan did not receive the appointment, he remained friends with Hayes, sending him, from time to time, long letters of unsolicited political advice that Hayes, in his replies, mainly ignored. In July, 1878, Bryan wrote Hayes that Maxey, who was Bryan's guest at the moment, was "inclined to sustain you

[66] Woodward, *Reunion and Reaction*, pp. 196–197, 204–205.
[67] *Congressional Record*, 44th Cong., 2nd sess., Feb. 28, 1877, p. 1992.
[68] *Carthage Panola Watchman*, March 29, 1877; Procter, *Reagan*, p. 216.
[69] *State Gazette*, April 4, 1877.
[70] Maxey to Marilda Maxey, April 6, 1877, Maxey Papers.
[71] Guy M. Bryan to R. B. Hayes, April 2, 1877, Maxey to R. B. Hayes, April 6, 1877, Richard Hubbard to R. B. Hayes, April 7, 1877, Rutherford B. Hayes Papers.

[Hayes] and will always do so when he thinks *you are right*, and will oppose you when you are wrong."[72] But, in truth, Maxey did not wholly trust Hayes, and he wrote Bryan in December, 1878, when Bryan was trying again to persuade Hayes to appoint him to a government post, that "Mr. Hayes is a good man at bottom, the trouble is he has not the positiveness of character and continuity of purpose essential to a man in his position."[73]

[72] Guy M. Bryan to R. B. Hayes, July 22, 1878, ibid.
[73] Maxey to Guy M. Bryan, December 14, 1878, Guy M. Bryan Papers.

6. Maxey Takes Care of Texas Business in the Senate, 1877–1879

The West and the South made a common cause in the movement for the remonetization of silver, while the East, prompted by self-interest, opposed it.[1]

THE FIRST SESSION of the Forty-fifth Congress, which opened October 15, 1877, concerned itself with the perennial national problems of the monetary standard, free coinage of silver, greenbacks, tariff reform, and labor. At this session, Richard Coke, who had defeated Morgan Hamilton in the recent election eagerly joined his friend Maxey in the Senate.

Coke contrasted interestingly with Maxey. Both were tall, but Coke's frame was big and rugged, whereas Maxey's was slender and gave him an almost emaciated appearance. Maxey was fair; Coke had a large head with dark thick hair and olive skin. He was not interested in dress and frequently wore a long coat that flapped at his knees and an old black floppy hat. This apparel undoubtedly pained the fastidious Maxey. Coke had a bluntness of speech and manner that caused him some awkwardness in dealing with people. He always carried a heavy walking stick and used it to emphasize his points while speak-

1 Maxey in interview with the *Dallas Commercial News*, as published in the *Dallas Tri-Weekly Herald*, August 8, 1878.

ing. One listener said of him, "Old Coke just gets up on a stump and waves that big stick of his and bellers like a prairie bull but he wins his point."[2]

Maxey and Coke made their first cooperative senatorial effort in an attempt to improve the faltering relations of Texas with Mexico. Porfirio Díaz, who had come to power in Mexico in early 1876, was not able to control the Mexican revolutionaries, and they continued to indulge in their favorite pastime of raiding across the border into Texas. In June, 1877, Hayes, meeting the problem head on, issued orders to federal troops stationed on the border that, if necessary, they could cross the Mexican border to chase outlaws.[3] Hayes's strong policy was met with indignation in the United States, and some even accused him of wanting to annex portions of Mexico's territory.[4] It was also rumored that certain northern speculators, who had bought border claims for a few cents on the dollar, were actively supporting the annexation project. These speculators were not likely to profit by their transaction unless the U.S. government assumed the debt and gave Mexico a quittance for the few thousand square miles of sagebrush and bandits.[5]

On November 6, Maxey brought to the attention of the Senate a report about a violation of international law that had occurred August 11, 1877, on the Rio Grande frontier. He told of bands of armed Mexicans, organized on the soil of Mexico, breaking into the jail of Starr County, Texas, and releasing two Mexican prisoners—one who had been confined for murder and the other for horse stealing. The released prisoners were than carried back into Mexico by the invaders —a clear violation of international law. Maxey pointed out that this was only one of a series of such outrages and that the people of Texas were in danger of losing their possessions and their lives. Since negotiations were being carried on in Mexico City by the State Department, Maxey offered a resolution requesting that the president communicate to the Senate any facts in his possession relating to the alleged unlaw-

---

[2] T. Henderson Shuffler, *Son, Remember.*
[3] Harry Barnard, *Rutherford B. Hayes and His America*, p. 443.
[4] H. J. Eckenrode, *Rutherford B. Hayes*, p. 282.
[5] The issue was discussed in the *New York Daily Tribune*, November 22, 1877.

ful rescue, if this were not incompatible with the public interest.[6] On the same day Maxey introduced another resolution authorizing the appointment of commissioners to ascertain on what terms a reciprocal treaty of commerce with Mexico could be arranged.[7]

On November 14 the State Department replied to the Senate in Executive Session that it was declining to make public in an official form the actual state of the negotiations being carried on at Mexico City.[8] When this was made known in open session of the Senate, Maxey made an able and earnest speech upon the general subject of U.S. relations with the people and government of Mexico. He began by retracing the history of Mexico and Texas and discussed particularly the problems of the Zona Libre. This belt of country, about seventeen miles wide, extended from the mouth of the Rio Grande for three hundred miles, bounded on the one side by the Rio Grande and on the other by an imaginary line. In 1859, the Mexican government had promulgated a law laying off that particular land, six leagues in width. Since goods could be carried to any of the towns in it without the payment of duty, this free belt was a rendezvous for smugglers and adventurers of every nationality. Attention of the Mexican government had again and again been called to the matter, by the State Department, and as far back as December 4, 1871, President Grant had referred to affairs on this border in his annual message. Maxey, in his speech, pointed out that the people of Texas were a part of the American Union and were demanding protection, that if they did not get protection from the general government they would protect themselves, and that if war ensued it would not be the fault of Texas. He continued:

It is said that we want more Territory. What a ridiculous absurdity! The people of Texas have common sense. . . . With a population flowing into our state annually of three hundred thousand, when the wealth of the state has been doubled in the last three years, when the next appointment for

---

6 U.S. Congress, *Congressional Record*, 45th Cong., 1st sess., November 6, 1877, p. 246.

7 Ibid.

8 Maxey discussed this event in an interview with a reporter from the *New York World*, November 15, 1877.

Congress will show between fifteen and twenty representatives on the floor of the other House for the State of Texas,[9] I ask if any wise man in Texas would endeavor to plunge this country into war whereby this great stream of wealth which is pouring into our state might be diverted into some other channel? It is foolish. Texas wants no war.

To those who had charged that Texas was anxious to acquire territory across the Rio Grande, Maxey retorted that Texas was already as large as "all New England, all the middle states, Ohio, Illinois and several thousand square miles thrown in for good count." "What good would it do to remove the frontier line from the Rio Grande to the Sierra Madre?" he queried. "It would be simply removing the line of contention, not the cause."[10]

At appropriate intervals during Maxey's long speech, Coke took the floor to present further documentary evidence that border relations between the United States and Mexico needed to be improved. At one point he reminded the Senate that the area they were talking about, that is, the land between the Rio Grande and the Nueces River, was a section of some forty thousand square miles—as large as the great state of Ohio.[11] Maxey concluded the speeches with a plea for the establishment of a new post on the Rio Grande along with the strengthening of the four posts already there.

Newspapers across the country carried articles for several weeks about Maxey's pronouncements. The *New York World* acclaimed his speech, describing him as a sound lawyer, a clearheaded and able statesman, and a soldier.[12] The *Houston Age* and the *Dallas Herald* also praised the speech and agreed with his views on frontier protection.[13] The *New York Herald*, however, expressed anxiety over his proposal that, if help was not forthcoming, Texans might start a war in order to protect themselves. Said the *Herald*, "We have no doubt

---

[9] Maxey was mistaken, the Forty-sixth Congress still had only six Representatives from Texas. See U.S., Congress, House, *Biographical Directory of the American Congress, 1774–1961*, p. 214.

[10] *Congressional Record*, 45th Cong., 1st sess., November 14, 1877, p. 392.

[11] Ibid., pp. 392, 394–395.

[12] *New York World*, November 15, 1877.

[13] The *Paris North Texan* quoted from the November 17 issues of the Houston and Dallas newspapers, November 24, 1877.

Senators Coke and Maxey are dreadfully in earnest in their demands for protection for the Texas frontier, and that they would go to war and annex the whole of the Northern states of Mexico rather than not make a fuss which will please, or which they suppose will please, their people."[14]

When Maxey turned his attention from the Texas frontier to vote against two Hayes nominations for the New York Customs House, he heard political repercussions from his home state. Haye's nominations were part of his efforts to end the political graft that had snowballed during the Republican's reign since the Civil War. The Customs House was a glaring example of need for reform, having been used extensively by Senator Conkling, the powerful New York Republican boss, to reward his faithful supporters. Conkling considered the Hayes nominations to replace his two principal political lieutenants, Chester A. Arthur and Alonzo B. Cornell, to be an attack on him.[15] Maxey's constituency was at a loss to understand his apparent support of Conkling, especially as the majority of the Democrats had voted for Hayes's nominations. Said the *Meridian Independent Blade*, "It appeared that he [Maxey] could be used by the worst enemies of the South."[16] The *Huntsville Item* said that Maxey had let Conkling "honeyfuggle" him on the New York appointments.[17] Perhaps Maxey, a member of the Senate Committee on Post Offices and Post Roads, was merely reacting adversely to Hayes's basic civil service policy of removing appointments to office from the control of senators and representatives.[18] In a speech at Galveston in July, 1878, after a renewal of the charges that he was in league with Conkling and against the general policies of the Democrats, Maxey said, in defense of his vote against the Hayes appointments, that the reasons that influenced him "were secrets of Executive Session which he dared not disclose."[19] It is also possible that Conkling and Maxey made a simple vote trade, with Conkling, a

[14] *New York Herald*, November 27, 1877, quoted in the *Galveston News*, November 28, 1877.
[15] Eckenrode, *Hayes*, pp. 264–269.
[16] *Meridian Independent Blade*, February 12, 1880.
[17] *Huntsville Item*, February 12, 1880.
[18] Barnard, *Hayes*, p. 453.
[19] *Galveston News*, July 6, 1878.

member of the powerful Committee on Commerce, agreeing to help with appointments in Texas or with appropriations on the river and harbor funds for Texas, in exchange for Maxey's vote to keep Arthur and Cornell.[20]

Much of the work of the Forty-fifth Congress related to the nation's financial problems. Maxey's study of these problems had convinced him that sound money was a sectional rather than political issue. Silver had fallen rapidly in value after its demonetization in 1873, and the silver-producing states, along with other western and southern states that were suffering from financial depression, demanded the repeal of the Act of 1873. To add to the discontent of these same states, Congress, in 1875, passed the Resumption Act. This act provided that after January 1, 1879, the government would exchange gold dollars for greenbacks and directed the government to acquire a gold reserve for redemption purposes. This was good for the interests of the creditor classes of people but not for agrarian-debtor groups.

In December, 1877, the bill of Richard P. Bland of Missouri (leader of the silver forces in the House) to provide for the reissue of silver dollars according to the terms of the act of January 17, 1837, and for their restoration to legal-tender status came before the Senate. Put before the Committee on Finance, whose chairman was William Allison of Iowa, the free-coinage clause was changed to permit the secretary of the treasury to purchase silver bullion at the market price, to the amount of not less than $2 million and not more than $4 million each month, and coin it in dollars. Though the House did not like the compromise, it passed the bill and sent it to President Hayes. Hayes sent it back with his veto on February 28, 1878, but, that same day, Congress overrode his veto and passed the bill.[21] The same day that the Bland bill reached the Senate, Senator Stanley Matthews of Ohio introduced a resolution that provided for the payment of interest on government bonds in silver.[22]

[20] Alwyn Barr to Louise W. Horton, September 25, 1969.
[21] Eckenrode, *Hayes*, p. 296.
[22] Charles C. Tansill, *The Congressional Career of Thomas Francis Bayard, 1869–1885*, pp. 207–208.

Bayard argued against the repeal of the Resumption Act, against the Bland-Allison bill, and against the Matthews resolution. He contended that all legislation that would remonetize silver and make it legal tender for all amounts of indebtedness, including payments of interest on government bonds, would affect seriously the whole banking and financial structure of the country.[23] He was hoping that when the resumption of specie payments began on January 1, 1879, a new stability would be brought to the American currency and that inflation would be curbed.[24]

Senators Allen Thurman of Ohio and Daniel Voorhees of Indiana had, at first, agreed with Bayard on the currency issue, but during the summer recess of 1877 they found their constituents favoring the silver men. Senator Voorhees concluded that there were two different minds in the country: "Those who desire money to be plentiful and cheap because they work for it, and those who desire it to be scarce and dear because they already have it."[25]

Maxey and all the Texas delegation except Congressman Gustavus Schleicher supported the westerners and southerners in their fight against resumption and for free silver coinage.[26] John Reagan spoke in the House on November 14, 1877, in favor of the repeal of the Resumption Act: "The course of those in favor of the repeal of the law providing for the resumption of specie payments on the 1st of January, 1879, and of those who have sought to remonetize silver and secure its free coinage, has been upon the floor denounced as demagoguery, has been denounced as dishonest, has been denounced as unpatriotic, and as communistic and agrarian. It has also been called repudiation."[27] Maxey, on December 6, spoke for the Matthews resolution, arguing that the Constitution established the double standard and made gold and silver mutually interchangeable, the unit of silver and the unit of gold having exactly equivalent values. Said he, "Let the debts of the country, public and private, be paid

[23] Ibid., pp. 205, 208, 209, 212, 215.
[24] Ibid., p. 211.
[25] As quoted from Wirt Armistead Cate, *Lucius Q. C. Lamar*, p. 309.
[26] Alwyn Barr, *Reconstruction to Reform*, p. 39.
[27] *Congressional Record*, 45th Cong., 1st sess., November 14, 1877, p. 412.

according to the contract, gold or silver coin, and not in a dollar which by a violation of the Constitution and laws and the rights of the people under contract, will have, if the silver bill is defeated, its purchasing power doubled since the date of the contract.[28]

Maxey's views on money were widely publicized in Texas—in the *Austin Daily Gazette,* the *Galveston Daily News,* the *Houston Telegram,* the *Dallas Herald,* and all the small-town newspapers of North Texas. On January 18, 1878, he spoke in the Senate again on the remonetization of silver, saying in part;

We have a tariff system fossilized a century ago and a financial condition growing worse every day. . . . Why should the silver production of Nevada excite the fears of anyone? How can this mere drop in the world's great bucket make it overflow? . . . A general diffusion of wealth among the masses is infinitely of more worth to our institutions than a concentration of wealth in the hands of the few. What we ought to do is to help lift the people on their feet. I shall vote for this measure most cheerfully, first, because for the reasons I have given, I believe the Constitution demands the double standard. Second, welfare of the people imperatively demands it and such a passage will be hailed with joy in every household.[29]

During the Senate recess, Maxey returned to Texas, and interested himself in state politics. In August, while visiting his old friend Judge John Jay Good in Dallas, he was interviewed by a reporter from the *Dallas Commercial.* The reporter wrote that he had found Maxey in the office of Judge Good, where he was enjoying a good cigar and making himself as comfortable as the state of the weather would permit. Asked to state his opinion of the relations of the northern and southern Democrats, Maxey replied:

The difference between the two wings of the party is not political but one of material interest. On all questions relating to internal improvements and the development of material prosperity the South and West usually act together. . . . The South and West are deeply in debt and the contraction policy bore very heavily on them because it caused a steady appreciation of money and depreciation of the prices of all commodities. On the con-

---

[28] *Congressional Record,* 45th Cong., 2d sess., December 6, 1877, p. 408.
[29] Ibid., January 18, 1878, p. 930.

trary the bonds worked favorably for the Eastern bondholder. Therefore the West and the South made common cause in the movement for the re-monetization of silver while the East, prompted by self-interest opposed it.[30]

The reporter then asked about the chances of Bayard to be named the Democratic presidential nominee for 1880. Maxey's answer carefully avoided any mention of Bayard:

The nominee of the party in 1880 will come from the West and Thurman or Hendricks will probably be the man. Tilden has seen his day and has no prospect for another nomination. Judge Thurman is recognized as the leader of the party in the Senate and is a very able man. As a leader he never attempts to drive the party but always consults the members before attempting any important move. This makes him very popular and secures the hearty cooperation of his fellow Senators.[31]

Meanwhile, information had reached Maxey that his old rival, Throckmorton, intended to use the Texas governorship as a springboard for election to Maxey's Senate seat in 1881, when his term would expire. Therefore, when the gubernatorial race began in June, 1878, Maxey did all he could to prevent Throckmorton's name being backed in Maxey territory. The three Democratic contenders for the governor's race were Throckmorton, R. B. Hubbard, and W. W. Lang (Master of the State Grange, an organization that had been taken over by the Greenbackers). Lightfoot wrote from Austin to Maxey: "Throckmorton and Hubbard are mixed considerably. . . . Reports from the West are not as favorable as they might be for T.—our county and Fannin [County] will be divided some but I will try to see that 'Brother T' does not get this and Delta counties. . . . It would not astonish me if Fannin County should instruct for Lang (and I wouldn't care much if they did)—though Hubbard is now the strongest anti-T man in the race and I will do all I can for him in this sec-

[30] The *Dallas Tri-Weekly Herald* republished the *Commercial's* interview, August 8, 1878. Judge Good practiced law in Dallas as a member of the firm of Good, Bower, and Coombes. See Walter P. Webb and H. Bailey Carroll (eds.), *Handbook of Texas*, I, 708.

[31] From the *Dallas Commercial*, republished in the *Dallas Tri-Weekly Herald*, August 8, 1878.

tion—in a quiet way."[32] By July the *Galveston News* had noted that Maxey was actively working against the election of Throckmorton for governor, but the *Gainesville Independent* defended Maxey, adding that "in fact we think Mr. T will be retired to private life by the Austin convention from which retirement he will not likely be called except by the Texas and Pacific as a lobby member of Congress or of the state legislature."[33]

While in Texas Maxey was wooed by a number of leading Texas industrialists who hoped to influence his actions in the Senate. In addition to a grand reception by Paris city officials, the Paris Band, Paris Rifles, and Paris citizens on June 22, he was invited to attend festivities at Galveston on July 4. The Galveston Cotton Exchange arranged for him to view the progress of the harbor improvements at Bolivar Point and afterward gave a dinner for him at the Tremont Hotel. Some of the dignitaries attending the dinner were Colonel W. L. Moody (president of the Cotton Exchange), Mayor D. C. Stone, Guy M. Bryan, W. P. Ballinger, DeWitt Giddings, and Major T. P. Ochiltree. Maxey's speech to the assembly was full of compliments for the progress made on the Galveston harbor. He advocated a bill in Congress for a line of steamers between Galveston and Rio de Janeiro to enlarge the market for the 700,000 bales of cotton and the 64 million bushels of wheat produced annually in Texas. Giddings, a Texas member of the House, also spoke at the banquet. He paid tribute to the labors of Maxey in obtaining $75,000 for the Galveston harbor improvements, pointing out how Maxey, when he saw that the bill would not be reached before the adjournment of Congress, had gone to each senator who had objected to the bill and persuaded them to give a "yes" vote. As a consequence, the bill had passed unanimously.[34]

In August when a Dallas reporter asked Maxey's opinion of the Texas and Pacific Railroad bill, Maxey said: "The lines [between the northern and southern Democrats] are not so clearly defined but still

---

[32] Henry Lightfoot to Maxey, June 1, 1878, Maxey Papers.

[33] *Galveston News*, July 5, 1878; *Gainesville Independent*, July 13, 1878.

[34] Circular inviting Paris citizens to greet returning Senator Maxey at the Paris railroad station, June 22, 1878; *Galveston News*, July 6, 1878.

the West will give it a large support. The bill is almost sure to pass the Senate but its fate in the House is more doubtful. Beck and Mc-Creary of Kentucky have recently become the bill's friends—they are not heartily in favor of the measure but in obedience to instructions from their legislature they will both vote for it."[35] Throckmorton had addressed the House on government aid to the Texas and Pacific on March 1, 1877, and Lamar had addressed the Senate on the same aid bill on May 22, 1878. But in 1879, when Lamar tried to enlist Maxey's aid in promoting the bill, Maxey still refused to work with Throckmorton.

The third session of the Forty-fifth Congress began on December 2, 1878, and the Senate opened quietly with a continuation of its unfinished work. Texas was in severe financial difficulties—even the state government was not operating on a cash basis.[36] Maxey wrote Marilda on December 14, 1878, that his own pockets were empty. Coke had earlier borrowed thirty dollars from him, and when Maxey asked for its return, Coke was chagrined and replied that he would repay the loan in "eight or nine days."[37] Chenoweth had also borrowed from Maxey and had been unable to repay. By dint of judicious saving, Maxey had been able to send Marilda nine hundred dollars. As was usual, she had been writing depressing letters to him expressing her dissatisfaction that they were so deeply in debt. He had replied that he knew the matter of debt was exceedingly unpleasant to her—that the panic of 1873 had found him in debt from which he was unable to extricate himself. "I ought to have a guardian or rather ought to have had, for I have shown no capacity for business except the slave's capacity to labor," admitted Maxey, and added, "My own judgment is that we will have harder times from about April till the new cotton crop comes in than we have had since annexation."[38]

[35] *Dallas Commercial* interview, republished in *Dallas Tri-Weekly Herald*, August 8, 1878.

[36] The panic of 1873 cast its shadow of depression over Texas until 1879. Texas had a large floating debt, weak state credit, and chronic annual deficiencies in the general revenue account. See Edmund Thornton Miller, *A Financial History of Texas*, pp. 416, 426.

[37] Maxey to Marilda Maxey, December 14, 1878, Maxey Papers.

[38] Ibid.

Shortly after Maxey and his senatorial colleagues returned to Washington, Texas Representative Gustave Schleicher died. The funeral cortege back to Texas was made up of Coke, Giddings, Hamlin of Maine, and Bayard of Delaware. (Maxey declined to go because of a flare-up with his old back pain.) In Texas, Bayard was met with special cordiality and respect. "I see the Texas papers seem much taken with Bayard," said Maxey in a jealous tone, evidently forgetting that he had been much smitten himself with the personality of Bayard when he had first met him.[39]

The Democrats, now a majority in the Senate, held a caucus to decide how to proceed with their bills so that the Republicans would have the least opportunity to vote them down. They decided that this could best be accomplished by tacking on amendments to the appropriation bills. Many of them, including Maxey, disagreed with this plan. He considered the procedure a needless circumvention since the Republicans, so far, had shown no disposition to filibuster, nor had the president shown signs of wishing to veto their bills. However, Maxey abided by the decision of his fellow Democrats and dutifully attached to the Post Office Appropriation Bill an amendment to establish a Brazilian steamship line from Galveston to Rio de Janiero. He asked Coke to speak on behalf of the amendment but then, when Coke made a good speech, Maxey spoke somewhat grudgingly of his efforts: "Coke made a good speech. Of course, he had to take issue on some minor points. He is not the author of the Galveston proposition but for all that he came to time on the main issue."[40]

Another bill in which Maxey took a special interest was one to reorganize the army, including a proposal to reduce its officers by more than three hundred. Most Democrats favored this bill, but Maxey had the foresight to see that a reduction of staff officers would cut down the number of military forces on the frontier, with the result that Texas would lose some of her protection. He made prompt efforts to call General E. O. C. Ord, commanding general of the Military Department of Texas, before the Senate Military Committee. Ord had

[39] Ibid., January 26, 1879.
[40] Ibid., February 21, 1879.

some three thousand troops stationed along the Texas southern and western borders and was able to give a report on the necessity of keeping a military force on the frontier. Maxey also received a promise from General Ranald Mackenzie, commander of the federal troops on the Rio Grande, that he would come to Washington and testify to the need of further protection.[41]

When the session ended Maxey made another expensive trip home, but he was back in Washington in time for the opening of the Forty-sixth Congress on March 18, 1879. Maxey was at last beginning to have some political influence. He was elevated to the chairmanship of the Senate Committee on Post Offices and Post Roads, a committee on which he had served since his arrival in the Senate in 1875. This position allowed him a clerk, and he chose William H. Gill of Texas, whom he considered a good business man, a fine scholar, and a good penman. With his brother-in-law, William E. Smith, in tow, Maxey had called on Postmaster General David M. Key and requested that Smith be appointed Post Office Inspector at Austin.[42] When Smith obtained the position, Maxey bragged a bit to Marilda by saying: "Judge Key is a strong friend of mine, he wants to make an appointment and told me he was satisfied Smith was the right man. . . . I do feel gratified that my wishes are greatly respected and I am getting to be pretty well known throughout the country. Now you know that I have been accused a good deal of vanity, I think you have twitted me with it. I always felt that if I had a fair show I could make my mark in any crowd and probably showed it."[43] During this time Maxey also used his influence in having Stillwell H. Russell (later tried and convicted of misusing federal funds) appointed a U.S. Marshal and in having the destitute Andrew Dorn appointed doorkeeper of the Senate.[44]

Maxey's heavy schedule of work began in earnest as the new session settled down to business. There were hundreds of letters and telegrams requiring his reply. On a typical day he attended the Sen-

[41] Ibid., January 12, 1879.
[42] Ibid., January 17, 1879.
[43] Ibid., May 23, 1879.
[44] Ibid., May 20, 1879.

Samuel Bell Maxey, his wife, Marilda, and daughter, Dora (Courtesy of the Maxey Museum, Paris, Texas)

Maxey Home in Paris, Texas (Courtesy of *The Paris News*, Paris, Texas)

Henry and Dora Lightfoot (Courtesy of the Maxey Museum, Paris, Texas)

Samuel Bell Maxey Long when a page in the U.S. Senate during the first Cleveland administration (Courtesy of the Maxey Museum, Paris, Texas)

ate Military Committee meeting until noon. He then was in the Senate until 3 P.M., at which time he moved to the committee room to work on reports and direct his clerk until 5 P.M. At five he returned to his private rooms and worked on speeches and reports until bedtime.[45]

Part of the Democratic strategy for the 1880 presidential campaign was to urge a congressional investigation into possible fraud in Hayes's election in 1876. The southern Democrats had a strategy of their own. Dissatisfied with the fulfillment of Hayes's tacit promise in 1877 to ease the enforcement of wartime and Reconstruction statutes—such as having federal troops at the election polls—they were determined to use their influence in Congress to remove these statutes from the law.

Meanwhile the Republicans were not really ready for the 1880 presidential campaign. They were divided among themselves—many hated Hayes for doing them out of favored political jobs through the civil service reform, some had not approved of his conciliatory compromises with the South, and others disliked his personality. But when Congress announced the appointment of a committee to look into possible fraud in the Hayes election, the Republicans rallied and reassembled behind him. They demanded a retaliatory investigation into the more recent 1878 elections where southern Republican congressmen had been replaced by Democrats.

When the Army Appropriation Bill had come before the House in February, 1879, southern Democrats were successful in tacking to the bill a rider, which, they hoped, would make the government remove federal troops from the polling places. But the bill was turned back by the predominantly Republican Senate, and the third session of the Forty-fifth Congress had ended without an appropriation being made for the army.[46] Hayes promptly called Congress into another session. This time, after a Democratic caucus where Senator Augustus Garland had urged the members to promote "no general legislation during the session but to concentrate on the appropriations bills and their

---

[45] Ibid., April 1, 1879.
[46] Barnard, *Hayes*, p. 482.

political riders,"[47] the Senate and the House passed an Army Appropriation Bill with the rider calling for the removal of federal troops at the polls and forbidding federal marshals to use civilian means to enforce election laws.

Maxey had written on March 26 his disapproval of the Democratic plan:

We had a caucus of the Democrats of the Senate and the House today with respect to the questions which divided the two Houses at the last session. I do not think the best plan was adopted. It would have been singular if it had been. My own opinion is that every proposition should have been presented in a separate bill. Had the Republicans manifested an unmistakable disposition to filibuster or had the bills passed and been vetoed by the President, then would have been the time to tack on to the appropriation bills. The caucus, however, determined to put them on the appropriation bills at the start.[48]

On April 21, Maxey made a speech in the Senate urging a free ballot, under state laws, and with no armed interference.[49] On the twenty-fifth, when the bill had been sent to Hayes, Maxey wrote, "He [Hayes] can in no way justify a veto but whether he will sign or not remains to be seen," and on the twenty-eighth he wrote: "How Mr. Hayes can do other than sign the bill I am not able to see. He will have to walk right over the Constitution to do it, but the Republicans have done that thing frequently, they know exactly how."[50]

After she had seen in the newspapers that the president had vetoed the Army Appropriation Bill, Marilda wrote Maxey: "I think the Democrats are in a rather close place. If they adjourn now the President will reassemble Congress from time to time until there is no telling where it will end. Then, if there is no appropriation made for carrying on affairs, you Democrats will bear the blame, and now, after such a bald stand, to back down would not appear well, so I think

[47] Tansill, *Bayard*, p. 230. During the first session of the 46th Congress, Maxey sat in the front right row of the Senate, between Senators Isham Harris of Tennessee and Augustus Garland of Arkansas.

[48] Maxey to Marilda Maxey, March 26, 1879, Maxey Papers.

[49] *Congressional Record*, 46th Cong., 1st sess., April 21, 1879, pp. 600–603.

[50] Maxey to Marilda Maxey, April 25, 28, 1879, Maxey Papers.

you all have got yourselves into a pretty mess."[51] Maxey wrote back on May 13:

I see that the President intended to veto the bill prohibiting troops at the polls as I thought he would. I think that rapid work, but it is with a vengeance to the country first and to the [Democratic] Party next, for both will suffer from the course pursued by the Democratic Party in Congress. Had this whole question been left until after the next Presidential election or until the next regular session of Congress, it would have been better in a financial view for the country and for the Democratic Party. For a party to take a bald stand in any position or on any part of the ground and then have to back right square out (not even permitted to turn around and walk out) always very materially injures it. I think this the blunder that will nip in the bud all the hopes of the Democrats ever entertained for 1880.[52]

Hayes did finally approve a version of the Army Appropriation Bill that forbade the use of the federal military at the polls.[53] Though Maxey had not approved of the Democratic strategy, he was forced to see that it had worked to some degree.[54]

When Congress passed a bill creating a new U.S. Judicial District in Texas, Maxey called on President Hayes to urge the appointment of his old friend from his days at court in East Texas, Captain Thomas J. Brown, for the judgeship. Among the Texas delegation, Throckmorton, Culberson, and Giddings also supported Brown's appointment. Coke and Mills had their own nominee for the position, Thomas Harrison; and Reagan wanted Reuben Reeves.[55] Maxey was particularly provoked at Reagan for not agreeing to the will of the majority. Maxey also tried to persuade certain non-Texan members of Congress to speak to Hayes on Brown's behalf. Congressman James

[51] Marilda Maxey to Maxey, May 1, 1879, ibid.

[52] Maxey to Marilda Maxey, May 13, 1879, ibid.

[53] Barnard, *Hayes*, p. 483.

[54] For a discussion of the effect of the Democratic strategy on the Democratic presidential campaign see Wirt A. Cate, *Lucius Q. Lamar*, p. 348, and Allan Nevins, *Abram S. Hewitt*, pp. 404–406.

[55] Thomas Harrison, a Houston lawyer, had been elected district judge of Harris County in 1866, and in 1872 he was a Democratic presidential elector. Reuben Reeves was an associate justice of the Supreme Court from 1864 to 1867, and again from 1874 to 1876 (Webb and Carroll, *Handbook of Texas*, I, 780; II, 455; Ben H. Procter, *Not without Honor*, p. 85).

Garfield of Ohio was one who agreed to talk to Hayes. As Maxey described it to Marilda, Garfield added that, situated as the Texas District was, "if he were President he would nominate a Democrat and that he would say so to Hayes."[56] But the choice of the Texas Democrats was to be unheeded, for when Coke and Maxey called on Hayes on April 5, Hayes informed them that he would not nominate a Democrat. Instead he assigned the position to Andrew P. McCormick, an able Republican lawyer in Texas.[57]

About this time, in May, 1879, Maxey and Coke became involved in a dispute with Bayard. The argument evolved from Bayard's position as chairman of the Senate Committee on Finance. The Warner Bill favored the bimetallist supporters (including Maxey and Coke), and when it was referred to the Senate Committee on Finance, Bayard immediately claimed the bill was so important that it should wait for prolonged discussion in the next session of Congress. Recognizing this as a maneuver to shelve soft money issues, at least temporarily, the supporters of the bill argued that the committee should take prompt action either for or against the bill and bring it out of committee. When Bayard refused to do this, Coke introduced a resolution in the Senate to discharge the Committee on Finance from any further consideration of the bill.[58] At a Democratic caucus, Coke charged the Finance Committee, composed of Bayard, Kernan, and three other Democrats, with smothering the bill. When Coke's resolution came before the Senate for a vote, Bayard and Kernan refrained from voting, but the three other Democrats on the committee voted for it—that is, to have the Warner Bill removed from their committee. Bayard then resigned from the committee. Maxey wrote of the affair to Marilda: "You will see a great deal about the failure of the Finance Committee to report back the silver bill. Bayard and Kernan made sixteen hand, mealy-mouthed jackasses of themselves. In my judgment the refusal was dictatorial and I have no compromises to make."[59] Maxey's reference to a compromise probably referred to the

56 Maxey to Marilda Maxey, February 21, 1879, Maxey Papers.
57 Ibid., April 5, 1879.
58 Tansill, *Bayard*, pp. 231, 233.
59 Maxey to Marilda Maxey, June 15, 1879, Maxey Papers.

many Democratic senators who had written Bayard asking him to withdraw his resignation from the Finance Committee. Thurman, Garland, and Joseph McDonald of Indiana had gone to see Bayard and asked him not to resign. Garland had asked Bayard to compromise by consenting to the bill being reported back to the Senate, either adversely or favorably, with a recommendation that its consideration be postponed until the next December.[60] Bayard had refused to comply with Garland's request.

Schlesinger, in the chapter titled "Yardsticks for Presidents" in his book *Paths to the Present*, rates Hayes's presidential record as winning "neither distinction nor discredit" and "standing midway between the best and the worst" of the presidents.[61] Barnard points out in his biography of Hayes that, since Hayes wished to consider himself a Whig, it necessarily followed that he must believe that the presidential office was subservient to congressional power.[62] However, in reality, Hayes was not able to allow himself to be dominated by Congress, and thus arose the great conflict between them. The struggle gained intensity during the Hayes-Conkling controversy in July, 1878, and a great clash between Congress and Hayes came over the sound money versus soft money issue. A majority of the Congress favored inflation as a cure for the depression.[63] Hayes used all his influence to prevent Congress from repealing the Resumption Act— the act that was the special terror of financially stricken Texans. Alwyn Barr explains the plight of these Texans: "The Resumption Act would force debtors to pay back dollars of greater value than those they had borrowed—a painful process to men struggling on new and rented farms. On the national level the senators from Texas and five of the six congressmen had joined other Westerners and Southerners against resumption and for controlled inflation through free coinage of silver."[64] When Hayes, abandoning the Whig doctrine that Congress alone should decide such issues, vetoed the silver purchase laws,

---

[60] Tansill, *Bayard*, p. 233.
[61] Arthur M. Schlesinger, *Paths to the Present*, p. 98.
[62] Barnard, *Hayes*, p. 459.
[63] Ibid.
[64] Alwyn Barr, "Texas Politics, 1876–1906," doctoral dissertation, p. 34.

he had the painful experience of having both Houses of Congress override his veto by more than a two-thirds majority.[65]

The long struggle between Congress and Hayes over the Army Appropriation Bill and its troublesome riders resulted in six vetoes from Hayes. The Democrats, who had decided to vote no appropriations unless the election laws were repealed, felt that there was more to Hayes's vetoes than his avowed objection to the propriety of rider legislation.[66] Therefore, when the appropriation for the Judicial Department came before Congress, the Democrats from both Houses caucused to work out some plan for passing it. Said Maxey: "The overwhelming majority of the Democrats in the senate believe that it is the duty as well as policy to make all the appropriations, recognizing that we have done all we can, and that the veto power is lodged by the Constitution in the President. Whilst I have great contempt for Hayes and know the ablest lawyers regard his last message silly, still he had the power."[67]

At the end of the session, in July, 1879, Maxey returned to Texas and promptly began a summer of writing and speaking on behalf of Texas Democrats. The Greenbackers, a new political party, had as its leading issue the demand that the general government issue more greenbacks or paper money and redeem all its treasury notes and outstanding bonds with such money.[68] The Greenbackers, made up of Republicans and dissenting Democrats, were busy organizing in Texas in preparation for the 1880 elections. When a member of the Democratic party organization at Dallas asked Maxey's opinion about how much threat the group might be to the Democrats, he replied:

There is no question as to the purpose of the Greenback party to thoroughly organize their forces and secure for the campaign of 1880 as many recruits as possible. The policy of that party, so far at least as this state is concerned, is essentially different from that of last year. Then, many of its

[65] Barnard, *Hayes*, p. 464.

[66] Ibid., p. 484.

[67] Maxey to Marilda Maxey, June 25, 1879, Maxey Papers. Hayes's last message had been on May 12, 1879, when he said that he vetoed the bill in question because of the propriety of the riders being attached (Barnard, *Hayes*, p. 483). See also Rutherford B. Hayes, *Letters and Messages of Rutherford B. Hayes*, p. 199.

[68] Roscoe Martin, *The People's Party in Texas*, pp. 22–23.

most pronounced advocates prided themselves on their democracy and claimed still to be good Democrats. By this special pleading good Democrats were drawn into the movement without intending to sever their relations with the party to which they had always belonged, and with whose general policy they were entirely satisfied.

Now, however, there is a complete change. Greenback papers and leaders proclaim that both the old parties are corrupt. . . . Greenbackers demand that party lines be drawn, let it be done.[69]

William Bramlette, a free-lance writer for newspapers in the Houston area, asked Maxey to write his views on national finance. Maxey complied with the request by restating his two favorite themes: (1) that it was desirable that the nation have unrestricted coinage of both silver and gold by the federal government and that the ratio between the gold and silver units be preserved, and (2) that the national banks should be retired as fast as the charters of the banks expect and that the bank papers should be replaced by currency issued by the government. Maxey said further: "Capitalists grow rich on fluctuation, the masses poor. This system which is that embodied in the Austin platform, and advocated by all Democrats in the great agricultural south and west, is planted square on the Constitution and avoids the grinding, despotic exactions of the single gold standard on one side and the wildly destructive theory of irredeemable fiat money on the other. It is rapidly gaining ground in the north and east and will, I trust, be the safe constitutional middle ground, occupied by the National Democratic party in 1880."[70]

At a Democratic rally at Cleburne on August 23, Maxey spoke for an hour and a half before an audience of four thousand people explaining the Democratic views on finance as opposed to those of the Greenbackers. The Greenbackers were given equal time to reply and Judge James M. Thurmond of Dallas spoke in rebuttal for two hours. When Roger Q. Mills spoke against the charges of the Greenback party, he was misunderstood by both groups. The Greenbackers claimed him as a convert and the old-school Democrats failed to understand his Democratic position. Mills had experienced difficulties

[69] Maxey to J. T. Dennis, August 3, 1879, Maxey Papers.
[70] Maxey to William Bramlette, August 5, 1879, ibid.

before with his speeches on this subject. In August, 1878, he had spoken at Marlin to support Coke, who was attempting to persuade Democrats to forego Greenback ideas. Mills had ended his speech by sounding as if he supported the Greenbackers. Said Coke, "Mills will be all right, he is fond of kicking a little against party traces, but always keeps inside."[71]

To clarify his own views on Texas finance, Maxey had written to Ashbel Smith, a land speculator and a past official in the Republic of Texas government, and one Maxey considered an authority on the financial affairs of the Texas Republic. Smith recommended Gouge's *Fiscal History of Texas* as the best financial history of Texas and urged Maxey to obtain a copy for study. "Gouge," said Smith, "was a New York financier and his comments on Texas though harsh and sometimes unjust were in their material facts in the main correct."[72] Smith complimented Maxey on a speech delivered in Paris and printed in the *North Texan*. "Your argument is unanswerable and needed by the times," said Smith. He continued, "It can only be regarded as one of the strange delusions that, like Salem witchcraft, take possession of the minds of people, that with American Continental money, the French Assignats, Texas Redbacks, Confederate money, irredeemable paper, whenever, wherever, by whomever issued in the world, the Greenback folly should get any of the least hold on the mind of the people."[73]

Maxey printed his views on Greenbackism in Texas in pamphlet form for the Texas Democratic campaign and as late as 1881 was passing it out among his senatorial colleagues. Senators Jackson of Tennessee and Voorhees of Indiana made a point of telling him that they agreed with his views as expressed in the pamphlet.[74] The final

---

[71] Richard Coke to O. M. Roberts, August 15, 1878, Oran Milo Roberts Papers.

[72] William M. Gouge, *The Fiscal History of Texas*, pp. 59, 99, 228, 232–233, 206, 207, 310.

[73] Ashbel Smith to Maxey, October 20, 1879, Maxey Papers. See also Herbert T. Hoover, "Ashbel Smith on Currency and Finance in the Republic of Texas," *Southwestern Historical Quarterly* 71, no. 3 (January 1968): 419–425.

[74] Printed speech on Greenbackism, 1880, Maxey Papers. See also Maxey to Marilda Maxey, October 10, 1881, ibid.

passage of the silver bill and its implementation had not had the effect on the economy that so many easterners had predicted. Instead, the credit of the government had gone up. Maxey hoped to see a flood of silver and gold coin throughout the country, a condition he felt would bring prosperity.

During August, 1879, Jean Valjean of the *Saint Louis Republican* came to Paris to interview Maxey. He was greeted with cordiality and invited for a stroll around the Maxey estate. Valjean later described the Maxey home as one of "real elegance set among other white cottages on a narrow shaded street."[75] In the orchard Valjean was given samples of ripe grapes, apples, peaches, pears, and pomegranates, all of which he declared excellent. They also viewed the vegetable garden with its many varieties before returning to the broad veranda of the Maxey home for the interview. When asked who would receive the Democratic nomination for president, Maxey became very guarded and reticent. He did admit that he supposed a candidate from the South was not to be thought of. This remark, when published, raised the ire of several Texas newspaper editors, who thought it was not a fitting remark by a U.S. senator from Texas.

Asked by Valjean about the possible nominee for the Republican presidential ticket, Maxey was more expansive. Said he, "Grant has no chance for the Republican nomination." When asked about the possibility of Conkling of New York, Blaine of Maine, Sherman of Ohio, or Edmunds of Vermont becoming the Republican nominee, Maxey described Conkling as having no personal magnetism, a trait Maxey considered necessary for any presidential nominee. "Blaine is very agreeable and has irresistible personal magnetism but he is too far East and has made mistakes in the senate," said Maxey. He described Sherman as selfish and proclaimed him a cunning politician who inspired little confidence. Maxey thought Edmunds had more reputation than any Republican in the Senate and one who, if nominated, would make a strong race.[76]

To Valjean's query about the chances of getting aid from Congress

---

[75] *St. Louis Republican*, August 9, 1879.
[76] Ibid.

for that great southern project, the Texas and Pacific Railroad, Maxey replied that there was no chance at all for the time being. He spoke with regret about a lack of harmony in southern delegations that hindered getting appropriations for their sections. No doubt he was remembering that Lamar and Matthews had failed to ask him and Coke to help with the railroad bill when it first came before Congress. According to Maxey, Stanley Matthews, at that time senator from Ohio, had killed the bill by making two fatal blunders. First, he had called the bill up without notifying his friends to be present, and, second, he had called it up at the time when the patent bill had precedence. Consequently the friends of the Texas and Pacific bill were forced to vote against consideration of Matthews's bill at that time. Maxey thought Matthews a good fellow but a poor manager.

Since the second session of the Forty-sixth Congress was not called until December 1, 1879, Maxey continued his speaking engagements in San Antonio, Houston, Austin, and Galveston. He wrote his West Point classmate Marcus J. Wright (who was busily gathering records of the Civil War for the War Department's compilation, *War of the Rebellion*) that he had been welcomed in each city in a manner "truly gratifying to one who had tried faithfully to do his duty."[77]

The newspapers throughout the state were discussing Maxey's accomplishments in the Senate and his prospects for reelection in 1881. His opponents were Throckmorton, Reagan, Roberts, Culberson, Hubbard, Mills, W. W. Lang, Thomas J. Devine (San Antonio attorney and railroad promoter), and J. W. Ferris (a Supreme Court judge). The *North Texan* explained why Maxey would win over his Democratic competitors by ticking off the shortcomings of the stronger ones —Roberts was too old, Reagan had made too many enemies, Culberson had a high position already, Devine would not press his claim with vigor. This left only Mills and Hubbard, who, the *North Texan* admitted, would make the race a tight one.[78]

Maxey had been dubbed the beaver of the Senate because he worked so steadily to get his bills passed. The *Texas Journal of Commerce*

[77] Maxey to Marcus J. Wright, November 7, 1879, Marcus J. Wright Papers.
[78] *Paris North Texan*, January 10, 1880.

quoted Governor Jones of North Carolina as having asked while
pointing to Maxey, "Who is that man?" North Carolina Senator Ransom had replied, "That man is Maxey of Texas who does more work
and gets more things done than any man in the senate."[79] An editorial in the *Texarkana Weekly Visitor* stated that when Maxey "set his
head on a measure or scheme nothing short of a Returning Board
would stop him."[80] The *Sherman Weekly Courier* praised Maxey but
pointed out that, in its opinion, his chief failing was a tendency to
want his own way and to ignore the advice of others.[81] Some newspapers pointed out Maxey's beaverlike action of sending out his printed congressional speeches to his constituents; others complained of his
lack of humility about his accomplishments. The *New York Truth*
noted that Maxey was apt to be reelected in the Lone Star State although there were quite a few other candidates for the senatorship,
the principal contestant in their opinion, being Reagan.[82] A few newspapers unfairly reported that Reagan and Coke were responsible for
pushing through Congress the bill that had obtained federal aid for
the Galveston harbor improvements. In reality, the entire Texas delegation had been prodded since 1876 by several Texans, including
Ashbel Smith, W. L. Moody, and Guy M. Bryan, to push the bill for
federal aid to harbor and coast improvements in Texas.[83]

   During the Senate recess Maxey had spoken to interested groups
in Houston and Galveston regarding their harbor improvements. In
November, 1879, he wrote a letter to H. G. Wright, U.S. Office of
Chief Engineers, giving a detailed account of the important harbors
of Texas and how he thought they could be improved. Wright replied, after studying the plans, that he agreed with Maxey's views
about Texas needing deep entrances to all the larger harbors. Wright
proceeded to give an estimate of the cost of improving the eight harbors that Maxey had named. The largest item was one of $200,000

[79] *Texas Journal of Commerce*, November 29, 1879.
[80] *Texarkana Weekly Visitor*, December 2, 1879.
[81] *Sherman Weekly Courier*, December 5, 1879.
[82] *Truth*, January 9, 1880.
[83] *Texas Journal of Commerce*, September 27, October 4, 1879.

for improving the entrance to Galveston harbor; the second was $150,000 for Pass Cavallo (Matagorda); others were for Aransas Pass, the ship channel of Galveston Bay, Sabine Pass and Sabine River, and the Trinity and Neches rivers—the total expenditure amounting to $618,000.[84] But the Forty-sixth Congress made no sizeable appropriation for these improvements in Texas.

[84] H. G. Wright to Maxey, November 15, 1879, Maxey Papers.

7. A Second Term in the Senate

In this country, thanks to free government, we have no heredi-
tary nobility, but we have a nobility far above any that earthly
title can give—the nobility God impresses on an honest man.[1]

MARILDA ACCOMPANIED her husband to Washington for the session of Congress that opened on December 1, 1879, and the
Maxeys began to take part in some of the official social activities.
When Marilda called at the White House on Mrs. Hayes's reception
day, she was appalled at the sight of the huge crowd of women who
were waiting to shake the hand of the First Lady. She wrote back to
Paris: "No doubt Mrs. Hayes is an excellent woman. She has hair as
black as any Indian you ever saw. . . . She wore a white crepe dress
and receiving with her were Mrs. Justice Harlan, Mrs. Secretary Ram-
sey and Mrs. Senator Randall. The White House is neat and some
of the rooms are real pretty. The furniture and carpets look old and
faded. The curtains to the windows nothing extra. . . . I saw a great
many hot house foliage plants in every room, but no flowers, although
there is a very fine conservatory attached to the mansion."[2] In February, 1880, Marilda donned her black lace dress and accompanied
Maxey to the Hayes's reception for the diplomatic corps, pronounc-
ing it "certainly the grandest affair of the kind I ever attended" and

[1] U.S., Congress, *Congressional Record*, 47th Cong., 1st sess., January 23, 1882,
p. 551.
[2] Marilda Maxey to Mary Long Terrell, January 13, 1880, Maxey Papers.

describing Mrs. Hayes as having "a sweet face and her manners remarkably winning, perfectly simple and natural."[3]

Maxey settled down to work in the Senate, where one of the first
considerations was the appropriations for post office services. Earlier
in 1879, Postmaster General David Key, in his annual report, had
called upon the Treasury for extra money to be used for the extension
of the star route mail service. This category of mail service referred to
the kind of delivery needed for the western frontier, where there were
neither railroad nor steamboat carriers, so that the Post Office Department made special contracts with individuals who guaranteed to deliver the mail along these difficult routes. In Texas at that time, 3.18
trips per week were made by star route contractors, 1.78 trips per week
made by steamboat, and 7.37 trips per week by railroad.[4] Texas congressmen urged the extension of the service to the sparsely inhabited
areas of Texas, arguing that the mail routes carried population with
them and helped in the building of settlements. Back in July, 1878,
Throckmorton and Giddings, Texas members of the House, had written a letter to Postmaster General Key asking for increased service
on the Fort Worth, Texas, to Yuma, Arizona, mail route. The letter
was endorsed by Maxey and Reagan, and congressmen from western
states as far away as California had added their petitions that the
route be established.

When Congress had not provided funds for the increase in inland
mail transportation, Key asked in December, 1879, for two million
dollars to sustain the star route service. When this request was debated in the Senate, Beck of Kentucky demanded a report from the
secretary of the treasury listing the appropriation for each star route
separately. The House, in an effort to handle the deficiency of funds,
presented a bill to do away with 107 star routes, main trunk and important lines mainly west of the Mississippi River.[5] Maxey was enraged at the regional injustice and said so in a speech, which he later
printed and distributed under the title *A Fair Play Is a Jewel, Equal*

[3] Marilda Maxey to Dora Lightfoot, February 14, 1880, ibid.

[4] U.S., Post Office Department, *Annual Report of the Postmaster General, 1879*,
pp. 1–20, copy, ibid.

[5] *Congressional Record*, 46th Cong., 2d sess., February 26, 1880, p. 1170.

and Exact Justice to All.[6] On March 25, the Senate passed a bill providing one million dollars for the star route deficiency, but when the bill reached the House there was much disagreement and discussion.[7]

A congressional committee had been set up earlier in 1879 to investigate the activities of Assistant Postmaster Generals Thomas J. Brady and James Tyner.[8] Reagan, suspecting that the management of the Post Office Department was not what it ought to be, insisted that it was the duty of Congress to remedy the department's great extravagance by refusing to appropriate funds for the increase in mail contracts. Maxey maintained, on the contrary, that it was the duty of the courts to find out if fraud had been perpetrated and the duty of Congress to see that the Post Office Department had funds to work with.

As the debate grew hotter on the appropriation for the star routes west of the Mississippi, congressmen divided, not into Democrats versus Republicans, but into East versus West and Southwest. The Texas, Arkansas, and Louisiana delegations supported the appropriation. Said the *Daily Arkansas Gazette*: "There was but one man in all three of the delegations named [Texas, Arkansas, and Louisiana] who turned his back on the people and voted with their enemies to strike down their mail service. This was Mr. Reagan."[9] Reagan had voted with Joseph Hawley of Connecticut and Joseph Cannon of Illinois to nonconcur in amendments to the bill. In the Senate, Coke and Maxey of Texas, Garland and Walker of Arkansas, and Jonas and Kellogg of Louisiana had worked to pass the appropriation; in the House, Culberson, Jones, Mills, Upson, Wellborn, and the entire Arkansas and Louisiana delegations had supported the bill. On June 9, the bill was finally approved. Although the star service was destined to receive unwanted publicity and a setback later during 1880 and 1881 and Maxey was to be accused at that time of having conspired with fraudulent mail contractors, the good that the services brought to the communities they served could not be undone. General

6 Maxey speech in the Senate, in *Congressional Record*, 46th Cong., 2d sess., March 15, 1880, pp. 1549–1554.

7 *Nation*, March 25, 1880, p. 223.

8 Harry Barnard, *Rutherford B. Hayes and His America*, p. 489.

9 *Daily Arkansas Gazette*, April 11, 1880.

William T. Sherman was to make the statement that the mail lines were the "skirmish lines of civilization" on the frontier.[10]

Barnard points out in his biography of Hayes that the scandal that arose over the star routes had been brewing since Grant's presidency.[11] In 1872 the House Committee on Post Offices and Post Roads had initiated a congressional investigation into star route matters, and the successive Forty-third, Forty-fourth, and Forty-fifth Congresses had examined the Post Office budgets rather thoroughly. But it was not until 1879 that the investigations involved the names of prominent senators and high government officials.[12] On March 25, 1880, the House Committee on Appropriations began hearing testimony in relation to the postal star service, particularly in regard to the activities of Assistant Postmaster Generals Thomas Brady and James Tyner in letting mail contracts. Some of the testimony seemed to imply that Postmaster General David M. Key had not been sufficiently vigilant.[13] Key, who had been appointed by Hayes in a good-will gesture to the South, resigned his position on June 1, 1880, although he continued to serve until August 24 of that year, when he was replaced by Thomas L. James. Maxey, alarmed by Key's resignation, rushed to Key's and Brady's offices and later wrote of his visits:

I went to the Post Office Department today. . . . at the instance of a great many people petitioning for increase of trips between Stephensville and Eastland pressed by Senator Davenport [of the Texas legislature], I had the service increased from tri-weekly to seven times a week. That won't hurt out there, not much. Whilst my hand was in, I saw Judge Key who told he he had ordered a dollar a day added to [William E.] Smith's per diem whilst traveling to take effect July 1. I also told him and Brady to see to it that the new Postmaster General did not interfere with my Texas appointments which they said they would look to. So that important point is provided against.[14]

[10] William T. Sherman to Maxey, June 4, 1881, Maxey Papers.

[11] Barnard, *Hayes*, p. 489.

[12] J. Martin Klotsche, "The Star Route Cases," *Mississippi Valley Historical Review* 22 (1935): 409.

[13] U.S., Congress, House, Committee on Appropriations, *Inquiry into the Postal Service*, 46th Cong., 2d. sess., 1880, H. Document 31, pts. 1, 2, and 3, pp. 1–874.

[14] Maxey to Marilda Maxey, June 2, 1880, Maxey Papers.

When Maxey returned to Texas in June, 1880, at the end of the second session, he began stumping for Allen Thurman, whom he wished to see nominated as the Democratic presidential candidate. He was well aware that Hubbard, Throckmorton, and others of the Texas delegation were supporting General Winfield Scott Hancock, the Texas Reconstruction benefactor, for the nomination. Although he greatly respected his old West Point friend Hancock, Maxey felt that Thurman was a more likely candidate. But when the Democratic national convention met on June 22 in Cincinnati, Hancock was nominated by Daniel Dougherty of Pennsylvania, and the motion was seconded by Hubbard of Texas. Thurman and Bayard were also nominated, but the first ballot showed Hancock with 171 votes, Bayard, 153½, and Thurman, 68½. The tide of the balloting then turned toward Hancock, who was proclaimed unanimously the Democratic presidential candidate.[15] On June 24, Maxey wrote Hancock that he would support him and that he knew Hancock would win. Hancock replied expressing gratitude for Maxey's good wishes.[16]

As the time grew nearer for the Texas legislature to either reelect Maxey or find a new man for the senatorial post, the Texas newspapers took their stand on Maxey. The *Dallas Times Herald*, backing Throckmorton, criticized Maxey for advocating the star route appropriations, asserting that, since he was the chairman of the Senate Committee on Post Offices and Post Roads, he should have known that the increase of pay on the contracts would open the doors to most glaring frauds. The *Galveston News*, backing Maxey, gleefully pointed out that Throckmorton was not without blemish in the star route investigation since his name had appeared on some of the mail route petitions.[17]

The third session of the Forty-sixth Congress opened on December 6, 1880, after Garfield's defeat of Hancock for the presidency. Washington began to prepare for Garfield's inauguration, but Maxey, absorbed in his own problems of being reelected to his seat, wrote to

---

[15] Frederick E. Goodrich, *The Life and Public Services of Winfield Scott Hancock*, p. 315.
[16] Winfield Scott Hancock to Maxey, July 1, 1880, Maxey Papers.
[17] *Dallas Times Herald*, August 14, 1880; *Galveston News*, August 15, 1880.

Marilda, who had returned to Paris: "A good many yet think that old Granny Roberts is going to be a candidate for the Senate. . . . I don't. . . . Others again think Reagan is lying in wait. No doubt he will come to the front if he sees any show. . . . I think it will be decided between Throckmorton and myself."[18] Maxey was mistaken in his belief that Roberts was not considering running. Olin Wellborn, an attorney who had moved from Georgia to Texas in 1871, had written to Roberts that he would help influence the Georgians in his congressional district (Dallas) for Roberts should he run for the seat in the Senate. Wellborn also promised to use his influence at the meeting of the Texas legislature.[19]

Maxey arrived in Austin on January 18, 1881, in anticipation of the meeting of the legislature, on the twenty-fifth that was to choose him or his successor. He had been suffering for days with his forever-recurring back pain. He took rooms at a nearby hotel and was immediately called on by many of the Texas senators and representatives. Throckmorton came to see him and was "as pleasant and gentle as a cooing dove," said Maxey, adding, "I shall return his call, of course, when I get able."[20] Maxey had not planned to attend the ceremonies of Governor Roberts's inauguration but, learning that Throckmorton was present and busy currying favor among the people, he hastily followed the advice of his campaign manager, Lightfoot, and put in an appearance. In the evening Roberts gave a levee, but Maxey, still feeling unwell, sent his regrets by Lightfoot.

On the morning of the twenty-fifth, after the roll call was taken in joint session of the Texas legislature, Charles Stewart of Harris County nominated Maxey, and Senator A. W. Terrell of Robertson County seconded the nomination. True to predictions he had made to Marilda, Maxey was elected on the first ballot, the Senate vote being twenty-two for Maxey, eight for Throckmorton, and one for former Governor E. J. Davis; the House vote was fifty-one for Maxey, thirty-four for

18 Maxey to Marilda Maxey, December 19, 1880, Maxey Papers.
19 C. B. Wellborn to O. M. Roberts, September 23, 1880, Oran Milo Roberts Papers.
20 Maxey to Marilda Maxey, January 18, 1881, Maxey Papers.

Throckmorton, one for Reagan, and five for Davis.[21] The *Houston Post* reported that the *Washington Post* and the Republican party's newspaper in Washington expressed gratification at Maxey's reelection.[22]

Maxey returned to Washington to finish out his term in the Forty-sixth Congress and then begin the special Senate session of the Forty-seventh. On March 5, the Senate began a fight over the loaves and fishes, as Marilda aptly described it.[23] Since the Republicans had gained enough new members to make a majority, they took over all the important offices and announced new standing committees—Maxey was replaced by Ferry of Michigan as chairman of the Committee on Post Offices and Post Roads. On March 23, the Republicans offered resolutions for five new appointments to the important administrative offices of the Senate. Republican George C. Gorham of Massachusetts, who was slated to be secretary of the Senate, was an intimate friend of William Mahone and Harrison Riddleberger, both senators from Virginia who had recently turned away from the Democrats. Riddleberger was being pushed for the post of sergeant-at-arms and Mahone was helping him. The Democrats fought back as well as they could, and Riddleberger's nomination afforded them special ammunition. Maxey spoke in the Senate against Riddleberger, comparing him to a "pitching mustang, who pitches out of the Republican traces whenever it suits him to pitch out." When several Republicans made reply that Maxey was trying to attend to Republican business, Maxey rebutted by saying, "As a question of party discipline, I was simply trying to understand how the Republican party could place a gentleman in such an important position who was in the habit of doing pretty much as he pleased on the questions of party nominations." This remark caused Republican Senator Logan to reply, "I know the Senator is quite a disciplinarian; he has been in former times and is entitled to much credit for that; but if he will be kind enough to allow

---

[21] Texas, Senate, *Journal*, 17th legislature, January 26, 1881, p. 38; Texas, House, *Journal*, 17th legislature, January 26, 1881, p. 61.

[22] *Houston Post*, February 3, 1881.

[23] Marilda Maxey to Sam Bell Long, March 27, 1881, Maxey Papers.

us to manage our own affairs in our own way, we shall not try to interfere with the management of his affairs in his way."[24] Of course, it was really too late for the Democrats. They had not held a proper course during the last session, when they were in the majority, and one by one they now had to yield all the important offices, but the harangue went on for six more weeks, ending only on May 20.

The newspapers across the country were giving much publicity to the alleged postal frauds, and Maxey returned to Texas to look into rumors that fraud had occurred in some of the postal delivery contracts. In early May a post office inspector, John A. Galbreath, had been sent to Texas to check on the star routes there. On May 31, he wrote from San Antonio to his superior in the Post Office Department in Washington giving a scathing account of the desolate country between Brackettville and Fort Davis which, according to him, was "uninhabited except by a few Mexicans and stockmen who are temporarily in that country. A crow going over it would have to take his rations along." Galbreath recommended that the route be canceled. He also reported that Maxey's Saint Louis friend, R. C. Kerens, was interested in postal contracts in Texas and had been able to get one of his relatives a job at San Antonio.[25]

In May several arrests were made in Texas by the U.S. commissioner. Three Texas men were charged with fraud for having given worthless bonds for star route contracts. The routes involved were Fort Griffin to Fort Elliott, Brackettville to Fort Stockton, and Fort Elliott to Meschita Falls.[26] The route from San Antonio to Corpus Christi was also under investigation by the attorney general. A Texan named Ellis gave evidence that J. B. Price, owner of an Arkansas newspaper and a friend of Maxey, was the contractor for the San Antonio to Corpus Christi route, and that Assistant Postmaster General Thomas J. Brady was also involved in the contracting. Brady was alleged to have manipulated mail contract bids so that the contract was awarded

24 *Congressional Record*, 47th Cong., spec. sess., March 24, 31, 1881, pp. 44–45, 137–138.

25 John A. Galbreath to P. H. Woodward, May 31, 1881, and June 2, 1881, in U.S., Congress, *House Executive Documents, 100–103: Star Route Investigations*, 48th Cong., 1st sess., vol. 25, pp. 35–36, 231.

26 *Galveston News*, May 7, 1881, newsclipping, John H. Reagan Papers.

to Price, having first conspired with Price to arrange for a kickback. Because no evidence was available to prove that money had passed between Brady and Price, the allegations were dropped.[27]

Among the newspaper clippings in the Reagan scrapbook are a great many pertaining to the investigation for evidence of fraud in the Texas star route contracts.[28] It is probable that Reagan, who had warned Congress against appropriating such large sums of money for postal routes, watched the investigations with interest and a feeling of "I told you so." The fact that he preserved so many newspaper clippings containing derogatory remarks about Maxey makes one suspect that Reagan had no real sympathy for Maxey.

The *New York Herald* urged that Maxey, along with Congress· men Page of California, S. B. Elkins of New Mexico, Money of Mississippi, and Blackburn of Kentucky should be asked to explain his senatorial conduct of having urged an increase in appropriations for the star route contracts.[29] In Texas, the *Sherman Courier-Chronicle* took up the cry against Maxey: "Senator Maxey has either been neglectful of his duties as Chairman of the responsible committee which he has the honor to hold or else he is the most easily hoodwinked senator we have ever heard of."[30] Said the *Austin Statesman*: "The *Statesman* never believed that Mr. Maxey acted against his convictions but it did believe that he should have been influenced by evidence nearly as strong then [1879] as now. . . . The question of his relatives and friends being given important supervision of postal routes and offices in this district may excite speculation in the minds of the suspicious but that must be all."[31]

Two of Maxey's enemies, ex-Governor E. J. Davis, the leader of the Texas Republicans and a man who believed that all Democrats and conservatives were rebels and would always remain so, and Levis J. DuPre, editor of the *Austin Democratic Statesman*, claimed that Assistant Postmaster General Brady had offered money to aid in Maxey's

[27] U.S., Congress, *House Document 38: Testimony Relating to Star Route Cases*, 48th Cong., 1st sess., pt. 2, vol. 22, p. 192.
[28] Reagan scrapbook, Reagan Papers.
[29] *New York Herald*, May 1, 1881, newsclipping, ibid.
[30] *Sherman Courier–Chronicle*, May 15, 1881.
[31] *Austin Statesman*, May 15, 1881.

reelection to Congress. Davis further implied that Maxey had money to invest in the mail contract business and that he had spent a night in Saint Louis at the home of R. C. Kerens, one of the star route contractors, in order to discuss the matter. Maxey found no opportunity to refute the accusation until the next session of Congress. In October, he chanced to see DuPre in Washington and charged him with having lied. Said Maxey: "There is not the slightest foundation for even a rumor of that sort for two reasons—first, I had no money to invest, second, if I had a million, I couldn't invest a cent here. The whole thing is a lie off the whole bolt." DuPre replied, "I could not have told Davis there was such a rumor for I never heard anything of the sort." Maxey's letter to Marilda telling of his conversation with DuPre commented further, "The lie is between them [Davis and DuPre] and of the two there is not much choice, if any."[32]

The insinuations stung Maxey to the quick. His honesty and integrity had been attacked, and he fought back in the only manner he could think of. He wrote to influential friends—to James B. Beck, Kentucky senator who had launched the star route investigations in the Senate, and to William T. Sherman, general of the United States Army—asking them outright if they knew any facts that implicated him in the fraud investigation. Both Beck and Sherman said they did not. A similar letter to Postmaster General Thomas James elicited the reply that should he or the attorney general discover any information touching upon Maxey in the course of the pending investigation, such information would "not be improperly used." Maxey had asked James for a statement that would exonerate him, and James's reply did not satisfy him. Sherman urged Maxey not to give the newspaper innuendos "a single thought. By one word on the floor of the Senate you can brush aside any such newsmen as you would a cobweb."[33]

Maxey's political enemies in Texas continued to grasp at half truths and spread malicious gossip. In July, the *Houston Post* reported that Maxey had influenced the postmaster general to replace Throck-

[32] Maxey to Marilda Maxey, October 9, 1881, Maxey Papers.
[33] Maxey to James B. Beck, Maxey to William T. Sherman, Maxey to Thomas L. James, May 30, 1881, copies; Thomas L. James to Maxey, June 13, 1881; W. T. Sherman to Maxey, June 4, 1881, ibid.

morton's good friend Captain Joe Walker, U.S. postal agent at Austin, with Maxey's own brother-in-law, William E. Smith. The *Post* published a letter purportedly written by Assistant Postmaster General Thomas Brady to Republican Marshal Stillwell H. Russell of Austin, in which Brady offered financial help in order to reelect Maxey to the Senate.[34] The indictment in the star route case brought by the government in February, 1882, against eight men, including Thomas J. Brady, contained no reference to any route in Texas.[35]

Beset on all sides by political enemies in Texas, Maxey was gratified to receive an invitation to speak again at the annual July 4 rally at Galveston. At the same time he received an urgent invitation from Tammany Hall to join with the Society of Tammany in its ninety-third celebration of the Fourth of July. Maxey declined the invitation from New York and attended the Galveston celebration. He was a guest in the home of W. P. Ballinger, who, with an interesting sense of proportion, recorded Maxey's visit in his diary:

July 2, 1881   General Maxey arrived today and is staying with us. . . . President Garfield was shot and wounded it is supposed mortally this morning at the railroad depot in Washington by a vagabondish lawyer theologian and stalwart politician named Guiteau possibly crazy. . . . The artillery serenaded Maxey tonight at my house—sent out champagne and had a pleasant evening—several little speeches. Told Maxey to refer to Garfield which he did appropriately.
July 3, 1881   Talked with Maxey or rather gave audience to him. Read one part of his speech for the 4th.
July 4, 1881   Heard Maxey's speech. Not much of 4th of Julyish but sensible and practical. Very good audience. . . . Maxey pleased with himself and everybody.
July 5, 1881   Maxey went out to examine the Harbor works . . . and returned much impressed—seems confident of success.
July 6, 1881   Gave dinner to General Maxey this evening. Company besides him, Colonel Mansfield, Major Fisher, Mr. Jenkins of the *News*, Captain Stafford, Hutchings, Seth Shepard, Gresham. . . . Maxey spoke

[34] *Houston Post*, July 21, 1881, newsclipping, Reagan Papers.
[35] U.S., Supreme Court of District of Columbia, *Record of the Star Route Trials*, p. 2051.

at the Cotton Exchange at 12 today. Very effectively. He is not an able man—but is earnest, simple, practical and industrious.[36]

Maxey had prepared his Galveston speech earlier, but, as Ballinger pointed out, the news of the near assassination of Garfield necessitated some changes. He inserted some appropriate remarks referring to the "fatal stroke against the President as a stroke against free government" and said that he saw a possibility that the uncertainties about the presidential succession might strengthen the "upholders of monarchs in Europe and the advocates of a strong government in America,"—a possibility that should be viewed with alarm by all Americans.[37]

Maxey brought this point up again during the special session of Congress following Garfield's death. In a speech before the Senate he urged the Senate Judicial Committee to consider provisions for the eventuality of a vacancy in the office of the president of the United States. He reported to Marilda after this speech that he had been complimented by several of his fellow senators. Edmunds of Vermont had told Maxey that he had studied the Constitution for the same grounds that Maxey had forwarded in his speech and had made notes of the same passages.[38]

Following the death of President Garfield on September 19, 1881, Chester A. Arthur was sworn in as president. George Frederick Howe states in his biography of Arthur that the immediate summoning of the Senate to a special session indicated Arthur's concern for "the possible contingency of his own sudden death."[39]

Maxey and his family had been vacationing at Eureka Springs, Arkansas, when they learned of Garfield's death and that Maxey should return to Washington. When the special session opened in October, the old animosities flared up over who was to be chosen Senate president pro tem and, though Maxey was no longer a Bayard

[36] W. P. Ballinger Diary, W. P. Ballinger Papers.

[37] *Galveston News*, July 5, 1881.

[38] Maxey speech in the Senate, in *Congressional Record*, 47th Cong., spec. sess., October 12, 1881, p. 540; Maxey to Marilda Maxey, October 13, 1881, Maxey Papers.

[39] George Frederick Howe, *Chester A. Arthur*, pp. 154–155.

admirer, he admitted to displeasure when Bayard lost out to radical fence-straddler David Davis for the position.[40] As the Senate settled down to organize committees, Maxey commented to Marilda that there no doubt would be many inside fights among the Republicans over post office appointments and other positions of power. And he added: "So far as I am personally concerned I have no desire for a chairmanship. Parties are too evenly divided. It will not be a sinecure to anybody."[41]

Much Republican pressure had already been put upon Postmaster General James to oust the Democrats from post office positions. In Texas, for instance, Ulysses S. Grant's sons, Jesse and Ulysses S., Jr., had been nominated as postmasters at Terrell and Brackettville.[42] E. J. Davis had asked President Hayes in January, 1881, to remove William J. Bryan, nephew of Guy M. Bryan, and replace him with a good Republican named Hackworth. Hayes had refused to remove Bryan, but Davis was now again pushing for removal of all Democratic post office appointees in Texas. Maxey and Coke called on Postmaster General James, and, though James seemed mildly reluctant, they insisted that their nominees remain on the list for affirmation. Still dissatisfied, they called on President Arthur but again received little satisfaction. Arthur said that he thought it would be indelicate of him to ignore President Garfield's nominations, unless some compelling reason, not known when the appointment was made, should present itself.[43]

The first regular session of the Forty-seventh Congress met on December 5, 1881. Texas, along with the nation, had gained some measure of prosperity by the end of the seventies, and an enormous government revenue was beginning to accumulate. This latter fact, according to Maxey and other southern Democrats who believed that the government should not hold large surplus funds, emphasized a need for reform. Maxey had managed to pull himself out of debt, and his new solvency allowed him the generous gesture of bringing

---

[40] Maxey to Marilda Maxey, October 13, 1881, Maxey Papers.
[41] Ibid., October 11, 1881.
[42] Richard Coke to Maxey, March 13, 1881, ibid.
[43] Maxey to Marilda Maxey, October 13, 1881, ibid.

Marilda, Sam Bell Long, Henry and Dora Lightfoot, and Marilda's companion, Etta Wooten, to Washington. The entourage of Texans first made a detour through New York and Philadelphia. In New York they were impressed with Central Park, the elevated train, and Broadway, filled as it was with wagons and carriages. In Philadelphia they saw the celebrated John McCulloch play in *Othello*, and they visited Girard College, the Academy of Fine Arts, and the Mint, where young Sam Bell saw "blocks of silver laying around on the floor" and "the scales where they weigh the gold."[44] They arrived a day late for the first session of the Senate, and then, while Maxey set himself to business, the others continued their sightseeing by visiting the Washington Art Gallery and the Smithsonian Institution, and by dining at Welcker's Restaurant. They found the new electric lights on Pennsylvania Avenue, though faulty at times, a marvel to behold. They watched for Garfield's assassin, Charles F. Guiteau, as they strolled along the avenue near the building to which he was brought each day for his trial. Lightfoot and Dora attended the trial, but Sam Bell was considered too young to accompany them.[45]

Guiteau's trial during January was the high spot of excitement for all of Washington. Etta Wooten, Marilda's companion, watched near the court house as Guiteau, crouching down between two policemen, was led each day from the police van. Henry Lightfoot attended the trial for several days. Young Sam Bell wrote his stepfather after the trial was over, "There ain't such a crowd around the Court House now that Guiteau has not been brought there any more and I guess he will be hung."[46] Nicer treats were in store for Sam Bell, who was allowed to accompany his uncle on visits to Attorney General Wayne MacVeagh and Secretary of War Robert T. Lincoln. He was permitted to converse with General Sherman and General Longstreet when he met them.

Marilda had set Thursday as her day to receive. She was dismayed when she had forty calls to return. Said she: "Etta and I have been since two o'clock calling. We made about seventeen calls this evening.

[44] Sam Bell Long to his mother, Mary Long Terrell, December 5, 1881, ibid.
[45] Ibid., January 11, 1882.
[46] Sam Bell Long to James L. Terrell, February 1, 1882, ibid.

We have so many more that this whole week will have to be spent returning calls." She attended a last memorial service for Garfield and wrote home: "It is to be hoped the Republicans have finished putting poor Garfield away. Today they held the last memorial services. . . . The House of Representatives was packed and jammed with people of all classes and conditions, the great and the small. Etta and I sat on the steps of the gallery."[47] Marilda wore her old dolman cloak all winter in order to save money to buy furniture and carpets in Saint Louis on her way back to her beloved Texas home in May.

Maxey meanwhile had settled down to work. Like others in the Senate, he felt that the mark of a good congressman was not how many bills he was able to introduce and get passed, but how well he attended to the concerns of his constituency. Maxey's endeavors could be likened to those of Abram S. Hewitt as described by Allan Nevins: "Seeing that men who tied themselves to one object, like W. R. Morrison with tariff reform and John H. Reagan with railroad regulation, were doomed to heartache and disappointment, he [Hewitt] identified himself with many. This required immense and unremitting labor, but it brought compensations."[48] Maxey, following the example of many of his colleagues, often relied on outside suggestions about legislation. As Alfred R. Conkling expressed it in his book on Roscoe Conkling: "Comparatively few members of a legislative body draw up measures they offer. Such matters are frequently suggested by commercial bodies or manufacturers."[49] Certainly the most pushed legislation for Texas was the gigantic river and harbor bill, which was a collective effort of Texas industrialists. Even Reagan's railway regulation bill was the result of the combined efforts of the same industrialists.

Maxey turned his attention to a twenty-five–year–old North Texas border problem. Since the days of the Texas Republic there had been a running controversy between the federal government and the Texans living on the Red River border over the boundary line at the Red River. Sam Houston had protested in 1858 that the boundary line had

[47] Marilda Maxey to Mary Terrell, February 14, and 27, 1882, ibid.
[48] Allan Nevins, *Abram S. Hewitt*, p. 402.
[49] Alfred R. Conkling, *The Life and Letters of Roscoe Conkling*, p. 236.

been incorrectly established, but the Civil War had come close on the heels of his protest and the matter had not been officially brought up again.[50] Upon inquiry about the boundary matter at the Department of the Interior, Maxey discovered that the commission that had been assigned to survey the boundary before the Civil War had dissolved in 1862 without finishing the survey maps and without making a final report.[51] Maxey promptly offered a resolution in the Senate that the report and maps be finished. He hoped to use the report as the basis for a "bill to authorize the President of the United States, in conjunction with the State of Texas, to run and mark the boundary lines between the Indian Territory of the United States and the State of Texas, ascertaining and determining which is the principal Red River, the North Fork or the Prairie Dog Town Fork, and thus settle the question whether Greer County is part of Texas or part of the territory of the United States."[52] The Melish Map, Philadelphia edition, corrected to January 1, 1818, had been used to describe the boundaries in the treaty between Mexico and the United States in 1828. This same map was used by the survey commission in 1858. Texas claimed the North Fork of Red River to be the true Red River according to Melish's map. The area between the two forks of the Red River was Greer County, which was claimed by Texas but had been determined by the Department of the Interior to be part of the Indian Territory. The boundary bill that Maxey introduced after the report was made available passed the Senate on April 13 and was referred to the Committee on Territories. A month later, when the bill reached the House, Maxey called on Culberson, who told him that the bill had been changed somewhat from the one offered in the

[50] Texas Senator A. W. Terrell consulted an old San Jacinto veteran, John M. Swisher, who had some knowledge of the U.S. Commissioners' work on the boundary in 1862. See A. W. Terrell to Maxey, November 23, 1881, Maxey Papers. For Senator Houston's protest see U.S., Congress, Senate, *Congressional Globe*, 35th Cong., 1st sess., May 18, 1858, pp. 2210–2211; Llerena B. Friend, *Sam Houston*, p. 259.

[51] N. C. McFarland, commissioner, Dept. of the Interior, to Maxey, January 5, 1882, Maxey Papers.

[52] *Congressional Record*, 47th Cong., 1st sess., January 6, 1882, p. 258. Maxey kept Texas Governor O. M. Roberts informed on each step in the procedure on the boundary question. See Maxey to O. M. Roberts, January 7, 1882, Oran Milo Roberts Papers.

Senate. Complained Maxey: "Of course you know the House must find some point to differ with the Senate. The bill is very carefully drawn and can't be bettered but any bill that will settle the controversy is better than none."[53]

The boundary bill with its changes finally passed the House in 1884 but not before Thomas Reed of Maine tried to delete the part of the bill that stated that Texas was to be represented on the commission to be chosen for making the survey and report. When the bill came back to the Senate in 1885, in spite of Coke and Maxey's objections to the proviso that the federal government alone make the survey and that Texas need not be represented on the commission, the bill passed.[54]

At the same time that Reagan was attempting to gain support for his interstate commerce act to regulate the railroads, the Texas legislature was instructing Coke and Maxey to cooperate with Missouri congressmen in their efforts to help pass Senate Bill 60. This bill would allow the Saint Louis and San Francisco (Frisco) Railroad to extend westward through the Indian Territory. In October, 1881, Maxey begrudgingly had helped C. W. Rogers, second vice-president and general manager of the railroad, to persuade the Choctaws to allow a right of way through their land. In January, 1882, Maxey learned of a plot by Jay Gould and Collis P. Huntington of the Texas and Pacific Railroad. They were sending agents into the Indian Territory to stir up trouble so that the Department of the Interior would be induced to withdraw the Frisco's permission to go through.[55] The news soon came that Gould and Huntington had bought a controlling interest in the Frisco company, and Maxey felt it imperative to warn E. F. Winslow, president of the Frisco, that he did not believe the new owners were prepared to build the line from Fort Smith, Arkan-

[53] Maxey to Marilda Maxey, May 14, 1882, Maxey Papers. U.S., Congress, *Senate Executive Document 70: Texas Boundary Commission*, 47th Cong., 1st sess., 1882, series 1987, vol. 2, pp.1–3.

[54] *Congressional Record*, 48th Cong., 1st sess., May 26, 1884, p. 4496; *Houston Evening Journal*, June 13, 1884. In 1896 the United States Supreme Court ruled that the Texas boundary was the South, or Prairie Dog Town, Fork of Red River (Walter P. Webb and H. Bailey Carroll [eds.], *Handbook of Texas*, I, 195).

[55] Maxey to Samuel J. Kirkwood, Secretary of the Interior, January 4, 1882, Maxey Papers, Thomas Gilcrease Institute of American History and Art.

sas, to Paris. Maxey wrote to Winslow, "I would like to have a candid statement from you on this point, which may be, and I think is, important in its bearing on Senate Bill 60 ratifying the action of the Choctaw Council in granting right of way to your company." Winslow did not reply; instead, C. P. Huntington wrote Maxey on February 6, asking his help in passing Senate Bill 60. Maxey promptly flung back: "I beg to acknowledge the receipt of your carefully worded letter of yesterday in respect to the pending bill. . . . The friends of the bill had no sort of doubt when it was introduced that the company would, if the bill became law, build the road without unnecessary delay. Since the change of ownership, confidence has been very greatly shaken. They have no disposition to grant a valuable franchise to be *pocketed* for the benefit of those who think they can make more money by *failing* to build than by building." Huntington replied mildly to this attack that he and Gould would rather go slow in the matter and again asked Maxey to aid in the passage of Senate Bill 60.[56] Maxey tried but had infinite trouble pushing the bill, the Republicans in particular opposing it, and by April he had worked so hard that he could not rest day or night.[57] The amended Senate version of the bill finally reached the House, but none of the Texans could get it brought up and it was not to pass until 1886.

Maxey also worked hard for a reciprocity treaty of commerce between Mexico and the United States. President Grant in 1876 had been aware of the importance of such a treaty, and for years well-informed men in both Houses had tried to bring it about. President Hayes and Secretary of State William Evarts could not be persuaded to take initiative in this matter, but President Garfield's secretary of state, James G. Blaine, had seemed impressed when Maxey explained to him how such a treaty with Mexico could increase trade between the two countries. Blaine had asked Maxey to look through the existing

[56] Maxey to E. F. Winslow, January 26, 1882, C. P. Huntington to Maxey, February 6, 1882, Maxey to C. P. Huntington, February 7, 1882, C. P. Huntington to Maxey, February 9, 1882, Maxey Papers.

[57] For Maxey speeches on the bill, see *Congressional Record*, 47th Cong., 1st sess., April 3, 4, 11, and 12, 1882, pp. 2517–2528, 2563–2578, 2759–2768, 2801–2809, 2848–2857. Marilda wrote her niece that Maxey was so bothered he couldn't sleep (Marilda to Mary Terrell, April 5, 1882, Maxey Papers).

treaties with Mexico to find out what was lacking. Maxey, already prepared with such information, immediately launched an explanation. Blaine had demurred, claiming that he had pressing business, but promised that he would take up the discussion at another time. Instead came the end of Garfield's administration. Maxey now hoped that President Arthur and his secretary of state, Frederick T. Frelinghuysen, would make this treaty one of the events of Arthur's administration, and to his great satisfaction the treaty with Mexico was ratified in March, 1884.[58]

During the ten years after the Civil War the high duties levied on all commodities for revenue purposes gradually became transformed into a system of high duties almost wholly on protected commodities. In 1872, Congress voted a uniform cut of 10 percent from all the import duties, although this cut was strongly opposed by the Protectionists. In 1875, the 10 percent reduction was repealed, and duties were restored to their previous amounts.[59] Though in general Republicans were in favor of protection, they believed that the duties should be lowered some. Even carefully organized industries no longer opposed tariff revision. President Arthur recommended that a commission be appointed to examine tariffs, and most senators felt that a commission composed of tariff experts would be able to do a better job than would be obtained by congressional bargaining. On May 15, Congress authorized the appointing by the president of such a commission. Arthur appointed nine civilian experts, most of whom being from leading industries, such as wool, iron, steel, and sugar manufacturing, were manifestly protectionist, though not extreme.[60] It did not please Maxey when the members of the commission were announced. He wrote Marilda, now back at home, "Every man on the commission . . . is what they call *incidental* protection or undisguised protec-

[58] A review of Mexico–U.S. relations, including a statement on Maxey's efforts to improve them, was published in *New Orleans Times Democrat*, January 9, 1882, newsclipping, Maxey Papers. For details on treaty see U.S., Congress, *Executive Journal of the Senate*, March 11, 1884 (published in 1901), vol. 24, pp. 209–212, 380; Howe, *Arthur*, pp. 268–270.

[59] Charles C. Tansill, *The Congressional Career of Thomas Francis Bayard, 1869–1885*, pp. 61–66.

[60] Howe, *Arthur*, p. 219.

tion tariff men—several of them drawing heavy salaries from tariff users."[61] Before the Tariff Commission had even given its report, Maxey was wishing for a Senate adjournment so that he could return home. As far as he was concerned the Senate had safely disposed of matters of importance to Texas, and he wrote fretfully: "I very much fear that this tariff bill will raise the flood gates and turn loose an endless stream of tariff oratory—I am of the opinion that the Republicans were unwilling to go before the country without at least some reduction of taxes, as they have found that the country believes that the tariff commission was raised for the sole purpose of tiding over the fall elections without agitating the question."[62]

But while Maxey was longing for an adjournment, the matter of payment to southern contractors for mail deliveries prior to May 31, 1861, came before the Senate. This was an old problem; it had first been aired in the House in 1878. At that time Reagan, formerly postmaster general of the Confederacy, had stated that the Confederate government had not paid any of the claims of the southern mail contractors. Conger of Michigan had been able to prove from Reagan's own records, which were in the National Archives, that Reagan had indeed paid some of the southern contractors' claims. The unhappy results of this disclosure in 1878 had been an overwhelming defeat of the resolution to pay the claims, and, worse, the southern Democrats had been dealt a damaging blow. Now, on June 14, 1882, the same issue came before the Senate, and Conger was again quick to attack. The next day Maxey made a speech reviewing the history of the resolution and defending Reagan's part in the earlier House debate:

Mr. Reagan made a mistake in his recollection of events occurring many years before, as he himself frankly acknowledged on the floor of the House. I have known John H. Reagan for twenty-five years; and if he is not an honest and truthful man, I do not know where you can go to hunt one. His statement was made from recollection thirteen years after the events then under consideration. He had not the records, and the exact facts were

[61] Maxey to Marilda Maxey, June 8, 1882, Maxey Papers.
[62] Ibid.

misrecollected; but no one who knows him would attribute his statement to any other cause than fault of memory after the lapse of so many years.[63]

Maxey felt that Reagan could not say these things in his own defense. Garland of Arkansas and other southern senators complimented Maxey, and he wrote Marilda how Money of Mississippi had said, "In my opinion you wore Conger to a frazzle."[64] Maxey ordered a thousand copies of the speech for distribution, and when the resolution passed, he commented triumphantly: "Conger today went out at the little end of the horn. . . . He was afraid to call the ayes and noes as it was manifest he was badly beaten, even among the Republicans."[65] Reagan may have been pleased with the final passage of the resolution, but it is doubtful that he appreciated all the publicity Maxey got from it.

Reagan was soon in conflict again. On June 27, when the House debated a bill to regulate immigration, Congressman Van Voorhis of New York particularly favored a provision he believed would "prevent the flooding of the country with paupers through Canada."[66] Reagan disagreed, and the two exchanged sharp words of difference on the floor of the House. But Van Voorhis's keen intelligence and clever use of the English language bested Reagan. Reagan then attacked Van Voorhis through the House Committee on Commerce, of which Reagan was a member. The committee issued an official censure of Van Voorhis on July 20 charging him with an "unprovoked and unjustifiable attack upon their colleague, Mr. Reagan."[67] In his response to the unusual censuring action, Van Voorhis wrote: "You have given Mr. Reagan a character. He was sadly in need of one. If he don't lose it before he gets back to Texas it will doubtless be of use to him in his canvass for reelection. Such things help in far-off Texas."[68]

[63] *Congressional Record*, 47th Cong., 1st sess., June 15, 1882, p. 4921.
[64] Maxey to Marilda Maxey, June 17, 1882, Maxey Papers.
[65] Ibid., June 19, 1882.
[66] Van Voorhis to the House Committee on Commerce, July 27, 1882, published in the *Rochester Democrat and Chronicle*, July 30, 1882, newsclipping, Reagan Papers.
[67] Ibid.
[68] Ibid.

The debate on the rivers and harbors bill closed in the House on June 15, 1882. It was classified by many members of Congress, including Reagan's enemy Van Voorhis, as the worst rivers and harbors bill ever presented by the House Committee on Commerce. When it arrived in the Senate it was managed by Samuel McMillan of Minnesota, whom Maxey charged with mismanagement, complaining that the cumbersome and large bill had been loaded with amendments by greedy senators. "Were it not for the very great interest people have in it, I wouldn't care what became of it," declared Maxey.[69] On July 13, the bill passed the Senate with a vote of 38 to 23, but on August 1, President Arthur vetoed it. On the following day it was passed over his veto.

Following the indictment of February, 1882, the government had brought Stephen W. Dorsey, ex-senator from Arkansas; John W. Dorsey, his brother; Thomas J. Brady, second assistant postmaster general; John R. Miner, law partner of Stephen Dorsey; and others to trial for conspiracy to defraud the government on mail contract routes. On August 1, Maxey, along with a number of other senators and representatives, was summoned to appear as a witness for the defense in the star route trials.[70] The defense attorneys proposed to prove that it was the general policy of Maxey and the others to increase mail facilities in the West and the Southwest. But the judge declined to admit Maxey's testimony on the ground that none of the Texas routes were involved in the indictment.[71]

When the session of Congress finally ended, Maxey packed his books and prepared to go home. He was disappointed that the Frisco bill had not got before the House, but on the whole he was pleased that it, along with the Texas boundary bill and the Texas frontier defense claim, all of which he had introduced, had successfully passed the Senate. That the Texas newspapers gave him no credit for these accomplishments had galled him for some time and he had complained, "If any Senator from any state in the Union except Texas

[69] Maxey to Marilda Maxey, July 12, 1882, Maxey Papers.
[70] U.S., Supreme Court of the District of Columbia, *Record of the Star Route Trials*, vol. 2, p. 2051.
[71] Maxey to Marilda Maxey, August 1, 1882, Maxey Papers.

had done for it what I have done for Texas, his party papers would have been full of it."[72]

Two months after his return to Paris, Maxey began to complain of heart flutters and went to Hot Springs, Arkansas, to effect a cure. He refused to speak and campaign for John Ireland, who was running for governor, referring to him as "Humble John" to Marilda and Lightfoot. But he liked Ireland's opponent, Oran Milo Roberts, no better, calling him "O.A." (Old Alcalde) and "Dictator."

Several things were on Maxey's mind. He was fretting about where to buy land that would increase in value when the railroads came through the country. Also, when he returned to Texas, a check on his political friends revealed that none of them had read or cared much about the documents he had sent so laboriously from Washington. Even at his own law office in Paris he had been obliged to kick out of the way an accumulated stack of his documents—unopened.

[72] Maxey to Marilda Maxey, June 26, 1882, ibid.

8. Under President Arthur

I am of the opinion that we had better take care of our own
schools and not depend on Federal aid accompanied by Federal interference.[1]

THE NATIONAL ELECTIONS in the fall of 1882 gave the Democrats
the upper hand in Congress. Newspapers and local and national
organizations had been urging civil service reform in the national government, and the "sharp reverse suffered by the Republican party in
the elections of 1882 was partly the fruit of public indignation over
the refusal of Congress to promote civil service reform."[2] As the new
session of Congress opened in December, Maxey reported to Marilda:
"Our Republican brethren are struck with a very strong desire to
work. The lashing they received last fall has done them good. We now
work all day Saturday and I think the recess will be short and ought
to be."[3]

Civil service reform was begun in the Senate with the passing of
the Pendleton Act, which contained a provision for the president to
appoint a small, bipartisan commission to aid him in making and ex-

---

[1] Maxey to Marilda Maxey, March 21, 1884, Maxey Papers.
[2] George Frederick Howe, *Chester A. Arthur*, p. 204.
[3] Maxey to Marilda Maxey, December 17, 1882, Maxey Papers.

ecuting rules and regulations covering appointments to the federal Civil Service.[4] Many of the senators, including Voorhees of Indiana and Maxey, saw limitations involved in any bill that was set up to provide civil service reform and believed the Pendleton Act to be an inadequate effort.[5] Bayard, on the other hand, supported the bill and thought it a workable solution to the problem. Maxey commented acidly on its passing: "The Civil Service Act was passed today. I was against it, of course. Coke made a talk saying it was 'utterly worthless for any good purpose'—yet voted for it! That is the difference between us—nothing could induce me to vote for a measure I regarded as utterly worthless. Seeing it was bound to pass I administered a very bitter pill to the Rads in the way of an amendment which was adopted. That dose will do to throw up to them if they try on anymore political assessments."[6] Maxey's amendment to the bill was meant to protect government employees by prohibiting them from "paying out their earnings to any senator, representative or Territorial delegate or person acting for such." He believed that the amendment would "effectually put a stop to the political assessment business, so far as these Congressional committees are concerned."[7] Both Senate and House passed the bill with the amendment and on January 16, 1883, the Pendleton Act became law.[8]

The next item of business in the Senate was a tariff bill. The Tariff Commission's proposed law maintained substantial shelter for manufactured articles by reducing duties on raw materials. It cut most deeply the rates on sugar, molasses, and other necessities and retained high duties on luxuries. "The net government income would be reduced by such a law by about one-fifth."[9] Maxey took part in the many speeches made during the debate on this bill. Bayard and Beck of Kentucky also made speeches—Beck so many that jokes were made at

---

[4] Howe, *Arthur*, p. 208.
[5] Ibid.
[6] Maxey to Marilda Maxey, December 27, 1882, Maxey Papers.
[7] U.S., Congress, *Congressional Record*, 47th Cong., 2d sess., December 27, 1882, p. 643.
[8] Howe, *Arthur*, p. 208.
[9] Ibid., p. 222.

his expense—and the debate continued.[10] Maxey commented: "It is clear that the Republicans want so to adjust the tariff as to leave all the protected interests untouched. I have been taking . . . my share in the proceedings in the Senate and I have the satisfaction of knowing that I am always listened to respectfully and generally win."[11] On January 23, he spoke in the Senate on the proposal:

I have seen some disposition occasionally on the part of gentlemen to push this thing through, but is it expected that we are to do it without debate? How was the bill got up? Each one of these great protected industries was represented on this Tariff Commission by a representative man, and the special schedule for that industry was assigned to the special man who was interested in it and who was expected to uphold that industry. When a bill of that kind comes here, and there is involved in the bill $250,000,000 taxes, is it expected that those of us who represent the people who have in large part these taxes to pay are going to let it pass without debate, and folding our hands make no effort?

I say that every one of these schedules from beginning to end ought to be shown up, that the people may understand it perfectly well. I say that where the people have this money to pay they should know why they have to pay it. And when an industry is protected as you call it to the extent of prohibition, they ought to know why this protection should extend to prohibition.[12]

As the seemingly endless debate went on, Maxey was sure that the Senate could not finish by March 4, the proposed date for adjournment. "Perhaps," said he, "it is far better not to finish."[13] When the discussion of the tariff on cotton ties came before the Senate, he made a plea for a reduction of the tariff on them, especially those used for baling purposes. But the Senate Tariff Committee, composed of Republicans Morrill, Sherman, and Aldrich and Democrats Bayard and Beck, all of whom were against reduction, were watching Maxey's efforts closely. Maxey wrote of his actions: "Enough Republicans had promised to vote with me to secure its passage. I think Mr. Morrill

[10] Ibid., p. 224; Charles C. Tansill, *The Congressional Career of Thomas Francis Bayard, 1869–1885*, p. 308.
[11] Maxey to Marilda Maxey, January 12, 1883, Maxey Papers.
[12] *Congressional Record*, 47th Cong., 2d sess., January 23, 1883, pp. 1485–1486.
[13] Maxey to Marilda Maxey, January 24, 1883, Maxey Papers.

must have suspected this for he caved in and thereby spoiled half a dozen speeches. Coke, whose main effort appears to be in lumbering off occasionally a heavy prepared speech, told me after I had beat the fight that he had prepared to make a big speech. Beck, Vance of North Carolina and company of course would have to have spoken.[14] In the meantime I quietly carried off the coonskin and sent the people of the South half a million dollars annually."[15]

On February 3 Maxey spoke again in the Senate, this time on behalf of a reduced tariff on cotton yarn. Later he wrote Marilda: "I made what I think was a first rate short talk in exposing specific tariff duties in the cotton thread schedule today. . . . I have certainly been a useful man in the bill, and successful."[16] When William B. Allison of Iowa, a member of the Tariff Commission, gave some erroneous data relative to the cotton, Maxey asked in the Senate whether Allison and the commission had personally examined the cotton tariff schedule. Allison admitted that they had not but had used the expert advice of a Boston manufacturer and a New York expert, whereupon his competency as a member of the commission was challenged. The *Boston Post* took note of Maxey's astute questioning in the matter.[17]

On February 8, Maxey proposed to the Senate that the admission of books be made duty free. Soon afterward Beck made a successful plea for the reduction of tax on tobacco. The disenchanted Maxey spoke against Beck's motion and wrote later to Marilda: "Beck with his usual selfishness yesterday got the tobacco tax reduced to 8 cents per pound. It was a great mistake and has very much shaken my faith in his sincerity about tariff reduction. He has been loud mouthed in professions and yet he knows perfectly well that this useless and uncalled

---

[14] The Democratic senators, especially Beck and Bayard, frequently spoke persuasively and induced Republicans to vote for even larger reductions in individual tariffs. Morrill, a Republican, suspected that Maxey was preparing such a trap. By making a sudden capitulation to Maxey's proposals he cut short Maxey's Republican supporters. See Howe, *Arthur*, p. 223.

[15] Maxey to Marilda Maxey, January 28, 1883, Maxey Papers.

[16] Ibid., February 3, 1883.

[17] *Congressional Record*, 47th Cong., 2d sess., February 3, 1883, p. 1650; Maxey referred to a *Boston Post* article, no date given, in Maxey to Marilda Maxey, February 6, 1883, Maxey Papers.

for reduction of the tobacco tax will be a stumbling block in the way of tariff reduction now or hereafter, but he would sacrifice the prospects of the Democratic party for his own aggrandizement in Kentucky."[18] On the twelfth, George F. Hoar of Massachusetts and Maxey differed openly over the tariff on barbed wire, with Maxey winning the argument as the Senate voted to reduce the tariff.[19]

When the completed Tariff Bill was sent back to the House on February 27, the House, questioning the constitutional power of the Senate to amend their bill, returned it to the Senate and asked for a conference. The Senate appointed its Tariff Committee (Democrats Beck and Bayard and Republicans Morrill, Sherman, and Aldrich) as members of a conference committee. But when the Democratic House members on the committee did not appear for the conference, the Democratic Senate members used it as an excuse for refusing to serve longer on the committee. Other Democrats, including Maxey, were then asked to be conferees, but they all asked to be excused from the assignment.[20] Finally, Senators William Mahone of Virginia and James McDill of Iowa agreed to serve, and the committee produced a report in which certain duties were reduced (though in no case greatly), such as those upon wool, cheaper grades of cotton cloths, iron, steel rails, and copper. On the other hand, on many articles, duties already high were raised. This report was passed into law in the Senate on March 2 and in the House on March 3, 1883, and was approved by President Arthur.[21]

Maxey went home to Paris and during April traveled about Texas visiting his Democratic supporters. In May he went to the popular oasis Hot Springs, Arkansas, joining Senator George C. Vest of Missouri and Congressman William C. Oates of Alabama who were taking the waters. Reagan was there also, trying to rid himself of a carbuncle on his neck. Maxey, complaining of his old lumbago causing a pain in his legs and back and of a sore throat that would not heal, took the baths and whiled away the time between treatments by read-

[18] Maxey to Marilda Maxey, February 11, 1883, Maxey Papers.
[19] Congressional Record, 47th Cong., 2d sess., February 12, 1883, pp. 1703–1705.
[20] Ibid., March 1, 1883, p. 3466.
[21] Howe, *Arthur*, p. 225.

ing George Bancroft's *History of the Constitution* and by going fishing with Vest.

Later in the summer Maxey made a trip to Saint Louis where he visited R. C. Kerens and C. W. Rogers of the Saint Louis and San Francisco Railway. He attempted to interest them in a scheme an inventor had brought him for a new railroad-car coupler. In September, Maxey received a letter of thanks from Bayard for reports Maxey had sent him on the territory and resources of East Texas. This had been a calculated move on the part of Maxey to effect a favorable influence on Bayard concerning the need of East Texas for the Frisco line. In his letter to Maxey, Bayard mentioned that, as chairman of the Senate Committee on Railroads, he had found among the records of the committee an inquiry from the much-respected Texas Senator Thomas J. Rusk and he wondered if Maxey would like to have the letter. Bayard remarked that Rusk was "one of our best men—solid—and true but with a strange mystery around his inner life."[22] Rusk, who, along with Sam Houston, had been elected to the Senate in 1846, had been an ardent proponent of railway construction in Texas.[23] After the death of his wife in 1856, Rusk had become despondent, and he finally committed suicide in 1857. No doubt it was to this period of Rusk's life that Bayard was referring.

Tragedy struck the Maxey household in October when Dora, now mother of two children, was stricken with cancer. Marilda took her to physicians in New York, who pronounced her disease incurable. Maxey wrote her there: "I hope Dora will meet whatever may be necessary bravely. Tell Dora not to be uneasy about the children. May the Lord be merciful to her."[24] Marilda, numb with grief, returned to Paris with the beloved daughter.

While still in Texas, Maxey was interviewed by the *Galveston News* and reviewed some of his political stands in the Senate. He quoted Henry Clay and professed to agree with Clay's principles that taxes make the rich manufacturer richer and the poor consumer poorer. He went on record as opposing the repeal of the whiskey, beer,

---

[22] Thomas F. Bayard to Maxey, September 22, 1883, Maxey Papers.
[23] Walter P. Webb and H. Bailey Carroll (eds.), *Handbook of Texas*, II, 517.
[24] Maxey to Marilda Maxey, October 16, 1883, Maxey Papers.

and tobacco taxes. Replying to the reporter's query about whether he felt Tilden should again be the Democratic nominee in the coming presidential election, Maxey allowed that he had got enough of Tilden and believed that Thurman would be a good selection. Asked about the chances of Joseph E. McDonald of Indiana for the nomination, Maxey replied that, although he had unbounded faith in McDonald, with whom he had served six years in the Senate, he feared the constant talk of the old ticket (Tilden and Hendricks) handicapped McDonald at home in Indiana, since Hendricks was justly popular there. Maxey affirmed that he was against the nomination of Samuel J. Randall of Pennsylvania, Tilden's favorite, pointing out that he [Randall] was a protective tariff man and that tariff reform would be an issue in the presidential campaign.[25]

During the fall Maxey was also approached by a group of Texas Democrats who wanted President Arthur to nominate William P. Ballinger to a district judgeship in Texas. Said Maxey: "Undoubtedly he [Ballinger] would be the best selection but I have no idea that Arthur will nominate him or anybody else but an Arthur man. He [Arthur] wants to be President and of course wants to secure the vote of the Southern delegation in the National Convention. The appointing of a first rate judge is of very secondary consideration with his sort."[26] Ballinger's opponent for the judgeship was Texas Senator William K. Homan, whom Maxey liked better personally. But despite his own preference, after his return to Washington in December, Maxey accompanied Tom Ochiltree (a new member of the House) when he called on President Arthur and asked that Ballinger be nominated. After the interview with Arthur, Maxey wrote: "Arthur made no promises. I divided my sermon into three heads; first, Ballinger, second, Homan, third, Fernanst Evans. . . . Arthur in my opinion will not appoint any Democrat."[27]

The Democrats had won a majority in the House, and before the

[25] *Galveston News*, November 1, 1883.

[26] Maxey to Marilda Maxey, October 16, 1883, Maxey Papers.

[27] Ibid., December 9, 1883. William K. Homan was an old friend of Maxey from Burleson County. Fernanst Evans was probably the son of Republican Ira H. Evans. Arthur's nominee was Andrew Phelps McCormick, a Texas Republican. See Webb and Carroll, *Handbook of Texas*, I, 575, 830.

first session of the Forty-eighth Congress opened, a Democratic caucus was held to select a new Speaker of the House. The everhopeful,
now elderly Samuel S. Cox, who had wished to be Speaker since 1875,
insisted upon placing his name in the contest. His action annoyed
Maxey and other Democrats who were hoping this vote would help
them assess the comparative strength of the revenue men and the protectionists. The issue was clear enough though, when the final vote
in caucus was overwhelmingly for John G. Carlisle of Kentucky, an
ardent supporter of a more drastic reduction of tariff duties.

As the new Speaker began arranging the committees in the House,
the usual jealousies surfaced among the Democrats. Among the Texas
delegation there arose a dispute as to whether Roger Mills or John
Hancock should be placed on the Committee on Ways and Means.
Maxey commented: "I think Mills is entitled to the place and in every way a better and more representative man than Hancock. But I
understand that Hancock will have New York backing, which is likely, for although he is sound on tariff his notions about national banks
are not in accord with our people but suit capitalists." Maxey felt that
Carlisle's choice for this committee (from which any tariff bill would
proceed) would be influenced by whether the potential member was
a supporter of Carlisle's views on tariff reduction. And so, when Mills
was selected, Maxey interpreted the choice as an indication that the
committee would endorse strong revenue reform. Maxey wrote,
"There can be no doubt and if any member of the Democratic side
fails, he has simply deceived the Speaker."[28]

When the Senate organized, Maxey was placed on all his old committees. The Committee on Post Offices and Post Roads, whose chairman was Republican Nathaniel P. Hill, had a new committee room
on the gallery floor of Congress. The arrangement was pleasing to
Maxey for he had not liked the old committee room on the first floor,
which was "too convenient to respectable loungers."[29] The Senate had
recently passed a resolution to provide each senator with a clerk, and
he was also delighted to again have this aid. The swearing-in ceremony was a particularly pleasant occasion when Henry B. Anthony

[28] Maxey to Marilda Maxey, December 9, 24, 1883, Maxey Papers.
[29] Ibid., December 11, 1883.

of Rhode Island (a special friend of Maxey and of Ambrose Burnside) was sworn in for his fifth term. As a mark of respect to Anthony every senator stood while the oath was administered. "He is looking very pale, and has fallen off very much," wrote Maxey. "I don't think he will live long. Anthony is a gentleman."[30]

The Republicans, who still held the majority in the Senate, agreed in caucus to reorganize the officers of the Senate. "I suppose our Democratic employees will have to walk the plank," complained Maxey. But the Democrats had been pleased to observe that the Republicans were disagreeing among themselves about the nominations.—Maxey's letter to Marilda continued gleefully, "A fuss in the happy family is very consoling."[31]

Among Maxey's more pleasant duties was the welcoming of his friend Charles Stewart of Houston as a new member of the House. It was Stewart who, in 1881, had placed Maxey's name before the Texas legislature in nomination for the Senate. Not so pleasant was a request for help from Andrew Dorn, the ever-present office seeker. "He is the most helpless man I know, yet he is an honorable, good man, but a fearfully and wonderfully made hanger-on for office," complained Maxey. In an effort to place Dorn he called on James W. Wintersmith of Texas, the new doorkeeper of the House. Failing there, he appealed to the self-serving Coke, explaining later to Marilda: "Coke, in matters of this sort doesn't appear to know how to manage. I think that through Logan I may be able to save him [Dorn]." When applications to Logan and to the Texas delegation in the House also brought no job for Dorn, Maxey persuaded Coke to split the cost of a train ticket back to Texas for Dorn "on the principle I suppose that those who had done most for him should continue in well doing, and we did it very cheerfully and the blessings of peace from the most persistent office seeker. The rest of the session will amply repay us." When Governor Ireland sent Dorn back to Washington the following summer to look after the collection of funds owed Texas from the Frontier Defense Appropriation, Maxey and Coke were shocked. Maxey wrote Marilda that Coke had said, "Maxey, what in the name

[30] Ibid.
[31] Ibid., December 13, 1883.

of the Lord did Ireland send old Dorn on that business for?" Maxey could not answer, but he too felt that "it is a tremendous mistake. The state has over one million dollars involved and I worked hard and successfully to get matters in such shape to give the state an opportunity to get her dues. You might as well send me to teach Dutch."[32]

Another office seeker was Maxey's brother-in-law, William E. Smith, who had been injured in line of duty as a postal inspector. Smith, who was a hanger-on and a bit of a braggart about Maxey's influence, now asked Maxey to help him obtain a leave of absence for several months' duration. This necessitated a call on Postmaster General Walter Q. Gresham where Maxey learned that Republican Gresham and a Texas friend, a Mr. Malloy, were attempting to manipulate Smith in order to gain Republican influence in Texas.

In late April, 1884, Marilda, who had come to Washington with Sam Bell and Stella Wooten (Etta's sister), received news from home that Dora was much worse. She hurried back to nurse her, but Sam Bell, now fifteen, remained in Washington to continue his studies in a private school. He wrote in one of his many letters to "Muffod," as he called Marilda: "When Uncle and I came home yesterday after you all had gone, the room looked lonesome and we both wished you was [*sic*] here. Uncle and I slept together last night and got along very well although Uncle informed me of the fact that I had taken all the cover. . . . I went and recited my French lesson this morning. I went up to the Capitol and met Uncle there."[33] News about Dora's condition continued to be bad. Maxey wrote Marilda: "Poor child, her bright and joyous life and prospects in life are strangely clouded. The ways of Providence are inscrutable. We can only say, for it is beyond our comprehension, 'Thy will be done.' "[34]

During this time Mrs. Cadmus Wilcox, wife of Maxey's old West Point classmate, invited Sam Bell and Maxey to dinner. Also, although he rarely accepted evening engagements, Maxey accepted an invitation from Nathaniel P. Hill and enjoyed the social gathering, where he visited with Senators Morgan of Alabama, Plumb of Kan-

[32] Ibid., December 19, 1883, March 7, 1884, July 1, 1884.
[33] Sam Bell Long to Marilda Maxey, March 1, 1884, ibid.
[34] Maxey to Marilda Maxey, March 31, 1884, ibid.

sas, Dolph of Oregon, Gibson of Louisiana, Bowen of Colorado, and Blair of New Hampshire and Judge Schofield of the Court of Claims. Maxey, now fifty-eight years old, observed the wealthy senators and, comparing his financial lot with theirs, decided to take action to improve his fortune.

An opportunity to profit from investments had already arisen when, earlier in the month of March, Maxey and Senator Philetus Sawyer of Wisconsin were at work on a subcommittee. Maxey had mentioned how pleased he was that his stock in the Farmer's and Merchant's Bank in Paris had increased in value, adding that if more stock should become available he would increase the number of his shares, provided that he could find the necessary funds. Sawyer, a wealthy self-made man, was ever on the lookout for a good investment, and, as Maxey explained it to Marilda, proposed that Maxey "secure $10,000 to $15,000 worth of Paris bank stock," that Sawyer pay for all of it, yet allow Maxey "half of the stock at 6 per cent interest."[35] Since Maxey was a member of the board of directors of the Paris bank, he felt sure that he could arrange for additional stock to be released, but, to his chagrin, the other members of the board declined to do so. Hurt and offended, Maxey complained of this cavalier treatment, whereupon soon afterward, the directors did allow him to obtain $10,000 worth of stock, half of which he gave to Sawyer.

Another financial venture involved the purchase of land over which the railroad would pass. Walter Q. Gresham had, in 1879, purchased an interest in the Galveston railway system called the Santa Fe Railway Company (earlier called the Gulf, Colorado, and Santa Fe Railway Company).[36] Still holding his interest in the railroad in 1884, Postmaster General Gresham remarked to Coke one day that W. L. Moody, Maxey's staunch Galveston friend and a director of the Santa Fe, had reported to Gresham that the directors had voted to build two hundred additional miles of railway from Dallas to Paris. Coke divulged this piece of news to Maxey, who became very excited and

35 Ibid., March 8, 1884. Nevins, in his biography of Cleveland, charges that Sawyer was "interested in government chiefly as a means of enriching the lumber and railway interests of Wisconsin" (Allan Nevins, *Grover Cleveland*, p. 343).

36 S. G. Reed, *A History of the Texas Railroads*, p. 284.

sent word for Gresham to come to see him. Gresham came and when Maxey pressed for more details, after plainly telling Gresham that he wanted to invest in coal and timber interests and in bank stock with Sawyer's aid in financing, Gresham replied that he would probably want to put some money down himself. He agreed to tell Maxey definitely in about ten days whether the Frisco and the Santa Fe had pooled their interests so that the Santa Fe could build from Dallas to Paris and the Frisco from Fort Smith to Paris.[37]

Maxey promptly wrote Lightfoot to purchase land and bank stock as it became available and to say nothing to anybody. It was fortunate that about this time Maxey came into some funds of his own. An Austin concern approached him wanting to purchase, at three dollars an acre, 2,360 acres of land he held in the Panhandle. But Maxey was dismayed to discover that Coke was attempting to push through the Senate a bill to grant a charter to the Santa Fe to build north from Gainesville through the Indian Territory. Said Maxey: "Well, that isn't my particular business. If I had agreed to have taken hold, I would have done something. Of course I will not wear crepe if nothing is ever done."[38]

Maxey approached W. L. Moody for a loan, reminding him, "You were one of my stronger supporters in the legislature when I was first elected and you have been consistently for me ever since.[39] Moody responded by offering to assist Maxey in obtaining a loan from the bank in Galveston where Moody was the president. The loan could be had for 8 percent interest but would have to be renewed every four months. When Maxey demurred, Moody suggested that Maxey try to borrow money in New York and wrote a letter of recommendation to his old law partner who had moved there. Maxey used his Christmas recess to go to New York, where, using Moody's connections, he obtained a loan for twelve months at 6 percent interest payable semi-annually. Counting the money he had borrowed from Philetus Sawyer in order to buy the first $5,000 worth of bank stock in Paris, Maxey now owed $10,000, but possessed $20,000 worth of bank stock.

[37] Maxey to Marilda Maxey, April 28, 1884, Maxey Papers.
[38] Ibid., May 23, 1884.
[39] Maxey to Henry Lightfoot, May 24, 1884, ibid.

Maxey related to Marilda his experiences with the New York banks and pronounced his views on eastern finance: "There was, I presume, never more money in New York than now, but I have never seen such want of confidence in everybody and everything. There are millions of dollars locked up there lying idle. Railroad securities are all suspected and with them about everything else, except government bonds."[40]

Maxey paid a call on General E. F. Winslow, president of the Frisco, in order to push the coalition between the Frisco and the Santa Fe, and he later confided to Marilda, "I had a square talk with him [Winslow] about their intentions and said to him that the fate of this bill for extension [the Senate bill for right of way through the Indian Territory] would depend very much on his answers." Winslow assured Maxey that the Frisco intended to complete the railway bridge across the Arkansas River and thus come to Paris. Maxey, a bit over-optimistic about his influence in Congress, wrote Marilda, "He [Winslow] knows I won't let the bill pass til this is satisfactorily arranged."[41]

Two of President Arthur's particular interests in foreign relations were the reciprocity treaty with Mexico and the securing of a Nicaraguan Canal. The United States was now producing a surplus of manufactured and agricultural products and wished to sell them abroad. Arthur believed that exchanging favors with potential neighboring markets, like Mexico, was a good way to accomplish the sale of U.S. products. The Mexican treaty had gone before Congress earlier, but it was not until March 11, 1884, that it was ratified. Maxey had worked hard to see this treaty put into effect, as has been pointed out earlier. He thought it for the best interest not only of Texas but also of the entire country. He and Coke both made speeches before the Senate on March 11, urging ratification of the treaty.

On December 1, 1884, the United States, violating an earlier agreement with Great Britain that had pledged joint action in fostering construction of and in neutralizing political control of any means of interoceanic transport across Central America, signed a treaty with

---

[40] Maxey to Marilda Maxey, December 28, 1884, ibid.
[41] Ibid., December 27, 1884.

Nicaragua ceding a strip of land stretching across Nicaragua from sea to sea. Arthur submitted the Nicaraguan agreement to the Senate on December 10 and, after much debate in executive session, it looked as if the Senate favored ratification despite the risk of trouble with Great Britain. Maxey, an enthusiastic supporter of the treaty, was appointed chairman of a committee to inquire into all claims of citizens of the United States against the government of Nicaragua. But nothing came of the agreement. When Cleveland was elected president, he withdrew the treaty, thus ending the Nicaraguan adventure.[42]

When the Blair education bill, which provided for government money to be used to aid in the establishment and temporary support of common schools, came before the Senate, Maxey was very much opposed to the principles involved and described the bill to Marilda: "It is very extravagant but as it scatters a good many crumbs South, it will catch a good many Southern votes. I am of the opinion that we had better take care of our own schools and not depend on Federal aid accompanied by Federal interference."[43] In a speech before the Senate, Maxey pointed out that, when the money appropriated by Congress ceased to flow into the state schools, the state schools would then have no means to uphold their expensive system and would thus be worse off than before.[44] As Maxey spoke further against the encroachment of federal power and paternalism upon the states, Bayard added his voice of approval, but Lamar believed that the Blair bill would help the South. Some southerners, including many Texas newspaper editors, also approved of the bill and pushed their congressmen to work for its approval. Maxey wrote: "The *News* [probably the *Galveston News*] tries very hard to get a following against Coke and me on the school question but lamentably fails. Coke told me this morning that Governor Roberts wrote to him fully endorsing our course."[45]

The Morrison tariff bill, which provided for moderate tariff re-

[42] Howe, *Arthur*, p. 267.
[43] Maxey to Marilda Maxey, March 31, 1884, Maxey Papers.
[44] *Congressional Record*, 48th Cong., 1st sess., March 25, 1884, p. 2245.
[45] Maxey to Marilda Maxey, April 30, 1884, Maxey Papers.

form, did not have the total support of the Democrats, so that on March 25 a caucus was held in order to rally their support. Mills believed the Democrats would vote for the bill and thus enable it to pass the House, and he and Culberson spoke lengthily in favor of it. The Democratic leader of the House, Samuel Randall, was one who was a loud opponent of the bill. He tacitly sided with a group of eastern Republicans who, in an effort to help defeat the bill, had gathered at Philadelphia and received the backing of large manufacturing interests. When Lamar made an impassioned speech on behalf of the Morrison bill, his speech was hailed by the Republicans as a fine statement of the Democratic position.[46] When the vote in the House was taken, a totally Democratic vote of 151 lost to a mixed Republican and Democratic vote of 156 for defeat of the bill. Maxey analyzed the vote angrily:

The 156 vote was made up of the solid Republican vote reinforced by Randall and his gang. Whilst a mere fraction of the Democratic party entered into an unholy coalition with the Republican party and whilst the overwhelming majority of the Democratic party stood true to its colors, it will be difficult, I fear, ever to get the people to understand that they were slaughtered by a few unfaithful in the household of their friends. . . . While there is intense indignation in the Senate there is a difference of opinion as to the effect of this vote on the party. My own opinion is that it will have a damaging effect.[47]

At a Democratic mass meeting in Paris the following September, Maxey set forth his views on taxes and tariffs in more detail. He offered constitutional proof that Congress did not have the power to levy and collect taxes except to raise revenue for the support of the government. He went on to show that more than $100 million of surplus had been raised from taxing the people. "Yea, more than is necessary to pay the interest on the public debt, provide for the sinking fund, the current expenditures, extravagant as they are, and the enormous pension list," said Maxey. "Yet when the Democratic party pledges itself to reduce taxation to the actual needs of the govern-

[46] Wirt Armistead Cate, *Lucius Q. Lamar*, p. 397.
[47] Maxey to Marilda Maxey, May 6, 1884, Maxey Papers.

ment, economically administered, we are coolly told by Mr. Blaine
that 'on that question the two political parties are radically in conflict!' "[48] Maxey was incensed that the Republicans dared to compare
Blaine with Henry Clay—"that greatest of American statesmen," as
Maxey described him. Actually the only way in which Blaine resem-
bled Clay was in his notion that the great surplus of money in the government treasury should be distributed among the states.

In his speech to the Democratic meeting, Maxey also undertook to
discuss the tariff commission and the tariff laws. He pointed out that
the commission had been appointed as a sop to the complaints of the
people. "The great body of the Democratic party knew that the whole
thing was a humbug but it was seemingly so fair that some very worthy innocents, and all the so-called protective tariff Democrats, walked
into the trap," declared Maxey. He described the resulting tariff law
as the most "outrageous class legislation, the most oppressive that
ever blackened the statute book," since protective legislation like that
fostered and encouraged overproduction, which then resulted in the
reduction in the price of labor. This caused strikes and running of
the mills only half-time. Speaking of the interests of the people of
his own area, he turned to a discussion of the effect of protective tariff laws on farming interests. "Cut off a foreign market, build the
wall of protective tariff, and what becomes of the western farmer who
produces a surplus of 186,000,000 bushels after supplying all demands in the country?" asked Maxey. No forced collections were tak-
en up for the benefit of the cotton raisers, Maxey said, "but the cotton
raisers were forced to pay a toll to the producers of articles they needed such as iron tools, ploughs, wagons, gins, etc." He ended his
speech with a quote from a decision in the Supreme Court that stated
that it was unfair for the government to tax the property of the citizen in order to bestow aid upon favored enterprises and build up private fortunes.[49]

The Texas delegation in Washington had been instructed by the

[48] S. B. Maxey, *Address of Honorable S. B. Maxey of Paris, Texas, Delivered
before the Democratic Mass Meeting Held at Paris, Texas, September 20, 1884*, p. 15.
James G. Blaine was the Republican presidential nominee in the 1884 election.
[49] Maxey, *Address before the Democratic Mass Meeting*.

Texas legislature to continue to keep a close watch on appropriations for deep-water improvements for Texas. Some interested Galveston industrialists had conceived the idea of asking James B. Eads of Saint Louis (who had engineered the deep entrance at the mouth of the Mississippi River) to come before the Committees on Commerce of the Senate and House to explain his plan to improve Galveston harbor. This was to be followed by the Texas delegation's introduction of a special bill to obtain government aid to carry out the improvement. When Eads declined to appear before the committee, Maxey declared that it was a fortunate circumstance, saying: "The plan appeared to me Quixotic. Yet as the Galveston people insisted on it, we agreed, with the understanding that Eads was to appear and explain his plan. As he declines this, we concluded to decline him and rely on the usual appropriations."[50] James Eads was far too busy with obtaining federal aid for his "ship-railway" across the Isthmus of Tehuantepec, Mexico. His plan was to build a giant railroad that could carry seagoing vessels, thus taking the place of a canal.[51]

Reagan and Maxey worked together in an attempt to obtain at least some appropriations for the Galveston improvements. In June they persuaded Secretary of the Treasury Charles Folger to give an order to his chief of bureau for the preparation of statistics and a full statement of the necessity for improving Galveston harbor. The statistics were printed and distributed to the president and congressmen. On July 1 the River and Harbor Bill, complete with appropriations for Texas, passed the Senate without a division.[52] It was the first time since Maxey had been in the Senate that a struggle had not ensued before an appropriation was passed.

Maxey offered a bill to change the judicial districts in Texas with a view to encompassing and serving the Indian Territory, and the bill was referred to the Senate Judiciary Committee for further study.[53]

[50] James B. Eads to Maxey, March 17, 1884, Maxey Papers; Maxey to Marilda Maxey, April 3, 1884.

[51] *Dictionary of American Biography*, s.v. "Eads, James B."; Howe, *Arthur*, p. 272.

[52] *Congressional Record*, 48th Cong., 1st sess., July 1, 1884, p. 5229.

[53] Ibid., March 26, 1884, p. 2276. This was not the first time Maxey had offered this bill (see *Congressional Record*, 46th Cong., 1st sess., April 21, 1879, p. 592).

At the same time Senator Vest of Missouri presented a bill to create a court within the Indian Territory, probably at Muskogee. The rivalry between Maxey and Vest to get their bills out of committee and before the Senate became intense. Vest had the upper hand because he had an ally in Augustus H. Garland, who was a member of the Judiciary Committee and who wished to see the court established in Arkansas. In addition, both Vest and Garland were members of the Senate Committee on Indian Affairs.[54]

The already troubled waters of Maxey's court bill were further complicated by the demands of interested parties from Denison, Sherman, and Gainesville, Texas. They saw no reason why Paris should pluck the plum of having the U.S. Court of the Northern Texas District, and they appeared before the Senate Judicial Committee with papers and petitions that their city be chosen instead of Paris. "I can beat Vest and Arkansas if let alone," cried Maxey, "but these stabs from Texas people are hard to overcome." Maxey had begged House member Throckmorton to induce Sherman to withdraw its contention for the site of the court, but Throckmorton had made only a half-hearted response. Maxey continued his complaint to Marilda: "You know he [Throckmorton] wouldn't risk losing a vote by any such effort. What the honest views of Culberson and Throckmorton are I don't know. Throckmorton is between three fires [Denison, Sherman, and Gainesville were all in Throckmorton's voting district]. . . . Culberson having worked the bill through the House was happy over the accumulations of trouble in the Senate. . . . Accidentally or intentionally every trouble has been reserved for the Senate. Whether this has been a put up job is a question."[55] Determined to see the bill through at whatever cost to himself, Maxey wrote Lightfoot to increase his endeavors to get a protest against Vest's Indian court bill started in the Choctaw Nation. On June 5, Allen Wright of the Choctaws telegraphed Maxey that he was unable to obtain an official protest from

---

It had then been reported back adversely from the Senate Judiciary Committee and postponed indefinitely (*Congressional Record*, 46th Cong., 2d sess., Dec. 17, 1879, p. 135).

[54] Maxey to Marilda Maxey, May 6, 10, 18, June 11, 1884, Maxey Papers.
[55] Ibid., May 29, 1884.

the Choctaw Nation but that the general sentiment was in favor of Maxey's bill and opposed to that of Vest.[56] Matters were at a standstill while for six months the Senate committee refused to report either of the two bills out of committee.

Judge Reuben Gaines of the Sixth Judicial District of Texas visited Washington and called on Maxey demanding to know the state of the court bill and why Maxey was not following the lead of Throckmorton and Culberson, both of whom, according to Gaines, were being given credit in Texas for introducing and fowarding the bill.[57] Maxey placed all the papers concerning the bill in Gaines's hands and pointed out that there was no bill in the House reported from any committee for the organization of a court in the Indian Territory. Therefore he could hardly see how it was that Throckmorton and Culberson were doing so much for the bill. After Gaines's perusal of the situation, he went away enlightened though still not satisfied with the state of the bill. Said Maxey, "I am very glad he came, for the sole reason that it will probably teach some of our overzealous friends of the true situation."[58]

The session of Congress was over on July 7 and Maxey returned to Paris. When Dora died on July 12, the family went into deep mourning. In June, the Democratic state convention had been held to select Texas delegates to the national convention. Leaders of both the agrarian and "progressive" factions, as well as Coke and Seth Shepard, the latter an attorney for the Santa Fe railroad and a Texas senator, opposed sending another pro-Tilden delegation to the national convention.[59] When voting time came, the Texans split the first two ballots evenly between Bayard and Cleveland and on the third ballot went over to Cleveland.[60]

The Democrats held their national convention in July in Chicago. Richard Hubbard was chosen as temporary chairman of the conven-

[56] Allen Wright to Maxey, telegram, June 5, 1884, ibid.

[57] Throckmorton and Culberson were given credit for instigating the court bill in the *Dallas Weekly Herald*, January 31, May 22, July 24 and 31, 1884.

[58] Maxey to Marilda Maxey, July 1, 1884, Maxey Papers.

[59] Maxey to Marilda Maxey, June 16, 1884, ibid.

[60] Alwyn Barr, *Reconstruction to Reform*, p. 79; E. W. Winkler, *Platforms of Political Parties in Texas*, pp. 223–234, 217–220.

tion and Grover Cleveland was nominated for president. Pleased with this result, Maxey set about addressing Democratic mass meetings and pledging himself to work for the election of Cleveland. His address-es were similar to the one he had given at the mass meeting in Paris. He included his opinion that Congress did not have the constitutional power to levy and collect taxes except to raise revenue for the support of the government, and he denounced the Republicans for comparing Blaine to Henry Clay. He criticized the tariff commission and the tar-iff laws.

He went back to Washington on December 1. The caprice of the American popular voters kept both Republican and Democratic con-gressmen unsure about who would be in the majority from year to year, and more and more the business of Congress was conducted in committee rooms rather than on the floor. Many bills met the same fate as Maxey's judicial district bill and remained in committee for months. Even after receiving the recommendation of the committee to which they were consigned, they had to run a painful gauntlet before becoming law. Too, interests varied in each section of the country, so that the bills introduced by congressmen of one area vied with those of importance to other areas, in a flood of proposed legis-lation.[61] This was more especially true of the House, but like condi-tions, though less severe, existed in the Senate.

When the standing committees were announced in December, Max-ey kept his post as senior Democrat on the Committee on Post Offices and Post Roads (which now had a Republican chairman), and he be-came second in Democratic seniority on the Committee for Military Affairs. He was pleased to give up his place on the Committee on Ed-ucation and Labor, since he had never favored this assignment and had grown to positively dislike it when Blair had introduced the new education bill. He was the recipient of Republican courtesy when he was retained as chairman of the do-nothing Nicaraguan committee and given a room and a clerk. He took the honor saying, "When we [the Democrats] had power we made plans for a few of the oldest

[61] For a discussion of conditions in the nation and in Congress during this pe-riod, see James A. Barnes, *John G. Carlisle*, pp. 64–65.

Republican senators in service and now they return the compliment."⁶²

Reagan's interstate commerce bill regulating railroads passed the House on January 9. Maxey congratulated him and promptly set to work with Garland and Vest to get the Reagan bill placed before the Senate without reference to a committee, thus enabling the Senate to examine it at the same time as an interstate commerce bill introduced by Senator Shelby Cullom of Illinois.⁶³ Reagan's bill provided a law against known grievances against the consumer and placed in the courts the power to hear and judge the grievances. The Cullom bill was a permissive commission system for the ascertainment of grievances, but with no concrete way of enforcing regulation.⁶⁴ On January 20, Maxey made a speech in the Senate in which he pointed out the superiority of the Reagan bill over the Cullom bill for regulating interstate commerce.⁶⁵ When, on the next day, Coke spoke on behalf of Reagan's bill, Maxey complained that Coke's speech was good but very loud. When the Cullom bill passed the Senate on February 4, the disappointed Maxey wrote: "The bill as passed is no doubt very satisfactory to railroad men as without exception those generally counted as friendly to them voted for the bill as it passed and against the House bill. As I considered the Senate bill [Cullom's bill] as worse than no bill at all, I voted against it. The House will undoubtedly disagree to the Senate amendments and that will throw it in conference."⁶⁶ The struggle between the two bills continued until 1887, when they were sent to a conference committee, whereupon the Cullom bill, with some changes for the better, was finally passed. President Cleveland influenced this outcome by favoring the Cullom bill.⁶⁷

On January 8, 1885, Maxey and Coke called on President Arthur to ask him to pardon ex-U.S. Marshal Stillwell H. Russell of Texas, who, having been convicted of misusing government funds, had now served almost a year in prison. At his trial, Russell had slapped Assistant Attorney General Brewster Cameron, a matter that was not about

---

⁶² Maxey to Marilda Maxey, December 10, 1884, Maxey Papers.
⁶³ Ibid., January 9, 1885.
⁶⁴ Nevins, *Cleveland*, p. 355.
⁶⁵ *Congressional Record*, 48th Cong., 2d sess., January 20, 1885, p. 657.
⁶⁶ Maxey to Marilda Maxey, February 4, 1885, Maxey Papers.
⁶⁷ Nevins, *Cleveland*, p. 355.

to be forgotten or forgiven by Cameron or his relative, Attorney General Benjamin H. Brewster. Both Cameron and Brewster urged President Arthur not to grant Russell a pardon, but Arthur did grant it— one day short of Russell's full time. The pardon removed Russell's felony conviction and so had the effect of restoring his citizenship.[68]

As 1885 began there was great financial unrest across the nation. The sound-money men believed that the free coinage of silver was the main cause of the rapid depletion of the gold reserves.[69] "Not so!" cried Maxey and other Democrats from the West and the South who favored the silver coinage. Maxey attributed the unrest to high protection, which he felt caused overproduction, thus forcing the shutting down of mills and the discharge of hands; to good crops in Europe, which lessened the demand for grain and meats from the United States and hence reduced prices; to reckless and rascally management of railroad securities; and to bad management of banks, which resulted in bank failures.[70]

In the Senate, Maxey saw all around him the wealth of some of the nation's leaders—Senators James G. Fair of Nevada, Leland Stanford of California, Joseph Dolph of Oregon, John Jones of Nevada, Joseph E. Brown of Georgia, Philetus Sawyer of Wisconsin, and others —all of whom were personally wealthy and managed to manipulate their corporation interests while attending to their state's business in Congress.[71] In marked contrast Maxey pondered his debt of $10,000 and worried over his future should he not be reelected to a third term in the Senate. He felt great sympathy for the penniless Grant, and on January 14 he supported a bill authorizing the addition of Grant's name to the retired list of the army, though in 1883 he had voted against a similar bill. Now he even spoke before Congress recommending the bill and stating that his reason for having changed his mind had to do with Grant's most recent financial misfortune. He

[68] Maxey to Marilda Maxey, January 8, 17, 31, 1885, Maxey Papers; U.S., Department of Justice, *Exhibit No. 8: Case Against Stillwell H. Russell*, December 1884, pp. 1–212.
[69] Barnes, *Carlisle*, p. 86.
[70] Maxey to Marilda Maxey, January 11, 1885, Maxey Papers.
[71] Nevins, *Cleveland*, p. 343.

wrote later to Marilda: "Whilst he [Grant] was prosperous and, in the language of Mr. Conkling, 'The Nations of the earth stood uncovered before him,' I let him take care of himself. Now that he needs friends, I stand by him as he stood by me in the winter of 1865 when I needed friends."[72] The bill granting relief to Grant (and a pension to his widow should he die) was passed. Maxey, Garland, and Voorhees were among those who voted for the bill and Coke, Beck, Cockrell, and Saulsbury voted against it—Lamar and Bayard were absent. The *Nation* took notice of the "warm tributes to General Grant paid by Southern Senators Maxey, Jonas, George, Jones and Voorhees."[73] But not all of Maxey's constituents in Texas approved of his action, and when apprised of this he countered: "I have neither apology, explanation or excuse. . . . It would be better business to call upon the nine Democrats who voted 'no' for an explanation."[74] Grant died on July 23, 1885. Maxey called on Mrs. Grant in New York in the following December, and she and her daughter-in-law, Mrs. Fred Grant, received him graciously. Said Maxey of the visit: "Mrs. Grant was friendly as she always is, but not lively as she is naturally. She spoke of General Grant freely and was evidently pleased when I told her how the old Confederates at their reunions sympathized with her. She expressed herself very grateful for her pension. She said someone told General Grant before his death that she was entitled to it by law. She learned before his death that that was a mistake but she said that he felt so happy that this would secure her a living that she never undeceived him."[75]

Not among the many who were openly courting Cleveland as his inauguration approached, Maxey wrote Marilda: "Some of our friends are making pilgrimages to the rising Sun. As I have no special call . . . I shall wait til Mr. Cleveland is sworn in."[76] And on February 13, he noted:

---

[72] *Congressional Record*, 48th Cong., 2d sess., January 14, 1885, p. 684; Maxey to Marilda Maxey, January 19, 1885, Maxey Papers.

[73] *Nation*, January 20, 1885, p. 66.

[74] Maxey to Marilda Maxey, January 22, 1885, Maxey Papers.

[75] Ibid., December 31, 1885.

[76] Ibid., February 4, 1885.

Next Tuesday we will count the electoral vote and I shall enter the House for that purpose with far more satisfaction than I have ever done before. We had a number of anxious statesmen last week to make a pilgrimage to New York to fall down and worship the rising Sun. Well, I think they don't feel so well. I am happy to hear that Cleveland had the good sense to hear all these people had to say and say nothing in return. I abhor flunkeyism and toadyism. I shall treat Mr. Cleveland with the respect he is justly entitled to but as I recognize no earthly superior, I shall treat him precisely as I would any other gentleman occupying the social position of a gentleman.[77]

On the eighteenth, Maxey wrote: "Cabinet rumors fill the air but I suppose it is simply good guess work. Some of the guesses, notably Bayard for Secretary of State and Garland for Attorney General, are probably correct. There is a very general desire here that Judge Thurman should have a place in the Cabinet."[78] Continuing this letter, Maxey commented that "the result [electoral count] was announced so that Mr. Cleveland may rest quite easy about his inauguration. Everything passed off without a word of dissent to the vote of any state. The galleries, as usual, were crowded. We began the count at 12 and at 1:25 it was concluded and the Senate returned to the Senate Chamber and resumed work. What a difference between February, 1876, and February, 1885! You [Marilda] were here during the Tilden trouble and know all about it."

A short time later Maxey wrote his wife that he was tired after twelve years of service in the Senate and felt like taking some rest when his present term was out. "The position of senator is greatly coveted by the ablest men in the land and it is one of which any man may well be proud," explained Maxey, adding further, "I do not regret having served, for I have gained a reputation throughout the land which I could not have done had I continued the practice of law any-

[77] Ibid., February 13, 1885.
[78] Ibid., February 18, 1885. Cleveland's advisers decided against a cabinet position for Thurman because they considered him too old and also feared he might consider himself so important that he might try to run against the President in the next election (John S. Hare, "Allen G. Thurman: A Political Study," doctoral dissertation, pp. 298–299).

where, much less in a town no larger than Paris."[79] Perhaps his weariness arose from the fact that his name had been mentioned only briefly in Texas as a possible candidate for Cleveland's new cabinet. He had seen men like Garland and Lamar forge ahead of him, and even John Carlisle, who had entered the House only in 1877, had gained the coveted honor of being Speaker of the House.

[79] Maxey to Marilda Maxey, February 24, 1885, Maxey Papers.

9. Under President Cleveland

Mr. Cleveland made a big mistake last February when he
undertook to tell Congress before he was inaugurated what it
ought to do about silver and a bigger one when he put his
nonsense in his message.[1]

T HE INAUGURATION of Cleveland, the first Democratic president
since James Buchanan twenty-eight years earlier, was a grand and
festive affair. The formal ceremony took place on March 4, 1885, in a
special session of the Senate in the presence of the diplomatic corps,
Supreme Court justices, House and Senate members, the General of
the Army, the Admiral of the Navy, President Arthur, and President
Pro Tem of the Senate George F. Edmunds.[2] Marilda sat in the gallery and watched, and later she accompanied Maxey to the president's
reception, where Miss Cleveland assisted her bachelor brother in receiving his guests. Marilda later pronounced the raw-boned Miss
Cleveland "plain" and added that she believed "no amount of White
House could make Miss Cleveland pretty."[3] Little else was accomplished in the month before the Senate session ended on April 2,

[1] Maxey to Marilda Maxey, December 27, 1885, Maxey Papers.
[2] James A. Barnes, *John G. Carlisle*, pp. 90–91.
[3] Marilda Maxey to Sam Bell Long, date unknown, but mentioned in a letter from
Sam Bell Long to Marilda, March 22, 1885, Maxey Papers.

except for the chairing of the new standing committees. The Republicans, exercising their right as the majority in the Senate, placed Republicans in the chairmanships. Maxey was assigned to the Committees on Indian Affairs, Military Affairs, Post Offices and Post Roads, and Coastal Defense.

The Committee on Indian Affairs had a job to do almost immediately. Earlier, in 1884, President Arthur's secretary of the interior, Henry M. Teller, had brought the Senate's attention to what he termed the wide abuses of leasing Indian lands for cattle grazing, particularly in the Indian Territory. Several events caused Teller's action. Some of the Indians had complained to him that they had dissented when the vote in the Indian Council was taken on leasing their lands. Another complaint had come from the black freedmen who were adopted citizens of the Indian Tribes but not eligible (according to the Indians) to receive any of the Indian profits from leasing the land. And, finally, Helen Hunt Jackson had publicized these complaints in her book *Ramona*, which dealt with the ill-treatment of the Indians by the government.[4]

Maxey had brought up the welfare of the Indian at the previous session of Congress. He had mentioned especially the Indian Territory's need for a court closer than the existing one at Fort Smith and the need for federal laws for civil processes within the Indian Territory, saying:

I happen to know, from living in close contiguity to that country, that there is an immediate and pressing necessity for an investigation, not only of this but of other important matters by the Committee on Indian Affairs. Now can that be done without sending a committee or sub-committee to the Indian Territory? [He added:] I have heard a great many criticisms about the leases in the Indian Territory just north of me. Lands are rented there for a price greatly less than is paid for corresponding graze lands in my state; and I think there is much dissatisfaction among the Indians growing out of the leasing of the lands in such large bodies, as well as such low figures.[5]

[4] For a discussion of Teller's part in Indian affairs, see George Frederick Howe, *Chester A. Arthur*, p. 213.
[5] U.S., Congress, *Congressional Record*, 48th Cong., 2d sess., December 9, 1884, pp. 12, 13.

On January 5, 1885, Maxey had introduced a bill to amend Section 2117 of the Revised Statutes to render valid the leasing of lands occupied by Indian Tribes or Nations (the statute as it stood being regarded as invalid).[6] The bill was referred to the Committee on Indian Affairs, which was instructed by resolution on February 23 to continue its investigation by touring the Indian Territory during the next Senate recess.[7]

In April, Cleveland sent General of the Army Philip Sheridan to the Indian Territory to invite the Indian tribes to lay their complaints before him. After a brief investigation, Sheridan advised Cleveland to expel the cattlemen who were leasing the land for their great herds. On May 18, Maxey and two of his fellow members of the Committee on Indian Affairs—Chairman Henry L. Dawes of Massachusetts and James K. Jones of Arkansas—set off by rail from Saint Louis to investigate the situation. Before leaving Saint Louis they took the testimony of a black freedman, Albert Burgess, who declared that the blacks who went to the Indian Territory after the treaty of 1866 were not treated well.[8] They moved through the lands occupied by the Creeks, Cherokees, and Chickasaws, Maxey writing from Muskogee on the nineteenth:

We start to Tahlequa tomorrow to take testimony. It is about twenty-eight miles from here and we will go in a spring wagon. You remember we passed through there moving to Texas. Senator Dawes, Jones of Arkansas and myself are the only members of the committee present, but we are enough for effective work. It is impossible to say yet how long we will be at work or how many points we will visit. This country is now at its prettiest. The grass is as fine as I ever saw and the scenery beautiful. This place is in the Creek Nation. We will retain the railroad car until we get through.[9]

Three more members of the committee joined them at Muskogee

<hr/>

[6] Ibid., January 5, 1885, p. 429.
[7] U.S., Congress, Senate, Committee on Indian Affairs, *Report 1278: Resolution of the Senate*, 49th Cong., 1st sess., February 23, 1885, series 2362, vol. 8, pt. 1, p. 1.
[8] Ibid., May 18, 1885, series 2363, vol. 9, pt. 2, p. 3.
[9] Maxey to Marilda Maxey, May 19, 1885, Maxey Papers.

—Benjamin Harrison of Indiana, John J. Ingalls of Kansas, and John T. Morgan of Alabama (a substitute for Wade Hampton of South Carolina). The testimonies they took from black freedmen indicated that, as Teller had reported, the blacks' main complaint against the Cherokees was that they were not given full citizenship rights by the Indians. Because of a Cherokee law that only those freedmen who came into the Territory at a certain time in 1866 (or for a period of six months afterward) were to be made full citizens, the blacks did not have the same rights and privileges as the Cherokees. In particular they were not able to share in the money paid by the cattlemen for leasing the Cherokee land. The blacks also complained to the committee that blacks who were on the Union side during the war were treated less well than those who were on the Confederate side, and that the schools were segregated. They claimed that the teachers in their schools were not as good as those in the Cherokee schools. But when Maxey asked, "Is there any difference in the pay of the teachers and are the teachers white?" one black admitted that the pay was the same and that the teachers in both the Cherokee and the black schools were white. But, he said, "The Cherokees learn faster than the colored children."[10]

On the twenty-sixth Maxey wrote from McAllister: "We will leave in the morning for Caddo and after finishing there will stop at Denison and take the testimony of the Chickasaws whom the people at Denison promise to have there. Thence it is the design to run to Henrietta, the farthest point that can be reached by rail in the direction of the lease troubles and take testimony about that. I do not feel able to travel in rough conveyances by land, so I will, if they conclude to go further, turn back from that point. The testimony taken I think valuable and to my surprise very intelligent."[11] A Choctaw senator, who had formerly been a judge and a sheriff, and several cattlemen who leased Indian lands awaited the arrival of the committee at Denison. Among the Texas cattlemen were E. F. Ikard, whose brother William had brought Hereford stock to Wichita, Clay, and Archer

[10] Senate, Committee on Indian Affairs, *Report*, May 20, 1885, series 2363, vol. 9, pt. 2, p. 15.
[11] Maxey to Marilda Maxey, May 26, 1885, Maxey Papers.

counties in 1876; Daniel Waggoner, who in 1850 had taken a small herd of longhorns and located in Wise County, expanding the Waggoner Ranch until it occupied parts of six other counties; E. C. Suggs of Irion County, who owned with his brother, J. D. Suggs, the huge O H Triangle Ranch; and F. P. Knott, a Collin County rancher. Maxey's astute questioning brought out from the cattlemen several important facts: (1) Secretary of the Interior Teller and Senator Coke had both looked over and approved the lease agreement that the cattlemen had made with the Indians on December 23, 1884; (2) the Indians had counseled together for two or three years before they decided to sign the lease agreement; and (3) the cattlemen were leasing the land at six cents per acre, which was more than some Texas land leased for and was, according to the cattlemen, a very fair price considering how many cattle the Indians ate. Also, the cattlemen had agreed to hire a certain number of Indian horsemen at $25 per month.[12]

From Henrietta the committee took the train back through Fort Smith, Arkansas, and Caldwell, Kansas, for testimony from the Creek tribe, before parting company in Saint Louis on June 7, 1885. In the formulation of the committee's final report, Maxey's vote for moderation was overridden by Republicans Dawes, Harrison, and Ingalls, and northern Democrat Dwight M. Sabin. These members of the committee, having preconceived notions from the outset of points they wanted to make (that is, that the Indians were mistreated and misused by the southwestern cattlemen and others who stood to profit from them), had spent an inordinate amount of time taking the testimony of persons who would verify their opinions. Thus the committee's final report suggested that all the contracts for leasing the Indian lands for grazing be canceled.

Since Congress had let out on April 2, 1885, and was not to reconvene until December 7, the committee's final report was sent to Secretary of the Interior Lucius Q. C. Lamar. Lamar, imbued with the Democratic spirit of reform, urged President Cleveland to take the advice of the Senate Committee on Indian Affairs and of General Sheridan and drive out the cattlemen who were leasing the Indian

[12] Senate, Committee on Indian Affairs, *Report*, May 29, 1885, series 2363, vol. 9, pt. 2, pp. 318–336.

lands.[13] Cleveland proclaimed a forty-day notice to stockmen to drive their cattle out of the territory and forbade the fencing in of public lands. And Lamar set up a new set of strict rules regarding the leasing of public lands, an act that enraged some people who accused him of favoring the poor man over the wealthy one. Many stockmen, forced to move their herds to the overgrazed ranges in the Southwest just before one of the bitterest winters in years, lost thousands of heads of cattle. Allan Nevins has described well how westerners fumed at these regulations.[14]

Public sentiment had begun to turn against the professional friends of the Indians, particularly the Indian agents, in 1882 when Teller was secretary of the interior. It now grew worse. Many of the agents had been keenly concerned for the Indians. They had furnished beef when the Indians were starving and had provided supplies and teachers to the Indian schools. Now their posts were abolished, and during the winter of 1886 Maxey worked to get the federal government to pay the money it owed them. The Indians had also lost the revenue from their grazing lands and were able to put the lands to little use because they lacked the capital and know-how to stock their ranges. Maxey, trying to help the Indians gain an income, introduced a bill to allow the Indian Nations to lease lands for mining purposes, especially for coal mining.[15] This bill was referred to the Committee on Indian Affairs but there it stopped.

Maxey spent the rest of the summer and early fall resting and fishing, at home and at Hot Springs. He felt too tired to push hard in his campaign to be reelected. When Marilda pointed out to him an article in the *Brownwood Democrat* about the possibility of his reelection in 1887, he was pleased with the compliments to himself but reiterated his inclination to let "others settle it among themselves."[16] Texans from far and wide approached him with nominations to take to

[13] For further discussion of this material, see Wirt Armistead Cate, *Lucius Q. C. Lamar*, pp. 443–445; Allan Nevins, *Grover Cleveland*, pp. 229–230.

[14] Nevins, *Cleveland*, pp. 229–230. See also, Ernest Staples Osgood, *The Day of the Cattleman*, pp. 217, 241.

[15] *Congressional Record*, 49th Cong., 1st sess., February 11, April 29, June 3, 1886, pp. 1327, 3957, 5182; 49th Cong., 2d sess., February 19, 1887, p. 1854.

[16] Maxey to Marilda Maxey, June 30, 1885, Maxey Papers.

Cleveland, especially for post office positions and for U.S. marshalships. Richard Hubbard wanted to be made minister to Japan, a position Maxey finally wangled from Cleveland.[17] But not everyone liked Hubbard in his new position; for instance, his somewhat pompous air greatly irritated Henry Adams, who, after visiting the Japanese legation and meeting Hubbard, wrote of him that he was the "pompousest, dodgasted old Texan jackass now living."[18] R. F. Cook, editor of the *Austin Statesman*, wanted a consulship (most any would do), and Maxey's old friend James Chenoweth wanted to be made first auditor of the Treasury.[19]

Cleveland's cabinet, when he finally announced it, was not particularly strong, but Cleveland had made an important gesture to the South by naming Lamar as secretary of the interior and Garland as attorney general.[20] Maxey was mildly pleased with all the cabinet appointments except that of Postmaster General William F. Vilas, who ignored all of Maxey's requests. But Maxey put his own political influence to the test by contacting all his friends in Congress, who in turn brought such pressure on Vilas that he confirmed all Maxey's nominations. The victorious Maxey later remarked, "Vilas has learned that he can't afford to disregard my reasonable requests and I never make any other."[21] Maxey was surprised to find that people from every direction who had nominations pending in the Post Office Committee wrote to him for help, especially Democrats in states having Republican senators. There remained little doubt that every large post office was a center for the systematic distribution of spoils.[22]

As the new year began, Republican senators, chief among them Edmunds, Hale, Ingalls, Sherman, and Harrison, looked for a way to hamstring Cleveland on his more important appointments. They demanded an explanation for his removal of Republicans from certain

[17] Richard Hubbard to Maxey, August 7, 1885, ibid.
[18] Harold Dean Cater, *Henry Adams and His Friends*, p. 167.
[19] R. F. Cook to Maxey, November 2, 1885, Maxey Papers. Maxey mentions Chenoweth in Maxey to Marilda Maxey, Decmber 10 and 14, 1885, ibid.
[20] For good descriptions of Lamar and Garland and the questionable abilities they brought to their cabinet posts, see Nevins, *Cleveland*, pp. 197, 294–295.
[21] Maxey to Marilda Maxey, December 12, 1885, January 8, 1886, Maxey Papers.
[22] Nevins, *Cleveland*, p. 199.

offices and forced the fight into the open so that it looked for awhile as if Cleveland might have to yield. On January 15, a worried Maxey, along with Senators Harris and Vest as a committee on behalf of the Democratic senators, called on the president to learn what course he proposed to take in view of the threatened action of the Republicans. Cleveland was open and friendly to Maxey and his two colleagues and talked freely. He denied the right of Republican senators to question him, considering their action an invasion of his rights. Maxey concurred in this opinion, saying: "He [Cleveland] denies, and with reason, their right to question him . . . Section 1768 of the Revised Statutes, 2nd edition, . . . confers upon the President the unqualified power to suspend at his discretion, etc., the law does not require him to assign a reason, therefore they have no legal right to demand one. We will have a polly parrot of a time over this one."[23] Although the Democratic senators, including Maxey, made speeches in the Senate and rallied to the president's side in the matter, it was really Cleveland alone who waged the fight against the Republicans and won.[24]

The main problems Congress had to deal with were tariff, labor, and the silver question. Though Maxey did his best to carry out the wishes of the farmers and laborers of his constituency, his efforts were not enough to keep his supporters from following the trend in Texas and in the nation as a whole toward the division into class groups according to wealth. In his speeches Maxey tried hard to reach the farmer and laborer but the label of Bourbon Democrat was too firmly attached to him.

Every senator, including Maxey, felt that he must go on record with his views on silver coinage. On January 14, Maxey made his plea in the Senate that nothing should be done that would affect the monetary, or paying, value of the silver in circulation. He repeated the arguments he had put forth in 1878 that silver coinage helped the poor man who had debts to pay. Other Democratic senators—Beck, Vance, Vest, Brown, Pugh, Eustis, and Voorhees—joined the push for the silver cause, but silver continued to fall in price.[25] "The financial East

[23] Maxey to Marilda Maxey, January 15, 1886, Maxey Papers.
[24] Nevins, *Cleveland*, p. 264.
[25] Ibid., p. 278.

did not understand the extent to which the silver movement had already taken possession of the country," wrote Barnes in his biography of John Carlisle.[26]

The Blair bill of 1880, which suggested giving matched state funds to the South and allowed "separate but equal" segregated schools for black and white, was caught up from 1884 until 1888 in a parliamentary impasse. Though it passed the Senate several times, it was never allowed to come before the House for want of someone to be recognized to bring it up for consideration.[27] Though Maxey did not mistakenly believe as Coke did that the Blair bill would promote mixed schools, he continued to strongly oppose it and tried to counter the bill with a suggestion of his own. On February 16, 1886, in a speech before the Senate, Maxey had his final say on the bill:

I have on several occasions favored the application of the proceeds of the sales of public lands to educational purposes. . . . I have thus dwelt on the points I have endeavored to establish, first, because I am fully impressed with the admonition of Mr. Jefferson that a frequent recurrence to fundamental principles is essential to the perpetuity of free government and it is necessary to warn the people against the dangers of centralization; second, because a departure from those principles has been the fruitful source of usurped and dangerous legislation. While it is never pleasant to disagree with any gentlemen with whom I usually act and with some I now differ, yet I can not yield my conscientious convictions; and while I yield to no man in my devotion to the cause of education, and have proven it by a life-long support of state measures, having that end in view, I will never consent to the transfer of this state duty to the general government. . . . Mr. Sherman of Ohio declared that if Congress had the power to make the appropriation for the bill, Congress had the power to follow that appropriation and direct the appropriation. It is because this is true that I warn my brethren that they are favoring a measure which centralizes vast and far-reaching power in the hands of the general government to the detriment of the states and the people.[28]

[26] Barnes, *Carlisle*, p. 104.

[27] Ibid., p. 153; Daniel W. Crofts, "The Black Response to the Blair Education Bill," *Journal of Southern History* 37, no. 1 (February 1971): 41–66.

[28] *Congressional Record*, 49th Cong., 1st sess., February 16, 1886, pp. 1644–1645. The gentlemen with whom Maxey disagreed were Senators Coke, William H. Crain of Texas, Beck, and Lamar.

Maxey voted against the Blair bill as unconstitutional and impolitic. But he believed that, as the federal government chose to place the black in the position of a ward of the nation, it had best do something to fit him for the duties and privileges to which it had called him. He felt that this could best be effected through education and by selling public lands to obtain funds for education as the federal government had always done heretofore.[29]

By the end of March 1886, Maxey had begun to fear that Paris had been done out of the railway line through connivings between officials of the Frisco and the Santa Fe. Three months earlier he had been assured by C. W. Rogers of the Frisco that the company intended to build a line to Paris and only needed an extension of time on their charter to proceed. From Saint Louis Maxey had gone to New York, where he had warned Winslow of the consequences of deceit by the Frisco. He had written to Marilda, "I told him that the President of the Santa Fe insisted on right of way beyond Paris to Red River and that our people did not understand the object because it had always been the understanding that the junction was to be at Paris, whereas if it was north of Paris, so far from helping us it would be directly against our best interests."[30] Maxey had already placed before the Senate a bill for an extension of time on the Frisco charter. His Republican opponents, especially Harrison of Indiana, insisted that Maxey's extension bill be referred to the Committee on Indian Affairs, but Maxey, by now fully aware of the political complexion of that committee, held out that the bill should go first to the Committee on Railroads. He felt sure it would be reported favorably there, and thought it unlikely that the Republicans in the Committee on Indian Affairs would "try to override the report of their brother Republicans in the Railroad Committee."[31]

Jay Gould of the Texas and Pacific had been instrumental in a failure of the efforts of the Santa Fe to gain an outlet to Saint Louis. Maxey now feared he saw a calculation of the Santa Fe directors to circumvent Gould by connecting with the Atchison and Topeka at

[29] *New York World*, April 14, 1880.
[30] Maxey to Marilda Maxey, December 15, 1885, Maxey Papers.
[31] Ibid., December 8, 1885.

a point other than Paris. He angrily confided to Marilda that the building of a rival town fitted in with his opinion of the usual policy of railroad companies. "A more cold blooded selfish policy was never conceived by Jay Gould and this too in direct conflict with what [railroad attorney] Luley told me at St. Louis and what he professed to want to do in his interview with me here. I trust, however, that the company will yet do something in the neighborhood of right."³² He telegraphed to stockholders W. Sealy and W. P. Ballinger of the Santa Fe and complained of the unfairness, whereupon Ballinger tried to explain in a letter: "Really, I could do nothing in the world about it. . . . We [Galveston] need the connection between the Santa Fe and the Atchison and Topeka. Please defend us all you can. We like you most affectionately though possibly some of our most effective 'workers' may have other committals."³³ When he received Ballinger's reply, Maxey wrote Marilda that Paris people should "gobble up" all the available points on the Paris and Great Northern "down to and including the station at the river and then if Santa Fe seeks a connection, bleed it without mercy. . . . In the next place we will or ought to have, if that game is played, more fine cattle, fine hogs, mules, horses, and invaluable citizens than any county on earth ever had, and juries will be apt to think so with conspicuous unanimity."³⁴

The Frisco bill passed the Senate and was sent to the House. On May 21, Culberson of Texas tried to get unanimous consent in the House to call up the bill, but Robert M. LaFollette of Wisconsin, archenemy of Maxey's friend Philetus Sawyer, objected. Maxey did not like LaFollette and described him to Marilda as a "radical lunatic." There was dissension among the Texas members of the House over several matters, and it extended even to passage of the Frisco bill.³⁵ Wellborn, determined that he, not Culberson, would bring the

---

³² Ibid., April 29, 1886.

³³ W. P. Ballinger to Maxey, April 30, 1886, ibid.

³⁴ Maxey to Marilda Maxey, May 1, 1886, ibid. The Great Northern Railway Company was incorporated in 1881 by three Lamar County residents (S. G. Reed, *A History of the Texas Railroads*, p. 424).

³⁵ In December, 1885, William H. Crain and Charles Stewart had quarreled over which of them was to become a member of the House Committee on Rivers and Har-

bill before the House, had gone to LaFollette, a member of the House Committee on Indian Affairs, and induced him to object when Culberson brought up the Frisco bill. Two days later Wellborn called up the bill and asked unanimous consent for its passage, which was granted.[36] Culberson was very angry and told Maxey that he did not understand LaFollette's actions, since the House Committee on Indian Affairs unanimously had reported the bill favorably. Culberson felt that he would now be charged in Texas with carelessness or want of influence. Maxey, incensed at Wellborn's trickery, hunted up one of his friends of the *Galveston News* and asked him to publicize Culberson's efforts to bring the bill before the House.

The passage of the bill for the Frisco right of way through the Indian Territory was hailed by C. W. Rogers and by John O'Day (an attorney for the Frisco) as good news, and they promptly sent congratulatory telegrams to Maxey. He sent them on to Marilda with instructions: "Lay them away. I have an idea that O'Day is the dog who told Dunn I was opposed to the bill and this is a good club."[37]

Maxey had been at work for four years on the Frisco bill, and he confessed to joy and relief that it had now passed both Houses. But trouble was not yet over. Several bills pertaining to the right of way through the Indian Territory had passed the House at about the same time. One, which had originated with the Arkansas delegation with Poindexter Dunn of the House leading the push, omitted any provision for paying some very small tribes (who had bought land from the Cherokees) for the right of way through their lands. When the bills arrived on Cleveland's desk and this omission was noted, there were rumors that Cleveland had some thought of vetoing all the bills granting right of way. Senators Berry and Jones of Arkansas became much exercised. Winslow wrote Maxey expressing fears for the failure of the Frisco bill. Maxey considered it prudent to see two of Cleveland's cabinet members, Secretary of the Interior Lamar and

---

bors. Maxey had asked Speaker of the House John Carlisle to appoint Stewart, which was done (Maxey to Marilda Maxey, December 12, 1885, Maxey Papers).

[36] Ibid., May 23, 1886.

[37] Ibid., May 23, 1886. Poindexter Dunn of Arkansas worked on the Frisco bill in the House.

Attorney General Garland, to make gentle inquiries about the matter. Actually three members of the president's cabinet—Bayard, Garland and Lamar—had supported the Frisco bill while they were in the Senate. Cleveland had now submitted the question of veto of the bill to Lamar, as the Indian Bureau was part of the Department of the Interior.

When Maxey called upon Lamar he was forced to remind Lamar that he had been a member of the Senate Committee on Railroads that had reported the original bill and that the committee had at that time made an exhaustive study of the constitutionality of the proposal in relation to the pertinent treaties, the decisions of the Supreme Court, and the right of eminent domain. He also reminded Lamar that the bill had passed the Senate by a two-thirds majority (and five to spare), and the House by over three to one, and that the time limit for finishing the building of the railroad had been extended. At the end of Maxey's recital, Lamar remarked, "That is settled." As noncommittal as Lamar, Maxey promptly bid him "Good morning!" in a pleasant manner and proceeded to hunt up Garland.[38] Garland, unlike Lamar, had forgotten none of the details of the Frisco bill. He remembered his speech in the Senate in favor of the bill, and he recalled having voted for it. He promised Maxey that he would speak to Cleveland immediately in regard to approving it.

While awaiting Cleveland's decision, Maxey wrote Marilda: "Grover, I suppose, is now too happy to go into the veto business. He officially promulgates today that he and his 'gal' will tie next Wednesday evening in the Blue Room. As it will be more than ten days from the time he received the bill to next Wednesday, he can sign or let it alone just as he pleases and I don't suppose he will crowd his ponderous brain with many thoughts of vetoes just now."[39] On June 2, Maxey wrote triumphantly, "His [Cleveland's] wedding present he sent me today in the shape of an approval of my bill was very acceptable."[40]

Maxey was very much aware of the squeeze put on the citizens of

[38] Ibid., May 27, 1886.
[39] Ibid., May 29, 1886.
[40] Ibid., June 2, 1886.

Texas by the railroad monopoly. It was with this thought in mind that he secured the passage of the Denison and Washita Valley Railway bill through the Senate. "By the connection of that road of Denison with the Frisco, it gives the people on the Central [Houston and Texas Central Railroad] a competing line with the MoPac system at Denison," wrote Maxey, and continued, "I think I have not worked in vain this session. These two roads [the Frisco and the Denison and Washita] will be of incalculable value to the people of Texas."[41]

Maxey's court bill of March 26, 1884 (to establish a district court at Paris for the Indian Territory) had been referred to the Senate Judiciary Committee, but that committee suggested that the bill should go to the Senate Committee on Territories. When, in December, 1884, the bill was considered by the Committee on Territories, whose most influential members were Vest, Garland, and Harrison, it was reported back unfavorably to the Senate. On April 26, 1886, Maxey managed to get the bill referred again to the Judiciary Committee, where it fared even worse when it was turned over to a subcommittee composed of Vest, Ingalls of Kansas, and Allison of Iowa. The discouraged Maxey wrote on April 27:

Yesterday morning I made an argument on behalf of our court bill before the Committee on the Judiciary. The bill, with its usual fatality was referred to Vest, Ingalls and Allison of Iowa as sub-committee. I felt decidedly blue when I heard that Vest was on the sub-committee—I however concluded to have a talk with him which I did. He evidently softened. He has exhibited a bitterness against the bill which is wholly unaccountable to me. Coke also talked with him and says Vest told him that he didn't see how he could get over what I said and left the impression on Coke's mind that his opposition had given way. I also talked with Ingalls and Wilson [of Iowa] and am satisfied that they will raise no opposition if Vest don't. I talked with George [of Mississippi] this evening and he told me he was with me straight out. Coke says he will talk with Pugh [of Alabama]. I have no doubt that Pugh is right. I shall take occasion to interview the committee generally and unless I am unusually unfortunate I will get a favorable report. The last time you know it went to the Committee on Territories when Vest, Garland and Harrison had it all their own way. This

41 Ibid., May 23, 1886.

time the Arkansas senators are on our side—we have got rid of Garland. I have never had any bill which has given me so much anxiety and now I am in constant fear that Coke of the committtee will be called home on account of his wife's sickness. If I do get through I will deserve a blue ribbon.[42]

But on May 17, Maxey wrote that Vest apparently had not softened and was still holding out on reporting favorably on the bill. And on the twenty-fifth he wrote that he believed all the Republicans on the subcommittee were favoring Vest's court bill over his.[43] On July 3, the Judiciary Committee passed the buck by referring both bills back favorably to the Senate.[44] During the next session of Congress, Maxey attempted to get the bill before the Senate, but each time Vest was ready with an objection and a threat of debate. In February, 1887, having been defeated for a third term in the Senate, Maxey realized he would not have time to see the bill to a favorable conclusion. "I wouldn't have the worry I have had about that bill again to have the Supreme Court of the United States located on the southeast corner of our homestead," he wrote. "The seven years itch would be a luxury by the side of it."[45]

In 1886 the restlessness of labor was involving the nation in turmoil. In April, while Maxey was negotiating with officials of the Frisco and the Santa Fe, railroad strikers belonging to the Knights of Labor confronted railway deputies with violence at Fort Worth, Texas, the Farmer's Alliance (a cooperative organization) joining them in a sympathy move.[46] Other labor strikes and violence were taking place across the nation, and on May 4 the Haymarket Riot occurred. This riot grew out of two major causes—a lockout of over a thousand employees at Cyrus McCormick's reaper works at Chicago and a prolonged and radical agitation in the city. Maxey wrote of the situation: "Strikes and mobs are becoming fearful. . . . The nihilistic friendship

[42] Ibid., April 27, 1886.
[43] Ibid., May 17 and May 25, 1886.
[44] *Congressional Record*, 49th Cong., 1st sess., July 3, 1886, p. 6480.
[45] Ibid., February 21, 1887.
[46] Nevins, *Cleveland*, pp. 347–348; Maxey to Marilda Maxey, May 1, 1886, Maxey Papers.

displayed in Chicago yesterday will have to be put down. . . . These men are not laborers, they are not Americans—they are the lowest stratum of society who want to overturn all law, disrupt society, disregard the marital relation which they boldly complain, and support themselves in idleness on what honest men have worked for."[47] He sympathized with the Knights of Labor, who had been confused in the public mind with the nihilistic element, and said in further analysis of the difficulties: "There is widespread belief which has altogether too much foundation in fact, that corporations want to squeeze the greatest possible number of drops of sweat out of the laboring men for the least possible amount of money. This opens a field for the demagogue and Communist and instead of concentrating public opinion against this crying evil until it is broken down by the power of public opinion, they throw their whole weight in the direction of discontenting working men."[48]

Despite remarks he made to the contrary, Maxey had begun to give some thought to his reelection to the Senate. He had lost some ground, for one of his backers, the *Galveston News*, was now boosting A. W. Terrell for his place in the Senate. When Terrell criticized Maxey's use of patronage to strengthen his political position, Maxey tartly replied that his political strength along the coast did not depend upon patronage.[49] But he was careful to comply with Roger Mills's request to appoint one of Mills's friends as postmaster at Corsicana, fearing that failure to do so would move Mills's supporters to spread the word in Texas that Maxey was losing his political influence.[50] In addition, Maxey courted the Texas Knights of Labor, at least to the extent of delivering to the Senate no less than five petitions from them, as well as sending word to his Texas supporters to pay especial attention to their needs.[51] Maxey also circulated among the Texas delegation (composed of Throckmorton, Hills, Hancock, Reagan, Jones, Culberson, Wellborn, James Miller, and, of course, Coke) seeking their

[47] Maxey to Marilda Maxey, May 5, 1886, Maxey Papers.

[48] Ibid., May 3, 1886.

[49] Alwyn Barr, *Reconstruction to Reform*, p. 123.

[50] Maxey to Marilda Maxey, April 23, 1886, Maxey Papers.

[51] Ibid., April 23, May 15, 25, 1886; *Congressional Record*, 49th Cong., 1st sess., 1886, pp. 1232, 1808, 1937, 2518.

advice and their assurance that each of their districts would vote for his reelection. Throckmorton, Culberson, and Wellborn announced decidedly that they were for him. Mills and Jones talked privately with him and gave advice on what they thought would be good points in management of his canvas for relection, so by inference at least, they were for him. But Maxey was no dreamer, and he wrote Marilda: "I have no doubt that Mills is for me as the race stands . . . if he sees no opening for Mills to come in. . . . I have had it in my power to help everyone of them [the Texas delegation] and have done it cheerfully and a good deal of it this session. Reagan will be for me against Terrell or Ireland or anyone else except Reagan."[52]

The presidential campaign of 1884 had been characterized by much mud slinging by both sides. The average American grew contemptuous of the private life of Cleveland even before he was elected president, and some of Maxey's remarks, which are uncharacteristic of his usual gentlemanly attitude, reflect this general feeling. When he received a wedding announcement from Cleveland, who had married his pretty young ward, Maxey wrote to Marilda: "We received from the White House by tonight's mail a notification that Grover and Fanny had set up housekeeping. They are now billing and cooing at Deer Park, a station as you may remember on the B and O on the top of the Alleghany and a nice cool place they have for their business."[53] On June 12, he reported:

I called on him today for the first time since his marriage. . . . Common courtesy demanded that I should present congratulations so I told him that I was delighted to welcome him among the staid married men, that I had been trying on married life near thirty-three years and liked it as far as I had been, that I hadn't troubled him until today taking it from my own experience that he didn't care to be bothered with too much company for the last ten days or so. He enjoyed it very much and said he had been generally welcomed by his married friends into their circle.[54]

Maxey attended the presidential reception on June 15. He went with James Miller, a member of the Texas delegation, whose wife,

[52] Maxey to Marilda Maxey, May 15, 1886, Maxey Papers.
[53] Ibid., June 4, 1886.
[54] Ibid., June 12, 1886.

like Maxey's, was at home in Texas. Maxey wrote Marilda of his impressions of the evening:

The crowd was . . . simply immense. Grover and Fanny stood near a door entering the Blue Room—G next the door, Fanny on his right. The Marshal of the District announced the guests as they entered. Grover was all smiles. Fanny did her level. She is really a very pretty young woman and did her part up in a blue rag. She had on her wedding dress, a V, and a good large one from her neck downward, front and rear—not my style, but I suppose fashionable. After squeezing through to the august couple, we squeezed out again without the slightest degree standing on the order of the squeeze, and struck for fresh air.[55]

But Sam Bell wrote home to his Aunt Marilda that "Uncle went to the President's reception the other night and seemed taken with Mrs. Cleveland. All these senators and representatives seem to be 'mashed' on her. I think their wives had better move an adjournment and take them home."[56]

Maxey watched the growing movement in Texas of the Farmer's Alliance and the Knights of Labor and was wise enough to see that it probably would be impossible for him to overcome their bias against him in the coming Senate election. He wrote on July 5: "The political situation in Texas is very different from any I have ever known before. Those who have to face the music in this canvas have before them a race in which the influence of the Knights of Labor and the Farmer's Alliances cannot be foretold. . . . I think it is very difficult at this time to determine how far the Democratic party is to be controlled by the policies of the Knights of Labor and the Farmer's Alliances."[57]

With the connivance of Reagan and some of the other Texas congressmen in Washington, Reagan's home district convention at Palestine nominated him for the Senate race. Reagan afterward coyly explained to Maxey that his nomination was really the work of his old enemy John Y. Gooch, who wanted Reagan's place in the House. So-

---

[55] Ibid., June 16, 1886.
[56] Sam Bell Long to Marilda Maxey, June 17, 1886, ibid.
[57] Maxey to Marilda Maxey, July 5, 1886, ibid.

berly Maxey replied to Reagan that he supposed it was the old story: "The man who wanted your place couldn't kick you downstairs and thought this was a way to kick you up."[58]

When the first session of the Forty-ninth Congress ended on August 5, 1886, Maxey went to Texas to begin four months of intensive canvassing. Lightfoot was still Maxey's campaign manager and had a proposed agenda ready. Beginning in the districts near home, Maxey worked his way across the state and by the end of October arrived in Houston. He spoke at Houston and Galveston and drew good crowds. The potential candidates, besides Maxey, for his Senate seat were Ireland, Mills, Reagan, Hancock, and Terrell. In his speeches Maxey reiterated the proposal he had made in the last session of Congress to sell federal lands and distribute the funds for educational purposes to states according to the rate of illiteracy. When Terrell attacked the plan, Maxey defended the constitutionality of his education bill. He also announced that he was for Reagan's kind of railroad legislation and against monopolies, strikes, and the entry of the Knights of Labor and the Farmer's Alliance into politics.[59] Hancock, in his campaign, skirted criticism of the railroad commission and of federal aid to improve Texas harbors and stuck to subjects of general improvements in Texas. Reagan, of course, had gained tremendous backing in East Texas and other farming areas from his railroad regulation bill in the House. By the end of December, Maxey summed up his progress by saying: "The newspapers appear to have gone over to Reagan. Well, that is all right. I don't think they help or hurt anybody. Their vacillating course in the senatorial race has disgusted sensible people. . . . I suppose Mr. Lightfoot will go to Austin pretty early in January. I think it wise to be in on the ground early and get personally acquainted with every member and make all necessary arrangements with influential men."[60]

Meanwhile a new session of the Senate had opened on December 6 and on the seventeenth Maxey reported the fate of Reagan's version of the interstate commerce bill (which had passed the House in January,

[58] Maxey related to Marilda what he had replied to Reagan, ibid., July 7, 1886.
[59] Barr, *Reconstruction to Reform*, pp. 123–125.
[60] Maxey to Marilda Maxey, December 30, 1886, Maxey Papers.

1886, by a small margin) and Cullom's bill (which had passed the Senate in February, 1886, by a large majority). Cullom's measure had been the one accepted, but Reagan would not admit the defeat. Commented Maxey, writing of the affair: "The conference report on Interstate Commerce has been made to the Senate and if Reagan can get consolation from it, he is easily satisfied. His buro, as Culberson calls it, has been hard at work trying to show that the Senate conferees had yielded to him. If they lost a point, I fail to see it. He will have to contradict Cullom's statement accompanying the report from beginning to end before he can sustain his buro," and on the twentieth, as Reagan continued to give out that his bill had won, Maxey wrote: "Reagan is using every exertion to have the impression go out that his bill was the one reported. Nothing is further from the facts."[61]

Maxey arrived at the Driskill Hotel in Austin on January 12. The *Galveston News* reported that Ireland was taking jabs at Reagan by saying that the federal government could not correct railroad abuses and that such matters should be left to the state.[62] Reagan, clean-shaven and with his grey hair touched up to appear darker, openly courted the Grangers and went so far as to stay at the Avenue Hotel in Austin, where the Granger element was most often found. Maxey, also courting the Grangers, appeared just a bit less studiously neat and fashionable than usual in order not to offend the most confirmed Granger member. Rumors were rife that there were a lot of Republicans from Washington in Austin to put in a good word for Ireland, and the *Austin Statesman* took both Maxey and Reagan to task because they had temporarily abandoned their posts in Washington.[63] Maxey wrote on January 15: "My friends have been pouring in in a continuous stream. So far I clearly have the lead—Reagan is unquestionably next, Ireland next, and then Terrell with a small following. Ireland seems to have gathered some of Terrell's strength. Terrell is evidently blue. I called on Judge Reagan and he returned the call this

[61] Ibid., December 17, 20, 1886. For a discussion of Reagan's reactions to the Cullom bill see Ben H. Procter, *Not without Honor*, pp. 255–256, 258.

[62] *Galveston News*, January 14, 1887.

[63] *Austin Daily Statesman*, January 25, 1887. See also *Galveston News*, January 15, 1887.

morning. Terrell called on me night before last and I returned his call. . . . I hear no talk of a dark horse."[64]

Maxey had little time to himself. On the night of the twentieth he attended the inauguration ball for Governor Lawrence Sullivan Ross and circulated among the guests for an hour or so. The next night he was invited to the meeting of the Grand Commanders of the Knights Templar, who were holding their annual convocation in Austin. On the twenty-first he went to the State Capitol and visited with the members of both houses of the legislature.

When the legislature met on January 25, the senatorial battle began with a formidable array of speakers on behalf of the candidates. Maxey led on the first balloting, but the *Statesman* ventured to say that he had polled his full strength and would lose thereafter.[65] After four more ballots without a result being reached, Terrell's name was withdrawn and Reagan was in the lead. Gossip flew that neither Maxey nor Ireland were willing to drop out so that Reagan could win.[66] The railroad contingents continued to push Ireland, and on the twenty-ninth the *Statesman* reported that the senatorial struggle was a stubborn lock—that there was a see-saw arrangement between Maxey and Reagan, the Reaganites always keeping a weather eye open that their end did not get lower than the Maxey end.[67] It angered Maxey's supporters when Ireland, though he was losing votes, would not withdraw. Finally, on February 1, Reagan received a clear majority of the votes and won the Senate seat. Said the *Galveston News*: "Maybe there is something of poetic fitness in the result. The oldest, officially and chronologically, of the old children reaching and beseeching for the senatorial bauble has had it finally awarded to him."[68]

The influence of the East Texas farm members on their state congressmen had been sufficient to throw support to Reagan. Perhaps the whole story is not to be found in the records. In any event, Maxey sincerely believed that Reagan had used deceit to win. "I feel that the

[64] Maxey to Marilda Maxey, January 15, 1887, Maxey Papers.

[65] Texas Legislature, *Senate Journal*, 20th legislature, 1st sess., January 25, 1887; *Statesman*, January 26, 1887.

[66] *Statesman*, January 27, 1887.

[67] Ibid., January 29, 1887.

[68] *Galveston News*, February 2, 1887.

course I took in the canvas was honorable," wrote Maxey on February 12, "and that my positions were right and I would prefer defeat with such a record to success by crooked methods."[69] Throughout the harassing balloting Maxey had remained so quiet and mannerly that the *Galveston News* had been prompted to comment that he had conducted himself in every way to make his enemies as well as his friends admire him.[70]

Cleveland's first painstaking effort to select proper men for the newly legislated Interstate Commerce Commission was to name Thomas M. Cooley of Michigan as chairman.[71] Through the efforts of Senators Beck and Lamar, a move was made to place Maxey's name in nomination for a place on the commission.[72] Beck suggested to Coke that he go immediately to see the president to help further Maxey's appointment, but Coke dallied, saying that he wished to have the sanction of the entire Texas delegation before he acted. Reagan did not wish to endorse Maxey and gave as excuse the fact that Mills had already asked for his endorsement for a place on the commission. As chairman of the Texas delegation, Maxey was asked to call a meeting—he did so and then notified the delegation that he would not be present. After secret balloting at the meeting, Maxey won the nomination, and Reagan was asked to present the result to President Cleveland. Coke accompanied Reagan to Cleveland's office and later reported to Maxey that Reagan had made an admirable talk and that the president in turn spoke of Maxey in high terms. As one of their arguments in the resolution they presented to Cleveland the Texans urged that one member of the commission should be from Texas since Texas, though remote from the great centers of trade, was a large territory where the question of transportation was of importance.[73] T. P. Gore, later senator from Oklahoma, James Beck of Kentucky, James George

69 Maxey to Marilda Maxey, February 12, 1887, Maxey Papers. Maxey was probably referring to Reagan's deceit in pretending that his interstate commerce bill had been accepted.

70 *Galveston News*, February 1, 1887.

71 Nevins, *Cleveland*, pp. 355–356.

72 Maxey to Marilda Maxey, February 16, 1887, Maxey Papers.

73 Resolution to President Cleveland from Richard Coke and John Reagan, February 17, 1887, copy, Maxey Papers.

of Mississippi, James Pugh and John Morgan, both of Alabama, all spoke to Cleveland on Maxey's behalf and urged that the president not make his decision before March 4, since present members of Congress could not be chosen. Maxey remained aloof from all their efforts, saying: "I don't know and don't care much what will become of it all, further than in the irony of fate. It would be retributive justice that after the combinations made to defeat me, by railroad men, Knights of Labor and so on, I should be selected to carry out this measure."[74] An article in the *New York World* called attention to the fact that there were now about five hundred nominations for places on the railroad commission and mentioned some of the senators whose names were on the list—among them were Maxey, Clark of New York, Kernan of New York, and Williams of Kentucky.[75]

Marilda, who had believed that, at long last, she was about to regain her husband, was outraged at what she considered Maxey's new bid for a post in Washington. Maxey assured her that he had not uttered one word to anyone, including the president, about wanting an office, and added: "If Mr. Cleveland sees proper to appoint me, well and good, if not, well and good. I had just as soon be a free man for awhile as not."[76] On March 3, Maxey wrote his wife: "We are now in the last legislation day of the session. . . . I start home tomorrow . . . to look around to see what I will do for a living."[77] When the announcement was made of Cleveland's choices for the members of the railroad commission, Maxey's name was not among them. The only southerner on the commission was Walter L. Bragg of Alabama.

[74] Maxey to Marilda Maxey, February 16, 1887, ibid.
[75] *New York World*, February 17, 1887.
[76] Maxey to Marilda Maxey, February 21, 1887, Maxey Papers.
[77] Ibid., March 3, 1887.

10. Last Years: Maxey's Place
in Texas History

> In any other state I would have been recognized for my contri-
> bution to my party.[1]

M AXEY RETURNED to Paris and set to work in his law firm—
Maxey, Lightfoot, and Denton. Ben Denton, nephew of Marilda, was an active and young member of the firm. Lightfoot, prominent in Texas politics, attended to the firm's business in Dallas and
Austin.

The Prohibition Movement had gained momentum in Texas in
1887. Like Reagan and Culberson, Maxey was drawn into the prohibition camp, but speaking at a mass meeting in Fort Worth on June 30
he expressed the view that the next Democratic state convention
should not introduce the question of prohibition. Indeed, he felt that
to do so would be extreme folly. The leaders of the opposition or anti-
prohibition movement in Texas were Mills, Throckmorton, George
Clark, and James S. Hogg.[2] As August neared, the antiprohibitionists,
who appeared to be leading, took as their main theme for the convention the stand that the majority should not be allowed to force its will
on the minority in regard to moral and social conduct. Stung by this

1 Maxey to Marilda Maxey, December 13, 1880, Maxey Papers.
2 Walter P. Webb and H. Bailey Carroll (eds.), *Handbook of Texas*, II, 415.

undemocratic pronouncement, Maxey declared himself a Jeffersonian Democrat, willing to abide by what Jefferson had laid down as the cardinal principle of democracy; that is, as Maxey outlined it, "absolute acquiescence in the decisions of the majority, the vital principle of Republics, from which there is no appeal but to force, the vital principle and immediate parent of despotism."[3]

Meanwhile Sam Bell Long was enrolled at the University of Texas, where he planned to study law. He complained to his uncle that two of his friends seemed smitten by ex-Governor Roberts, now teaching at the law school, but, said Sam Bell (probably echoing his uncle's feeling): "I must say I am not. I can't see where his greatness comes in."[4] When Sam Bell's comprehension of mathematics flagged, Maxey wrote him: "The only difference in a sound argument in court and a mathematical solution is that one is naked logic, the other applied logic. A lawyer is always at a great disadvantage who does not understand surveying."[5]

Sam Bell made friends with the daughter of Governor Ross, who took him to the mansion to meet her father. Sam Bell had last visited the governor's mansion when the Maxey family had been guests of Governor Coke. As he looked about, he decided that the old house looked ten years older and was not as well furnished as it had been in Coke's day.

When the new State Capitol was dedicated in October, 1888, Maxey went to Austin, where he had been invited to speak. The Paris Light Guard including the Maxey Rifles Company (which had been formed in honor of Maxey) joined other state militia units in the dedication formalities. Maxey spoke in a large courtroom, and every available space, including the aisles, was filled. He spoke for one hour and forty-five minutes and began to say "in conclusion" when his audience interrupted him with cries of "go on, go on!" Flattered, he continued for some few minutes, but as he had fairly presented his argument, he soon sat down.[6]

---

[3] Maxey to the editor, *Fort Worth Gazette*, August 14, 1887.
[4] Sam Bell Long to Maxey, October 9, 1887, Maxey Papers.
[5] Maxey to Sam Bell Long, October 20, 1887, ibid.
[6] As described by Maxey, ibid., October 10, 1888.

The Republicans regained the White House with President Benjamin Harrison in 1888. Chenoweth, who had been first auditor of the Treasury under Cleveland, waited to be told when his resignation would be accepted. "The administration is going very slow," said Chenoweth to Maxey, "but I think will make a clean sweep. I am certain, however, they constitute by no means a happy family. I think the Democratic party will have but little trouble in returning to power four years hence—unless they exercise the very genius of mismanagement."[7]

H. M. Alden of *Harper's Magazine* asked Maxey to write a kind of biographical sketch of the development of the commonwealth of Texas to add to a series *Harper's* was doing on individual western states. Maxey was paid three hundred dollars for writing the article on Texas that appeared in the September, 1893, issue of *Harper's New Monthly Magazine*. He made a prior agreement with Alden that he should write the history of Texas as it had been made by "Anglo-American sagacity, courage and enterprise" and that he would not attempt to cover the history of Texas preceding the Anglo-American colonization. Maxey covered the lives of Stephen F. Austin, Sam Houston, Thomas Rusk, Ashbel Smith, and John Hemphill in his article and discussed the Alamo, the new Texas State Capitol, and the University of Texas. Guy M. Bryan, a descendant of Stephen F. Austin, helped Maxey immeasurably by sending him some of Austin's original correspondence. Bryan also wrote critically to Maxey about the writings of John Henry Brown and George Fulton, Sr., who had portrayed Austin's policies in a bad light.[8] Bryan urged Maxey not to refer to him [Bryan] either directly or indirectly in the *Harper's* ar-

7 James Q. Chenoweth to Maxey, May 4, 1889, ibid.

8 John Henry Brown's, *The Life and Times of Henry Smith*, published in 1887, contained a lettter from Fulton (Governor Smith's son-in-law and formerly on the editorial staff of the *Baltimore Sun*) praising Smith's part in Texas's achieving independence and indirectly criticizing Stephen F. Austin. Bryan had complained to Brown about his portrayal of Austin (Guy M. Bryan to J. H. Brown, February 25, May 30, December 23, 1887; and J. H. Brown to G. M. Bryan, January 7, 1888, Guy M. Bryan Papers).

ticle, for, said Bryan, "it will afford Brown and Fulton a pretext to assail your article."[9]

James Stephen Hogg was elected attorney general of Texas in 1886. Maxey did not admire him nor did he believe Hogg's knowledge of law was sufficient for the position. When Maxey's law firm represented the Houston and Central Railroad land titles in the Panhandle, Hogg, as attorney general, forced the railroads to sell their holdings to settlers within certain time limits. "I think Mr. Hogg has shown himself as ignorant of law as he did in the Drummer cases in which he fell sprawling in the Supreme Court of the United States," said Maxey. "His position is adverse to the statute of 1854 which he quotes without comprehending. . . . If he ever gets to the Supreme Court he will fall flat."[10]

When Leslie Waggener ran into difficulties after his remarks in his opening address as chairman of the faculty of the University of Texas in October, 1889, Maxey wrote him a letter of sympathy. Kentuckian Waggener had openly supported Coke and Maxey, "the noble men who have so long fought the battle of truth and justice in the Senate Chamber and in the Forum."[11] For these utterances Waggener was severely criticized by individuals and by the press, particularly the *Austin Statesman*.[12] Waggener later invited Maxey to give a speech at the university and the old pro Maxey could not resist having his speech printed up and distributed among his former senatorial colleagues.

Maxey missed his old friend General Joseph E. Johnston, who had made frequent trips to Washington from his home in Virginia and with whom Maxey had used to discuss literary figures, especially his favorite essayist Lord Macauley. But Sam Bell Long was at least as

[9] Guy M. Bryan to Maxey, October 9, 1889, Maxey Papers.
[10] Maxey to Sam Bell Long, October 23, 1899, Maxey Papers. The Drummer's Law required the payment of a license fee from any commercial traveler or drummer of trade. When out-of-state manufacturers challenged the law, Hogg as attorney general defended the State of Texas but lost (Robert C. Cotner, *James Stephen Hogg*, pp. 148–153).
[11] Leslie Waggener to Maxey, November 2, 1889, Maxey Papers.
[12] *Austin Daily Statesman*, October 21, 1889.

willing a listener. Maxey told Sam Bell: "I know of no essayist who is equal to Macauley. Nothing in any literature is comparable with Shakespeare. No philosopher of Greece or Rome has equalled Bacon. Those who understand the German believe that, in the lines of thought he has followed, Goethe is without a rival. In comedy nothing which has come to us from Greece compares with Molière, in tragedy Corneille, in beauty of expression with Racine."[13] Maxey read continually these latter works in the French language. His volumes were bound in fine leather and were a valuable part of his private library. Like his good friend Allen Thurman, he was well able to appreciate the humour of the French comedy and the pathos of the French tragedy. "The French are among the most accomplished people in the world, and are, to say the least, as far advanced in the arts, sciences and literature as any other nation," said Maxey.[14] He also admired the English historian James Anthony Froude and declared he agreed with Froude's opinion of the great leaders of Caesar's time. His attitude differed from that of Hamilton Fish, who, after having read Froude's *Caesar*, was half-vexed with Froude for proving Cicero to have been such a mean, self-seeking, faithless politician."[15] Though George Bancroft lived and wrote in Washington, Maxey made no mention of him in his correspondence, although he did read Bancroft's *History of the Constitution*.[16]

When a vacancy occurred on the Interstate Commerce Commission, Maxey's friends set to work to obtain the post for him and asked Reagan to write to President Harrison on Maxey's behalf.[17] Reagan did so reluctantly; since he had just resigned his seat in the Senate to accept control of the Texas Railroad Commission, he could hardly refuse. Governor Hogg and Secretary of State George W. Smith added their petitions for Maxey to Reagan's. Smith, a Republican and general manager of the International and Great Northern Railroad, wrote the president that though Maxey was a Democrat he was held in high

[13] Maxey to Sam Bell Long, January 22, 1890, Maxey Papers.
[14] Ibid., March 11, 1890.
[15] Allan Nevins, *Hamilton Fish*, p. 900.
[16] George Bancroft, *History of the Formation of the Constitution of the United States of America*.
[17] O. L. Pruden to John Reagan, September 8, 1891, copy, Maxey Papers.

esteem by the Republicans in Texas.[18] Maxey, however, did not receive the appointment.

During the summer of 1892 Texas Democrats listened to arguments about who would make the better governor, James Hogg or George Clark. Clark, a railroad attorney from Waco, had served as attorney general in 1874 and as a judge on the Court of Appeals in 1880. Hogg, a bitter enemy of the railroads, wanted a second term as governor. Clark claimed that Hogg's policies were driving capital from Texas.[19] Maxey read about and listened to both candidates and liked neither of them. Said he: "Hogg and Clark bid fair to have a polly parrot of a time at the Houston convention. . . . It would be infinitely better for the Democratic party to throw them out and select some able, safe, conservative man who possesses the confidence of the people."[20]

On October 28, 1892, Maxey resigned from the law firm of Maxey, Lightfoot, and Denton. In his place he put Sam Bell Long, now a graduate of the University of Texas Law School and proud possessor of a certificate from the State Bar. The day Maxey had longed for had finally arrived—he was free of debt and could live comfortably from his investments. The smell of politics continued to lure him, however, and he kept abreast of the political scene in Texas and in the nation.

When, in December, 1892, Roger Q. Mills, now a prominent member of the House of Representatives and the outstanding Texas member, was defeated for election as Speaker of the House, many Texans, including Maxey, were disappointed. They had been disappointed in April, 1891, when Hogg had not appointed Mills to fill the vacated Senate seat of Reagan; instead Hogg had appointed Horace Chilton, his old boyhood friend and first campaign manager. Mills, too, was unhappy that he had not received the honor of being appointed to the Senate vacancy. But when George Clark brought before the public the issue of Chilton's appointment over Mills and demanded that a special session of the legislature be called to discuss the appointment, Mills

[18] George W. Smith to Benjamin Harrison, September 15, 1891, ibid.
[19] John Stricklin Spratt, *The Road to Spindletop*, p. 218.
[20] Ibid., pp. 246, 303.

became alarmed.[21] He had no wish to become a part of George Clark's bid for the governorship of Texas against Hogg or to court the Populist cause. The Populists (as represented by the People's party of Texas, whose main strength lay in the Farmer's Alliance) aimed basically at opposing high property taxes, trusts, and monopolies. They advocated a graduated income tax and an economical government. In general they differed from the other Democrats (now termed Regular Democrats) in insisting that the federal government should have authority over problems that could not be taken care of by a single state government, such as those problems that involved several states at a time.[22]

By August, 1892, Mills had declared himself a supporter of Governor Hogg and endorsed the regular Democrats.[23] After deep consideration he had realized that his election to the coveted Senate seat depended upon the Texas legislature and that it would be comprised of a majority of regular Democrats. In December, 1892, Mills wrote Maxey: "No one can tell what may result in the present condition of the Democratic party in Texas. I am between two fires and may be brought down by the shots from one or the other or both. Clark is doing all he can to defeat me but so far as I can learn it is a tempest in a teapot. Many of those who supported Hogg are demanding that Federal offices shall be given to them alone, and that Clark's supporters be proscribed."[24]

Grover Cleveland was elected to the presidency for the second time in 1892. Maxey, having been persuaded to use his influence for several of his friends, joined the great army of men who swarmed to Washington to seek offices either for themselves or for others. In self-defense, Cleveland had issued a set of rules that he hoped would help fend off the office seekers; he ruled that he would not appoint anyone who had held office in his first administration.[25] Nevertheless, Cheno-

[21] Cotner, *Hogg*, p. 268.

[22] For a general discussion of Populism in Texas during this period, see Alwyn Barr, *Reconstruction to Reform*, pp. 143–146.

[23] Cotner, *Hogg*, p. 303.

[24] R. Q. Mills to Maxey, December 6, 1892, Maxey Papers.

[25] Allan Nevins, *Grover Cleveland*, p. 515.

weth approached Cleveland's new secretary of the treasury, John G. Carlisle, and asked to be reappointed as first auditor of the treasury. Carlisle wrote that, although Chenoweth came under Cleveland's rule, he had spoken to Cleveland about Chenoweth's excellent record. Cleveland was impressed by the amount and character of Chenoweth's work, and Carlisle thought it possible that some spot might be found.[26]

Maxey arrived in Washington in December, 1893, and took a room at the Riggs House. He wrote Marilda:

After breakfast I called to see Mr. Carlisle in the interest of Judge Cheno-weth and was told that he was not in his room and was at work on his report. I don't know whether it was true or not. I then went to the Senate, sent my card in to Coke, and he came out as friendly as he ever was and told me that Harris whose seat was next to mine and Coke's on his right was in the President's seat, Stevenson being absent, so we went in and my old friends on both sides flocked around to shake hands with me and to congratulate me on looking so fresh—said I was younger than when I left the Senate. I stayed there til about 4 o'clock. Mills met me as friendly as could be and I am to take dinner with him today. He proposes to go with me to see Cleveland and wrote a note to him yesterday to know when it would be convenient for him to receive us.[27]

Mills's support in Congress in October, 1893, of Cleveland's demand for repeal of the Silver Purchase Act had enhanced his influence with Cleveland. Apparently his influence was enough to override Cleveland's request that senators cease to escort office hunters into his office during the hours given to congressmen.[28] The next day Mills accompanied Maxey to Cleveland's office and, after saying to the president that Maxey had called to see him in regard to the marshalship of the Eastern District of Texas, left the coast clear for Maxey. Maxey wrote later of his interview: "Cleveland gave me all the time I wanted and

[26] John Carlisle to James Q. Chenoweth, March 4, 1893, copy, Maxey Papers.

[27] Maxey to Marilda Maxey, December 12, 1893, ibid. Referred to are Senators Isham Harris of Tennessee and Adlai E. Stevenson of Illinois (*Biographical Directory of the American Congress*, p. 290).

[28] Nevins, *Cleveland*, pp. 516, 547; Cotner, *Hogg*, p. 316.

I had a very free conference with him. Whether I accomplished anything remains to be seen. He received me most cordially and promised to give the case close personal attention."[29]

Seth Shepard, a follower in 1892 of the George Clark faction of the split Democratic party, was appointed an associate justice of the Court of Appeals in the District of Columbia. Shepard's adherence to the Texas group that had declared for Cleveland's policy of a gold standard had won him favor in Cleveland's eyes. Hogg's group, on the other hand, had repudiated the platform of the national Democratic convention and as a result fell short on federal patronage.[30]

Maxey called on Seth Shepard and asked that he accompany him to see Cleveland's new attorney general, Richard Olney of Massachusetts. Of their visit to Olney, Maxey wrote: "I would as soon try to decipher the countenance of an Egyptian sphinx as that of Mr. Olney. He gave me all the time I wanted and I suppose I was with him an hour." Of his efforts to persuade Olney to endorse the appointment of Sheb Williams of Lamar County, Maxey's friend and relative, as marshal of the Eastern District of Texas, Maxey said, "My own opinion is that his leaning is to Mr. Douglas of Sherman but it may be that I produced a favorable impression."[31] Almost every member of the Texas delegation in Congress had his own personal candidate for this position of marshal. Culberson, who disliked Williams and resented Maxey's intrusion into the affair, remarked that no appointment would be made until the time of the present marshal was out. About Culberson, Maxey commented: "I have no doubt the wish is father to the thought. Mr. Cleveland remarked that Mr. Culberson was very much opposed to Williams."[32] George Pendleton, a Texas member of the House, also asked Cleveland to disregard Culberson's opposition and appoint Williams. He explained that Culberson's op-

[29] Maxey to Marilda Maxey, December 13, 1893, Maxey Papers.

[30] Cotner, *Hogg*, p. 392; Webb and Carroll, *Handbook of Texas*, II, 601.

[31] Maxey to Marilda Maxey. December 14, 1893, Maxey Papers. Lemuel Hardin Williams, father of Sheb Williams, had married the sister of Maxey's brother-in-law Craft Irwin and had left Kentucky and come to Lamar County in 1857 with the Maxeys. See Alexander W. Neville, *History of Lamar County*, p. 98; Webb and Carroll, *Handbook of Texas*, II, 913–914.

[32] Maxey to Marilda Maxey, December 14, 1893, Maxey Papers.

position was because of the active support Williams had given Mills against Culberson when the Senate seat vacated by Reagan was up for grabs in 1892. Cleveland heard Pendleton out and then remarked, "Oh, that's it, is it?"[33] Williams got the job. At about this same time a federal court with jurisdiction over the southern portion of the old Indian Territory was established at Paris. This act of Congress was a compromise on the long debate over Maxey's court bill and that of Vest. The court at Paris became very busy with criminal cases and Marshal Williams's services were very much needed.[34]

Maxey's last years were as bright and as serene as his failing energies would permit. He had a great deal to make him happy—a devoted wife, work to do, boon friends, public honors—and he appreciated his blessings. He showed affection, kindness, and relaxed good humor to those around him. When he was called upon to make public speeches he spent much time in preparation. However, early in the spring of 1894 while in Austin, he was prostrated by an attack of gastrointestinal disease. The disease recurred in the spring of 1895, and a trip to Eureka Springs, Arkansas, failed to bring relief. He continued to weaken as the months went by, and late on August 15, 1895, he became very much worse. On the morning of August 16, he died.

His body was returned to Paris. Many of his old friends came from a distance to pay their tributes of respect. The funeral oration was simple, with passages from the Bible read by Robert C. Buckner, who had performed Maxey's wedding ceremony forty years earlier. General William L. Cabell delivered a eulogy at the graveside. Newspapers across the country reported Maxey's death. The *Washington Post* noted that Maxey had graduated from West Point with General Grant and described him as an outstanding, sincere, and frank man.[35] The New York papers, including the *Tribune, World, Sun, Times, Herald, Mercury,* and *Army and Navy,* carried notices of his death. The *Baltimore Sun* decribed Maxey as a "brave Southern soldier and

---

[33] Ibid. George Pendleton, Ellis County, Texas, was a member of the United States House of Representatives, 1893–1897 (Webb and Carroll, *Handbook of Texas,* II, 358).

[34] Frank W. Johnson, *A History of Texas and Texans,* V, 2354–2355.

[35] *Washington Post,* August 17, 1895, newsclipping, Maxey Papers.

United States Senator from Texas."[36] Giving the impression of having belatedly recognized Maxey's record, the *Boston Herald* reported that Maxey was a free trader and a regent of the Smithsonian Institution. The *Peoria Journal* pointed out that Maxey had pilloried John Sherman in 1877 in the Senate and forced the Ohio statesman to admit that the suspension of the coinage of the American silver dollar was a blunder and that it could be restored at any time.[37]

On June 11, 1896, Henry Lightfoot, Maxey's law partner for twenty years, read a memorial to Maxey before the Association of the Graduates of the United States Military Academy at West Point. He spoke of Maxey's admiration of Henry Clay, a warm personal friend of Maxey's father, and stated that during the years Maxey and Richard Coke represented Texas in the Senate, Texas was "more highly respected than it has ever been since the day of Houston and Rusk." Lightfoot continued:

Tall, dignified, commanding and soldierly in appearance, to a stranger he might seem proud and haughty, but unlike many other great men, the closer you became associated with him, the more you found to admire and love in his nature. He was uniformly courteous and polite and with his friends was a genial, affable, whole-souled, lovable companion. His personal integrity was never questioned, and at the bar, upon the hustings, or in the Senate Chamber, his word was a guaranty of truth, and even those who opposed him learned to respect his honesty and candor. He believed that the war ended at Appomattox, that "he was no friend of his country who would keep his country apart" and he had little patience with post bellum agitators who sought political preferment by stirring the embers of the past.[38]

Maxey was a plain man with simple talents. That so plain a man's life became intermingled with the dramatic occurrences of national history for twelve years and more is somewhat astonishing. He imposed upon himself a certain social isolation in Washington because he was poor and unable to return the social amenities offered him.

---

[36] *Baltimore Sun*, August 17, 1895.

[37] *Boston Herald, Peoria Journal*, both of August 17, 1895.

[38] Henry Lightfoot, *In Memoriam of General Samuel B. Maxey*, read before the Association of the Graduates of the U.S.M.A. at West Point, June 11, 1896.

Surrounded by wealthy men in the Senate, he never yielded to the temptation of bribes. His character and devotion to duty stood out among those with whom he worked in the Senate.

Intellectually, his chief characteristic was his doggedness in getting a thing correct. He was fond of saying that he had been a student all his life and that the scraps of time that many others threw away he used. He remarked that he never spoke on a question unless he understood it and to understand it often cost him a great deal of labor.

What did Maxey accomplish for his time? That he loved his adopted state, Texas, there can be no doubt. He was particularly well qualified to serve Texas during the difficult years from 1875 to 1880, while the bloody shirt was still being waved at the southerners in Washington. Being a Kentuckian by birth he lacked a typically southern accent or appearance, the merest glimpse of which seemed to set some northerners raving. He lacked the fiery Confederate flag-waving mannerisms of a great many of the southern congressmen and appeared disposed to let reason and moderation be his guidelines. He rapidly gained friends among the northern Republicans as well as among the Democrats, north and south, and perhaps this trait alone was his greatest asset and enabled him to make a contribution valuable to Texas. The name of Samuel Bell Maxey should be inscribed among the list of the great men of Texas, as are the names of Sam Houston, Thomas J. Rusk, John Hemphill, and Ashbel Smith. His name should be as well known in American history as those of Thomas Bayard and Allen Thurman.

BIBLIOGRAPHY

MANUSCRIPT MATERIALS

Adjutant General's Office Records, 1780–1917. National Archives, Washington, D.C. Record Group 94.

Army Mobile Units' Records. Returns of the Regular Army Seventh Infantry, Eighth Infantry, 1846–1848. National Archives, Washington, D.C. Record Group 391.

Ballinger, W. P. Papers. Typescript. University of Texas Archives, Austin. (There are some letters from Maxey in the main collection. Ballinger's diary contains numerous entries about Maxey and also gives a character description of Maxey.)

Bayard, Thomas Francis. Papers. Library of Congress, Washington D.C. (There are a few interesting Maxey letters in this collection.)

Beauregard, P. G. T. Papers. Library of Congress, Washington, D.C. (Main items are Civil War telegrams and orders to and from Maxey.)

Bragg, Braxton. Papers. Western Reserve Historical Society, Cleveland, Ohio. (Civil War telegrams and orders to Maxey.)

Bray, Eugene. "Historical and Genealogical Notes on the Maxey Family." Typescript, 1955. In possession of Mr. Eugene Bray.

Bryan, Guy M. Papers. University of Texas Archives, Austin. (The Maxey-Bryan, Bryan-Ballinger, Bryan-Coke, and Bryan-Hayes correspondence throws much light on the political times. The Maxey-Bryan correspondence is mainly about Galveston harbor improvements and post office appointments.)

Bryan, Moses Austin. Papers. University of Texas Archives, Austin. (Letters from Maxey about veteran affairs.)

Cherokee Nations Papers. Western Historical Collection, University of Oklahoma Library, Norman, Okla. (Contain a few letters from Maxey to Stand Watie.)

Cleveland, Grover. Microfilmed papers. University of Texas Library, Austin. (The Maxey letters in this collection are mainly recommendations for appointments of various individuals.)

Coke, Richard. Scrapbook. Archives Division, Texas State Library, Austin. (A disappointing collection of newspaper clippings.)

Coke, Richard. Governor's Letters, 1874–1876. Archives Division, Texas State Library, Austin.

Epperson, B. H. Papers. University of Texas Archives, Austin. (These papers contain some 1866–1868 Maxey correspondence.)

Hamilton, A. J. Governor's Letters; Executive Record Book; Proclamations of 1865. Archives Division, Texas State Library, Austin.

Hayes, Rutherford B. Papers. The Rutherford B. Hayes Library, Freemont, Ohio. (There are thirteen letters from Maxey. A letter from Guy M. Bryan to Hayes enclosing a Bryan to Maxey letter during the crucial Hayes–Tilden affair reveals that Maxey had a small part to play.)

Hogg, James Stephen. Papers. University of Texas Archives, Austin. (There are some Henry Lightfoot, as well as Maxey, letters in this collection.)

Hubbard, Richard B. Governor's Letters, 1876–1879. Archives Division, Texas State Library, Austin.

Ireland, John. Governor's Letters, 1883–1887. Archives Division, Texas State Library, Austin.

Ireland, John. Papers. University of Texas Archives, Austin.

Justice Department Records. Legislative, Judicial and Diplomatic Division. Extracts from Records of State Comptroller, Austin, Texas, relative to declaration of S. H. Russell. National Archives, Washington, D.C. Record Group 60.

Lamar County, Probate Court Records. Lamar County Courthouse, Paris, Texas.

Lathrop, Barnes F. "The Life and Character of John Ireland." Typescript. University of Texas Archives, Austin.

Lightfoot Family Papers. Archives Division, Texas State Library, Austin. (Contain about fifty-eight letters sent by Maxey between 1861 and 1865.)

Maxey, Samuel Bell. Papers. Distributed among three libraries—Archives Division, Texas State Library, Austin; University of Texas Archives, Austin; and the Thomas Gilcrease Institute of American History and Art, Tulsa, Okla. (The greater part of the Maxey Papers is held in the Archives Division, Texas State Library, where a printed inventory of the papers is available. This part consists of approximately ten thousand items, including the correspondence of Samuel Bell Maxey, his wife, and his father. A collateral collection, acquired as a part of the Maxey Papers, consists of correspondence of relatives who were members of the Lightfoot, Long, and Williams families. The papers of Samuel Bell Maxey consist of general correspondence, 1855–1895, and political, legal, and financial records. The most valuable parts of the collection are the Civil War correspondence [though some of the letters of that period have been siphoned off into the Lightfoot Family Papers and into the Maxey Papers at the Gilcrease Institute] and the correspondence of Maxey to his wife during the years he served in the Senate. The Thomas Gilcrease Institute holds the next largest collection of Maxey Papers. These cover the period from 1861 to 1865 and consist of some two hundred letters. The most important item in this collection is Maxey's "Confidential Correspondence" [1863–1864]. The University of Texas Archives has mainly a letterpress book and some telegrams of the period from 1862 to 1864.)

Pike, Albert. Papers. University of Texas Archives, Austin.

Reagan, John H. Papers. Archives Division, Texas State Library, Austin; and University of Texas Archives, Austin. (These papers are indispensable as source material.)

Roberts, Oran M. Governor's Letters, 1879–1883. Archives Division, Texas State Library, Austin.

Roberts, Oran Milo. Papers. University of Texas Archives, Austin. (Valuable source material.)

Sherman, William T. Papers. Library of Congress, Washington, D.C. (These papers yielded some ten valuable letters written by Maxey during the 1880's.)

Smith, Ashbel. Papers. University of Texas Archives, Austin. (The Smith-Ballinger, Smith-Bryan, and Smith-Reagan letters shed light on Texas and national affairs, especially during the 1880's.)

Smith, Edmund Kirby. Microfilmed papers. Ramsdell Collection, Barker Texas History Center, University of Texas, Austin.

Sutton, Mrs. Francena M. Narrative typescript. University of Texas Archives, Austin. (Useful for background material on the Indian Territory–Arkansas–North Texas area during the Civil War.)

Texas, House and Senate. Journal of the 14th Legis., 1st sess., 1874. Typescript. Archives Division, Texas State Library, Austin.

Throckmorton, James Webb. Papers. University of Texas Archives, Austin. (The Throckmorton-Epperson correspondence reveals important Texas events of the 1870's.)

United States Military Academy. Historical File. Archives and History Section, U.S.M.A. Library, West Point, N.Y.

United States Military Academy. Official Register of Officers and Cadets. Archives and History Section, U.S.M.A. Library, West Point, N.Y.

War Department Collection of Confederate Records. Old Military Records Division. National Archives, Washington, D.C. Record Group 109.

Watie, Stand. Papers. University of Texas Archives, Austin.

Wigfall, Louis T. Papers. University of Texas Archives, Austin. (Useful for Wigfall-Reagan-Ochiltree correspondence from Civil War years.)

Wright, George T. Family papers. University of Texas Archives, Austin.

Wright, Marcus J. Papers. University of North Carolina Library, Chapel Hill, N.C.

DISSERTATIONS AND THESES

Barr, Alwyn. "Confederate Artillery in the Trans-Mississippi." Master's thesis, University of Texas, 1961.

———. "Texas Politics, 1876–1906." Doctoral dissertation, University of Texas, 1966.

Brown, Walter Lee. "Albert Pike, 1809–1891." Doctoral dissertation, University of Texas, 1955.

Chamberlain, Charles K. "Alexander Watkins Terrell: Citizen, Statesman." Doctoral dissertation, University of Texas, 1956.

Hare, John S. "Allen G. Thurman: A Political Study." Doctoral dissertation, Ohio State University, 1933.

Hill, James L. "The Life of Judge W. P. Ballinger." Master's thesis, University of Texas, 1936.

McKay, S. S. "Making the Texas Constitution of 1876." Doctoral dissertation, University of Pennsylvania, 1924.

Roberts, Myrtle. "Roger Q. Mills." Master's thesis, University of Texas, 1929.

BOOKS AND ARTICLES

Abel, Annie H. *The American Indian as Participant in the Civil War.* Cleveland: Arthur H. Clark Co., 1919.

Allsopp, Fred W. *Albert Pike: A Biography.* Little Rock, Ark.: Parke-Harper, 1928.

Alumni of the United States Military Academy at West Point. *Register of Graduates of the United States Military Academy.* New York: West Point Military Academy, 1965.

Ambrose. Stephen E. *Halleck: Lincoln's Chief of Staff.* Baton Rouge: Louisiana State University Press, 1962.

Andrews, James Ray. *Genealogy of the Andrews-Maxey and Related Families.* Dallas: Acme Printers, 1963.

Appleton's Annual Cyclopaedia. 42 vols. New York: D. Appleton and Co., 1867–1903.

Bancroft, George. *History of the Formation of the Constitution of the United States of America.* 2 vols. New York: D. Appleton and Co., 1893.

Barnard, Harry. *Rutherford B. Hayes and His America.* New York: Bobbs-Merrill Co., 1954.

Barnes, James A. *John G. Carlisle.* New York: Dodd, Mead and Co., 1931.

Barr, Alwyn. "Confederate Artillery in Arkansas." *Arkansas Historical Quarterly* 22 (1961): 238–290.

―――. *Reconstruction to Reform: Texas Politics, 1876–1906.* Austin: University of Texas Press, 1971.

Beard, Charles A., and Mary R. Beard. *The Beard's New Basic History of the United States.* Garden City, N.Y.: Doubleday and Co., 1960.

Boatner, Mark Mayo, III. *Civil War Dictionary.* New York: David McKay Co., 1959. Reprint, 1961.

Boynton, Edward C. *History of West Point.* 2d ed. New York: D. Van Nostrand, 1871.

Brown, John Henry. *The Life and Times of Henry Smith: The First American Governor of Texas.* Dallas: A. D. Aldridge and Co., 1887.

Buck, S. J. *The Agrarian Crusade.* New Haven, Conn.: Yale University Press, 1920.

Caldwell, Robert Granville. *James A. Garfield: Party Chieftain.* New York: Dodd, Mead and Co., 1931.

Capers, Gerald M. *Stephen A. Douglas: Defender of the Union.* Boston: Little, Brown and Co., 1959.

Casdorph, Paul Douglas. "Norris Wright Cuney and Texas Republican Politics, 1883–1896." *Southwestern Historical Quarterly* 68, no. 4 (April 1965): 455–465.

Castel, Albert. *General Sterling Price and the Civil War in the West.* Baton Rouge: Louisiana State University Press, 1968.

Cate, Wirt Armistead. *Lucius Q. C. Lamar: Secession and Reunion.* Chapel Hill: University of North Carolina Press, 1935.

Cater, Harold Dean. *Henry Adams and His Friends.* Boston: Houghton Mifflin Co., 1947.

Chidsey, Donald Barr. *The Life of Roscoe Conkling.* New Haven, Conn.: Yale University Press, 1935.

Collins, Lewis, and Richard H. Collins. *History of Kentucky.* 2 vols. Covington, Ky.: Collins and Co., 1874. Reprint, Frankfort: Kentucky Historical Society, 1966.

Colton, Calvin. *The Life and Times of Henry Clay.* 2 vols. New York: A. S. Barnes and Co., 1846.

Confederate States of America. *General Orders of Army, Trans-Mississippi Department.* Houston: E. H. Cushing and Co., 1865.

Conkling, Alfred R. *The Life and Letters of Roscoe Conkling.* New York: Charles L. Webster and Co., 1889.

Connelly, Thomas Lawrence. *Army of the Heartland.* Baton Rouge: Louisiana State University Press, 1967.

Cotner, Robert C. *James Stephens Hogg: A Biography.* Austin: University of Texas Press, 1959.

Crofts, Daniel W. "The Black Response to the Blair Education Bill." *Journal of Southern History* 37, no. 1 (February 1971): 41–52.

Cullom, George W. *Biographical Register of the Officers and Graduates of the United States Military Academy at West Point, New York.* 2 vols. New York: D. Van Nostrand, 1868.

Cumberland, Charles C. "The Confederate Loss and Recapture of Galveston, 1862–1863." *Southwestern Historical Quarterly* 51 (October 1947): 109–130.

Cunningham, Frank. *General Stand Watie's Confederate Indians.* San Antonio: Naylor Co., 1959.

Daniell, L. E. *Personnel of the Texas State Government with Sketches of Representative Men of Texas.* San Antonio: Maverick Printing House, 1892.

Davis, Jefferson. *The Rise and Fall of the Confederate Government.* 2 vols. New York: D. Appleton and Co., 1881.

Duncan, Robert Lipscomb. *Reluctant General: The Life and Times of Albert Pike.* New York: E. P. Dutton, 1961.

Eckenrode, H. J. *Rutherford B. Hayes: Statesman of Reunion.* New York: Dodd, Mead and Co., 1930.

Elliott, Claude. *Leathercoat: The Life History of a Texas Patriot.* San Antonio: Standard Printing Co., 1938.

———. "Union Sentiment in Texas, 1861–1865." *Southwestern Historical Quarterly* 50 (July 1946–April 1947): 449–477.

Ellis, L. Tuffly. "The Revolutionizing of the Texas Cotton Trade, 1865–1885." *Southwestern Historical Quarterly* 73 no. 4 (April 1970): 478–509.

Fischer, LeRoy, and Lary C. Rampp. "Quantrill's Civil War Operations in Indian Territory." *Chronicles of Oklahoma* 46, no. 2 (Summer 1968): 155–181.

Fleming, Walter L. *Civil War and Reconstruction in Alabama.* New York: Peter Smith, 1949.

Flick, Alexander C. *Samuel Jones Tilden: A Study in Political Sagacity.* New York: Dodd, Mead and Co., 1939.

Friend, Llerena B. *Sam Houston: The Great Designer.* Austin: University of Texas Press, 1954.

Gammel, H. P. N., comp. *Laws of Texas, 1822–1897.* 10 vols. Austin: Gammel Book Co., 1898.

Goodrich, Frederick E. *The Life and Public Services of Winfield Scott Hancock.* Boston: Lee and Shepherd, 1880.

Gorin, Franklin. *The Times of Long Ago.* Glasgow, Ky.: Glasgow News Press, 1939.

Gouge, William M. *The Fiscal History of Texas.* Philadelphia: Lippincott, Grambo and Co., 1852. Reprint, New York: Augustus M. Kelley Publishers, 1968.

Gracy, David B., II, ed. *Maxey's Texas by Samuel Bell Maxey.* Austin: Pemberton Press, 1965. (Maxey's article was published in *Harper's New Monthly Magazine,* September, 1893.)

Gregg, Robert. *The Influence of Border Troubles between the United States and Mexico, 1876–1910.* Baltimore: Johns Hopkins Press, 1937.

Gresham, Matilda. *Life of Walter Q. Gresham.* 2 vols. Chicago: Rand McNally and Co., 1919.

Hall, Claude H. "The Fabulous Tom Ochiltree: Promoter Politician and Raconteur." *Southwestern Historical Quarterly* 71, no. 3 (January 1968): 347–377.

Hancock, Marvin J. "The Second Battle of Cabin Creek, 1864." *Chronicles of Oklahoma* 39 (1961): 414–426.

Hancock, Mrs. W. S. *Reminiscences of Winfield Scott Hancock.* New York: Charles L. Webster and Co., 1887.

Haney, Lewis Henry. *A Congressional History of Railways in the United States.* 2 vols. New York: A. M. Kelley, 1968.

Haworth, Paul Leland. *The Hayes-Tilden Disputed Presidential Election of 1876.* Cleveland: Burrows Brothers, 1906.

Hayes, Rutherford B. *Letters and Messages of Rutherford B. Hayes together with Letter of Acceptance and Inaugural Address.* Washington, D.C., 1881.

Heath, Gary N. "The First Federal Invasion of Indian Territory." *Chronicles of Oklahoma* 44 (Winter 1966–1967) : 409–419.

Hesseltine, William B. *Ulysses S. Grant: Politician.* New York: Dodd, Mead and Co., 1935.

Hill, Benjamin, Jr. *Senator B. H. Hill.* Atlanta: T. H. P. Bloodworth, 1893.

Hood, Fred. "Twilight of the Confederacy in the Indian Territory." *Chronicles of Oklahoma* 41 (Winter 1963–1964): 425–441.

Hoover, Herbert T. "Ashbel Smith on Currency and Finance in the Republic of Texas." *Southwestern Historical Quarterly* 71, no. 3 (January 1968) : 419–425.

Horn, Stanley F. *The Army of the Tennessee.* Norman: University of Oklahoma Press, 1959.

Horton, Louise. "General Sam Bell Maxey: His Defense of North Texas and the Indian Territory." *Southwestern Historical Quarterly* 74 (April 1971): 507–524.

———."Samuel Bell Maxey on the Coke-Davis Controversy." *Southwestern Historical Quarterly* 72 (April 1969) : 519–525.

———. "The Star Route Conspiracies." *Texana* 7, no. 3 (1969) : 220–233.

Howe, George Frederick. *Chester A. Arthur: A Quarter Century of Machine Politics.* New York: Dodd, Mead and Co., 1934.

Jillson, Willard Rouse. *Kentucky Land Grants.* Louisville: Standard Printing Company, 1925.

Johnson, Frank W. *A History of Texas and Texans.* 5 vols. Chicago: American Historical Society, 1914.

Johnson, Ludwell H. *Red River Campaign: Politics and Cotton in the Civil War.* Baltimore: Johns Hopkins Press, 1958.

Johnson, Robert Underwood, and Clarence Clough Buel, eds. *Battles and Leaders of the Civil War.* 4 vols. New York: Century Company, 1887–1888. Reprint, New York: Thomas Yoseloff, 1956.

Johnston, Joseph E. *Narrative of Military Operations Directed during the Late War between the States.* Edited by Frank E. Vandiver. Bloomington: Indiana University Press, 1959.

Johnston, William Preston. *Life of General A. S. Johnston.* New York: D. Appleton and Co., 1878.

Jones, Archer. *Confederate Strategy from Shiloh to Vicksburg.* Baton Rouge: Louisiana State University Press, 1961.

Kennedy, J. P. *Memoirs of the Life of William Wirt.* Philadelphia: J. B. Lippincott and Co., 1860.

Klotsche, J. Martin. "The Star Route Cases." *Mississippi Valley Historical Review* 22 (1935): 407–418.

Lightfoot, Henry. *In Memoriam of General Samuel B. Maxey.* Paris, Texas: Privately printed, 1896. (In Maxey Papers.)

Lomask, M. S. *Andrew Johnson: President on Trial.* New York: Farrar, Straus, 1960.

McElroy, Robert. *Grover Cleveland: The Man and the Statesman.* 2 vols. New York: Harper and Brothers, 1923.

McKittrick, Eric L. *Andrew Johnson and Reconstruction.* Chicago: University of Chicago Press, 1960.

McWhinney, Grady. *Braxton Bragg and Confederate Defeat.* New York: Columbia University Press, 1969.

Martin, Roscoe. *The People's Party in Texas.* 1933. Reprint, Austin: University of Texas Press, 1970.

Maxey, S. B. *Address of Honorable S. B. Maxey of Paris, Texas, Delivered before the Democratic Mass Meeting Held at Paris, Texas, September 20, 1884.* Paris, Texas: J. E. Ellis, 1884. (Printed pamphlet in Maxey Papers.)

——. *Address to the Annual Meeting of the Soldiers of the Mexican War of the State of Texas.* Paris, Texas: Privately printed, 1875.

Mayes, Edward. *Lucius Q. C. Lamar: His Life, Times and Speeches.* Nashville: Publishing House of the Methodist Episcopal Church South, 1896.

Merrill, Horace Samuel. *Bourbon Democracy of the Middle West, 1865–1896.* Baton Rouge: Louisiana State University Press, 1953.

Miller, Edmund Thornton. *A Financial History of Texas.* Bulletin no. 37. Austin: University of Texas, 1916.

Monaghan, James. *Civil War on the Western Border, 1854–1865.* Boston: Little, Brown and Co., 1955.

Mordecai, Samuel. *Richmond in By-Gone Days.* Richmond: G. M. West, 1856.

Neville, Alexander W. *The History of Lamar County.* Paris, Tex.: North Texas Publishing Co., 1937.

————. *The Red River Valley, Then and Now.* Paris, Tex.: North Texas Publishing Co., 1948.

Nevins, Allan. *Abram S. Hewitt.* New York: Harper and Brothers, 1935.

————. *Grover Cleveland: A Study in Courage.* New York: Dodd, Mead and Co., 1933.

————. *Hamilton Fish: The Inner History of the Grant Administration.* New York: Dodd, Mead and Co., 1937.

————. *Ordeal of the Union.* 2 vols. New York: Charles Scribner's Sons, 1947.

Nichols, James L. *The Confederate Quartermaster in the Trans-Mississippi.* Austin: University of Texas Press, 1964.

Nunn, W. C. *Texas under the Carpetbaggers.* Austin: University of Texas Press, 1962.

Oates, Stephen B. *Confederate Cavalry West of the River.* Austin: University of Texas Press, 1961.

Osgood, Ernest Staples. *The Day of the Cattleman.* Minneapolis: University of Minnesota Press, 1929.

Parks, Joseph Howard. *General Edmund Kirby Smith, C.S.A.* Baton Rouge: Louisiana State University Press, 1954.

————. *General Leonidas Polk, C.S.A.* Baton Rouge, Louisiana State University Press, 1962.

————. *John Bell of Tennessee.* Baton Rouge: Louisiana State University Press, 1950.

Pemberton, John C. *Pemberton: Defender of Vicksburg.* Chapel Hill: University of North Carolina Press, 1944.

Pike, Albert. *Report of Albert Pike on Mission to the Indian Nations.* 1861. Reprint, Washington, D.C.: Supreme Council, Ancient and Accepted Scottish Rite, 1968.

Polk, William M. *Leonidas Polk: Bishop and General.* 2 vols. New York: Longmans, Green and Co., 1915.

Poore, Benjamin Perley. *The Life and Public Services of Ambrose E. Burnside.* Providence, R. I.: J. A. and R. A. Reid, 1882.

————. *Perley's Reminiscences of Sixty Years in the National Metropolis.* 2 vols. Philadelphia: W. A. Houghton, 1886.

Procter, Ben H. *Not without Honor: The Life of John H. Reagan.* Austin: University of Texas Press, 1962.

Ramsdell, Charles William. *Reconstruction in Texas.* New York: Columbia University Press, 1910. Reprint, Austin: University of Texas Press, 1970.

Reed, S. G. *A History of the Texas Railroads.* Houston: St. Clair Publishing Co., 1941.

Richards, Ira Don. "The Battle of Poison Spring." *Arkansas Historical Quarterly* 18 (Winter 1959): 330–385.

Richardson, James D., comp. *Messages and Papers of the Presidents, 1798–1908.* 11 vols. Washington, D.C.: Bureau of National Literature and Art, 1908.

Richardson, Rupert Norval. *Texas: The Lone Star State.* 3d ed. Englewood Cliffs, N. J.: Prentice-Hall, Inc., 1970.

Roland, Charles P. *Albert Sidney Johnston.* Austin: University of Texas Press, 1964.

Roman, Alfred. *The Military Operations of General Beauregard.* 2 vols. New York: Harper and Brothers, 1884.

Rowland, Dunbar, ed. *Jefferson Davis, Constitutionalist: His Letters, Papers and Speeches.* 10 vols. Jackson, Miss.: Mississippi Department of Archives and History, 1923.

Schlesinger, Arthur M. *Paths to the Present.* New York: Macmillan Co., 1961.

Seitz, Don C. *Braxton Bragg: General of the Confederacy.* Columbia, S.C.: The State Co., 1924.

Shelley, George E. "The Semicolon Court of Texas." *Southwestern Historical Quarterly* 48 (April 1945): 449–469.

Sherman, John. *John Sherman's Recollections of Forty Years in the House, Senate and Cabinet.* 2 vols. New York: Greenwood Press, 1968.

Sherman, William T. *The Memoirs of General William T. Sherman.* 2d ed. 2 vols. New York: D. Appleton and Co., 1889.

Shuffler, T. Henderson. *Son, Remember.* College Station: Texas Agricultural and Mechanical College, 1946.

Smith, Edward C., and Arnold J. Zurcher. *Dictionary of American Politics.* 2d ed. New York: Barnes and Noble, 1968.

Smith, Justin. *The War with Mexico.* 2 vols. New York: Macmillan Co., 1919.

Smith, Theodore Clark. *The Life and Letters of James A. Garfield.* 2 vols. New Haven, Conn.: Yale University Press, 1925.

Smyrl, Frank H. "Unionism in Texas, 1856–1861." *Southwestern Historical Quarterly* 68, no. 2 (October 1964): 172–196.

Spencer, Edward. *An Outline of the Public Life and Services of Thomas F. Bayard.* New York: D. Appleton and Co., 1880.

Spratt, John Stricklin. *The Road to Spindletop*. Dallas: Southern Methodist University, 1955. Paperback reprint, Austin: University of Texas Press, 1970.

Stambaugh, J. Lee, and Lillian J. Stambaugh. *A History of Collin County, Texas*. Austin: Texas State Historical Association, 1958.

Stanwood, Edward. *James Gillespie Blaine*. New York: Houghton Mifflin Co., 1898.

Tansill, Charles C. *The Congressional Career of Thomas Francis Bayard, 1869–1885*. Washington, D.C.: Georgetown University Press, 1946.

Taylor, Richard. *Destruction and Reconstruction*. New York: Longmans, Green and Co., 1955.

Texas Almanac for 1873 and Emigrants Guide to Texas. Galveston: A. H. Belo and Co., 1874.

Texas Legislature. House. *Journal of the House of Representatives*. 16th Legislature, 1879. 17th Legislature, 1882. 20th Legislature, 1887.

———. *Members of the Legislature of the State of Texas from 1846 to 1939*. Austin, 1939.

———. Senate. *Journal of the Senate*. 16th Legislature, 1879. 17th Legislature, 1881. 20th Legislature, 1887.

———. *Records of the Secretary of State*. Secession Convention, 1861.

———. *Texas Reports*, vol. 39, 1874.

Thomas, Harrison Cook. *The Return of the Democratic Party to Power in 1884*. New York: Columbia University Press, 1919.

Tucker, Glenn. *Hancock the Superb*. New York: The Bobbs-Merrill Co., 1960.

United States. Congress. *Congressional Record*. 44th through 49th Cong., 1875–1887.

———. House. *War of the Rebellion: A Compilation of the Official Records of the Union and Confederate Armies*. Compiled under the direction of the Secretary of War. 4 series in 70 vols. (127 books and index). Washington, D. C.: Govt. Printing Office, 1880–1901. (Volumes used in this book are all from series 1.)

———. *House Document 38: Testimony Relating to Star Route Cases*. 48th Cong., 1st sess., 1884.

———. *House Executive Document 60: Mexican War Correspondence*. 30th Cong., 1st sess., 1847.

———. *House Executive Documents 100–103: Star Route Investigations*. 48th Cong., 1st sess., 1884.

———. Senate. *Congressional Globe*. 35th Cong., 1st sess., 1858.

————. *Senate Document 234: Journal of the Provisional Congress of the Confederate States.* 58th Cong., 2d sess., 1904.

————. Post Office Department. *Annual Report of the Postmaster General, 1879.* Washington, D.C.: Govt. Printing Office.

————. Supreme Court of the District of Columbia. *Record of the Star Route Trials: United States versus John W. Dorsey, John R. Miner, John M. Peck, Stephen W. Dorsey, Harvey M. Vaile, Montford C. Rerdell, T. J. Brady, and William H. Turner for Conspiracy.* 3 vols. Washington, D.C.: Govt. Printing Office, 1882.

————. *Proceedings in the Second Trial of the Case of the United States versus John W. Dorsey et al.* 4 vols. Washington, D.C.: Govt. Printing Office, 1883.

Vandiver, Frank E. *Mighty Stonewall.* New York: McGraw-Hill, 1957.

————. *Their Tattered Flags.* New York: Harper's Magazine Press, 1970.

Wallace, Ernest. *Charles DeMorse: Pioneer Editor and Statesman.* Lubbock: Texas Technological College Press, 1943.

————. *Texas in Turmoil.* Austin: Steck-Vaughn Co., 1965.

Waller, John L. *Colossal Hamilton of Texas: A Biography of Andrew Jackson Hamilton.* El Paso: Texas Western Press, 1968.

Webb, Walter P. *The Texas Rangers.* Austin: University of Texas Press, 1965.

Webb, Walter P., and H. Bailey Carroll, eds. *Handbook of Texas.* 2 vols. Austin: Texas State Historical Society, 1952.

Webster, Michael G. "Intrigue on the Rio Grande, 1875." *Southwestern Historical Quarterly* 74, no. 2 (October 1970) : 149–165.

West, Larry L. "Douglas H. Cooper, Confederate General." *Lincoln Herald* 81 (Summer 1969) : 69–76.

Wilcox, Cadmus M. *History of the Mexican War.* Washington, D.C.: The Church News Publishing Co., 1892.

Willey, William J. "The Second Federal Invasion of Indian Territory." *Chronicles of Oklahoma* 44 (Winter 1966–1967) : 420–430.

Williams, Charles Richard. *Diary and Letters of Rutherford B. Hayes.* 5 vols. Columbus: Ohio State Archeological and Historical Society, 1924.

Williams, T. Harry. *P. G. T. Beauregard.* Baton Rouge: Louisiana State University Press, 1955.

————, ed. *Hayes: The Diary of a President 1875–1881.* New York: David McKay Co., 1964.

Williamson, Edward C. "The Alabama Election of 1874." *Alabama Review* 17 (July 1964): 210–218.

Winkler, E. W. *Platforms of Political Parties in Texas*. University of Texas Bulletin No. 53. Austin, 1916.

————. ed. *Journal of the Secession Convention of Texas, 1861*. Austin: Texas Library Historical Commission, 1912.

Woodward, C. Vann. *Reunion and Reaction*. Boston: Little, Brown and Co., 1951.

Wooster, Ralph A. "Ben H. Epperson: East Texas Lawyer, Legislator and Civil Leader." *East Texas Historical Journal* 5, no. 1 (March 1967): 108–112.

————. *The Secession Conventions of the South*. Princeton: Princeton University Press, 1962.

Wright, Muriel H. "Biography of General D. H. Cooper." *Chronicles of Oklahoma* 32 (1954): 142–184.

————, and LeRoy Fischer. "Civil War Sites." *Chronicles of Oklahoma* 44 (1966): 158–215.

NEWSPAPERS AND PERIODICALS

Austin Daily State Journal, 1874.
Austin Democratic Statesman, 1874.
Austin Statesman, 1881.
Baltimore Sun, 1895.
Boston Herald, 1895.
Carthage Panola Watchman, 1877.
Clarksville Northern Standard, 1860–1865, 1872, 1873.
Daily Arkansas Gazette, 1880.
Dallas Times Herald, 1880.
Dallas Tri-Weekly Herald, 1878.
Dallas Weekly Herald, 1868, 1876.
Fort Worth Gazette, 1887.
Frankfort Commentator, 1826, 1827.
Frankfort Commonwealth, 1842, 1843, 1850.
Gainesville Independent, 1878.
Galveston News, 1861–1865, 1873, 1876, 1877, 1878, 1883.
Honey Grove Independent, 1876.
Houston Age, 1874.
Houston Daily Telegram, 1879.
Houston Daily Telegraph, 1861–1865.
Houston Evening Journal, 1884.
Houston Post, 1881.

Louisville Courier–Journal, 1874.
Meridian Independent Blade, 1880.
Nashville Banner, 1895.
Nation (New York), 1880, 1885.
New Orleans Times Democrat, 1882.
New York Daily Tribune, 1877, 1895.
New York Herald, 1881, 1895.
New York World, 1875–1878, 1880, 1895.
North Texas Enterprise (Bonham), 1874.
Paris North Texan, 1876, 1880.
Paris (Tex.) *Press*, 1874.
Peoria (Ill.) *Journal*, 1895.
Richmond Enquirer, 1862.
Rochester (N. Y.) *Democrat and Chronicle* 1882.
St. Louis Republican, 1879.
Sherman Courier–Chronicle, 1881.
Sherman Daily Courier, 1876, 1879.
Sherman Register, 1874.
Sherman Weekly Courier, 1879.
State Gazette (Austin, Tex.), 1861, 1874, 1887.
Street's Monthly (New York), 1880.
Texarkana News, 1877.
Texarkana Weekly Visitor, 1879.
Texas Journal of Commerce (Galveston), 1879.
Truth (New York), 1880.
Washington Post, 1895.

INDEX

Pittsburg Landing: 28
Pleasant Bluff, Ark.: 40
Plumb, Preston B.: 145
Poison Spring, Ark.: 37–38
Pope, Lucetta. SEE Bell, Lucetta Pope
Pope, Nathaniel, Jr.: 5
Pope, Nathaniel, Sr.: 5
Pope, William: 5
Poplar Mountain (Ky.): 7
Populists. SEE People's party
Porter, Fitz-John: 11
Portersville, Ala.: 34
Port Hudson: 32
Post Office Appropriation bill: 99
Post Office Department: 167
Post Offices and Post Roads, Committee on: 67, 100, 143, 155, 162
Prairie D'Ane, Ark.: 37
Price, J. B.: 120
Price, Sterling: driven from Springfield, 27; at Arkadelphia, 36; pursues Steele, 37, 38; invades Missouri, 40–42
prohibition: 184
Pugh, James L.: as pro silver, 168; and Maxey, 174, 183

railroads: and car coupler, 141; Gresham and, 146–147; Sawyer and, 146–147; monopoly of, in Texas, 174; legislation of, 179
Rainey, Frank: 54
Randall, Samuel J.: presidential nominee, 142; as Democratic leader of House, 150
Randle, Edward T.: 54
Randolph, Theodore F.: 65, 72
Ransom, Matt W.: 111
Reagan, John H.: as Confederate postmaster, 21; disenfranchised, 50; invited to Dora's wedding, 59; backs liberal Republican presidential nominee, 70; nominates Reeves, 103; as candidate for Senate, 110, 178, 181; and star route mail service, 115; Maxey and, 127, 177, 182 and n.; and payment of southern mail contractors, 132; and Van Voorhis, 133; physical description of, 180; resigns Senate seat, 188; as head of Texas Railroad Commission, 188
Red River: 36
Reed, Thomas: 129
Reeves, Reuben: 103 and n.
Republican party: factions in, 50; candidates of (1876), 76; in South (1876), 81; members of, in Texas, 180
Resumption Act: 93, 105

Richmond, Va.: 27
Riddleberger, Harrison: 119
Riggs House (Washington, D.C.): 191
Rio Grande: 60, 89. SEE ALSO frontier, protection of
river and harbor bill: and federal funds for Texas, 80; of 1882, 134; of 1884, 152; mentioned, 171 n.
Roberts, Oran M.: as attorney, 49; and Ireland, 73; as candidate for Senate, 110; as governor of Texas, 118; as professor, 185
Roberts, Samuel A.: 21, 49
Robinson's Creek: 33
Rodriguez, Joseph: 52–53
Rogers, C. W.: Maxey and, 141, 172; mentioned, 129, 170
Ross, Lawrence Sullivan: inauguration ball of, 181; and Sam Bell Long, 185
Rowell, Dora. SEE Lightfoot, Dora Rowell Maxey
Rowell, Thomas: 47
Rusk, Tex.: 42
Rusk, Thomas J.: 141, 195
Russell, Stillwell H.: as U.S. Marshal, 100, 123; pardoned by Arthur, 157

Sabin, Dwight M.: 165
Saint Louis, Mo.: 141
Saint Louis and San Francisco Railroad: and right of way, 129–130, 172; Maxey and, 141; and charter bill, 170–171
Saint Louis Republican: 109
Saline River, Ark.: 25
San Bois Creek (Ark.): 40
Santa Anna, Antonio López: 12
Santa Fe Railroad: in Galveston, 146; and Frisco line, 170; vs. Gould, 170–171
Sawyer, Philetus: and Maxey, 146; and LaFollette, 171
Schleicher, Gustave: 99
Schofield, John M.: 146
Sealy, W.: 171
secession convention (Austin): 17
Semple, James: 8
Shelby, Joseph: 37, 42
Shepard, Seth: 192
Sheridan, Philip: on "bandetti," 63; in Indian Territory, 163, 165
Sherman, John: Maxey and, 77; as Senator, 82, 167, 169
Sherman, William T.: Maxey and, 77; and star route mail service, 116, 122; and Sam Bell Long, 126
Sherman Courier-Chronicle: 121
Sherman Weekly Courier: 111
Shiloh: 28–29